Child Marriage in India

Child Marriage in India

Socio-legal and Human Rights Dimensions

Jaya Sagade

OXFORD
UNIVERSITY PRESS

OXFORD
UNIVERSITY PRESS

YMCA Library Building, Jai Singh Road, New Delhi 110 001

Oxford University Press is a department of the University of Oxford. It furthers the
University's objective of excellence in research, scholarship, and education
by publishing worldwide in

Oxford   New York

Auckland   Cape Town   Dar es Salaam   Hong Kong   Karachi   Kuala Lumpur
Madrid   Melbourne   Mexico City   Nairobi   New Delhi   Shanghai   Taipei   Toronto

With offices in

Argentina   Austria   Brazil   Chile   Czech Republic   France   Greece   Guatemala
Hungary   Italy   Japan   Poland   Portugal   Singapore   South Korea   Switzerland
Thailand   Turkey   Ukraine   Vietnam

Oxford is a registered trademark of Oxford University Press
in the UK and in certain other countries

Published in India by Oxford University Press, New Delhi

© Oxford University Press and Jaya Sagade 2005

The moral rights of the author have been asserted
Database right Oxford University Press (maker)

First Published 2005

ISBN 019 566890 1

Typeset in Garamond by Le Studio Graphique, Gurgaon, 122 001
Printed in India by Pauls Press, New Delhi 110 020
Published by Manzar Khan, Oxford University Press
YMCA Library Building, Jai Singh Road, New Delhi 110 001

To
My Mother

Contents

Foreword by Rebecca J. Cook   xi
Preface   xiii
Acknowledgements   xvii
List of Acronyms   xix
List of Tables   xxi

Introduction   xxiii
  The Term 'Child Marriage'   xxvi
  Focus on the Girl Child   xxvii
  Feminist Method   xxviii
  Human Rights Approach   xxxv
  Overview   xxxvii
  Conclusion   xxxix
  Appendix   xl

1. Dimensions of the Problem of Child Marriage   1
   in India: Causes and Consequences

   Introduction   1
   Marriage in India   3
   Child Marriage: The Demographic Context   4
   Reasons for Child Marriage   7
   Consequences of Child Marriages:
     Epidemiological Context   14

Other Consequences of Child Marriage   21
Barriers Faced by Adolescents   22
Summary and Conclusions   24

2. Legal Discourse on Age of Marriage   35

Introduction   35
Law Relating to Child Marriages   36
Child Marriage Restraint Act, 1929   43
The Indian Penal Code and the Minimum Age for
    Consensual Sexual Intercourse   63

3. Personal Laws, Legal Reform,   73
    and the Judiciary

Introduction   73
Personal Laws   74
Lacunae and Contradictions in Laws   85
Reforms in Law   86
Legal Literacy   90
Sensitizing the Judiciary   91
Brandeis Brief   92
Initiating Public Interest Litigation   92
The Role of Law   97
Conclusions   100

4. Child Marriage and International   111
    Human Rights

Introduction   111
Obligations of the Government to
    Implement Human Rights   113
Methodology   116
Evolution of International Human Rights   117
International Human Rights and Child Marriage   125

5. Human Rights Violated by   132
   the Custom of Child Marriage

   Introduction   132
   Right to Equality   132
   Right to Marry and Found Family   148
   Right to Liberty and Security   159
   Right to be Free from Slavery   163

6. The Girl Child's Right to Development: 175
   Adverse Consequences of Child Marriage

   Introduction   175
   Rights Affecting Reproductive Health   175
   Rights Affecting the Development of the Girl Child   192

7. Strategies and Future Action   208

   CEDAW and CRC: Need for Collaboration   208
   Strengthening International
      Normative Standards   209
   Strategies for Implementation of
      Human Rights at National Level   210
   Future Action   215

   Conclusions   221
   Select Bibliography   231
   List of Cases   250
   Index   253

Foreword

Jaya Sagade's book is an invaluable and timely resource for those working to eliminate child marriages. For too long, the issue of child marriage has not been sufficiently addressed by agencies working to improve the status of women and agencies promoting reproductive and sexual health. This book puts the issue squarely on the agenda of both groups.

It also poses a challenge to governmental agencies at state and national levels. Dr Sagade explains how child marriage is increasingly recognized to violate key constitutional and human rights principles, including the right to enter marriage freely, and freely to choose a marriage partner. She insightfully analyses how child marriage can also violate the rights of the girl child to be free from all forms of discrimination, inhuman and degrading treatment, and slavery.

The main burden of child marriage is born by girls especially because of the harmful consequences of premature pregnancy and childbirth. Pregnant girls are particularly vulnerable to prolonged obstructed labour resulting in stillbirth, obstetric fistula and sometimes pregnancy-related death. Moreover, married girls, compared with unmarried girls, are at increased vulnerability to HIV/AIDS.

The willingness of families to require and approve child marriage is conditioned by many factors, including family poverty, fear of female sexuality unconstrained by marriage, and lack of respect for social, cultural and religious norms that would discourage child marriage. On premature marriage, girls forfeit opportunities for education, training and economic self-reliance, which especially burdens them when their husbands are considerably older and die when the wives are young.

Federal legislation to prohibit child marriage has not been vigorously enforced, despite the urging of the Supreme Court of India, and marriages in defiance of the law remain valid. Dr Sagade endorses the approach of the Convention on the Elimination of All Forms of Discrimination against Women (the CEDAW Convention) that, despite the acknowledged cost to young girls in existing premature marriages, it is in the national interest that such marriages be legally considered null and void. The CEDAW Convention provides that

> The betrothal and the marriage of a child shall have no legal effect and all necessary action, including legislation, shall be taken to specify a minimum age for marriage and to make the registration of marriages in an official registry compulsory. (Article 16(2))

Nullification of such purported marriages is designed to deter them. Families giving their young daughters in premature marriage will be forewarned that their purposes will fail, and families receiving child partners for their sons will know that their sons will be neither married nor the fathers of legitimate children. Drastic though this approach may prove in families that retain the historic practice of child marriage, Dr Sagade argues that nothing less is likely to be effective for protection of young girls against the harsh physical, educational, social and economic consequences for them of a persisting practice whose time should have passed.

REBECCA J. COOK

Professor of Law, and
Faculty Chair in International Human Rights
Faculty of Law, University of Toronto

Preface

This book focuses on the issue of child marriage of young girls, which has been debated for more than a century in India but has never been considered as a serious threat to the life of young girls. It has remained a low or no priority subject for those who are in power. Though child marriage has been an offence in India since 1929, once solemnized such a marriage is valid and legal. This legal position has bothered me ever since I started teaching Family Law. When I decided to take a mid-career break to do further research on women's human rights, particularly their right to reproductive health, there was no better subject than child marriages of young girls and its effect on them.

The book analyses social, legal and human rights dimensions of the issue of child marriage of young girls from the feminist perspective. The book highlights the magnitude of the problem of child marriage prevalent in India, analyses diverse reasons for the continuation of the practice of child marriages, and focuses with the help of available social science data on the various adverse consequences on the health, development and personality of young girls. It brings to light the huge cost that society is required to bear due to the widespread practice of child marriage. It takes account of the legislative efforts made in the last decades of the 19th and initial decades of the 20th centuries and critically scans the present legislative provisions and judicial decisions.

Acceptance and recognition of interconnections between international human rights and constitutional provisions and domestic laws now has become quite clear. Arguments are often made at all levels by using the right-based paradigm. This book's major thrust therefore is on highlighting such interconnectivity. It analyses the harm caused to young girls due to child marriages, which results in violations of their human rights. It identifies those human rights expressed in the major international conventions, refers to the concluding observations, comments, general recommendations of the UN Charter based bodies and treaty based bodies established under the Conventions and locates similar provisions in the Indian Constitution. This book thereby attempts to demonstrate failure of the State to comply with its constitutional obligations.

Finally, the book suggests some law reforms and legal strategies to be carried out. It also recommends ways in which more responsive and responsible roles could be played by various actors and agencies at local, national, regional and international levels.

The approach of the book being interdisciplinary, it should interest students of law, social work, women's studies, sociology; researchers, policy makers, judicial officers, lawyers; NGOs, and all those who are interested in promoting human rights, particularly women's and children's human rights. Even health care professionals might find the book interesting, as one of the thrust areas of the book is the impact of child marriage on the reproductive health of young girls.

Recently a few voluntary organizations have taken up the issue and have started focussing on the ways and means for preventing child marriages. Occasionally one finds that audio as well visual media also highlight the government's lackadaisical attitude in addressing the problem and thereby creates awareness about the practice of child marriage. The National Commission for Women as well as the National Commission for Human Rights has addressed the problem of child marriage in the recent past. However, the government is not taking a responsive and responsible stand on the recommendations of both these commissions. It is now the responsibility of civil society to remain alert and active till some concrete steps are taken in the direction for providing justice to young girls.

One of the suggestions given in the last chapter for preventing child marriage is a public interest litigation (PIL) be filed in the Supreme Court. I am glad to note that recently such a petition has been filed by the Forum for Fact Finding Documentation and Advocacy—a Chattisgarh based voluntary organization seeking effective implementation of the Child Marriage Restraint Act, 1929. The Court has issued notices to the State governments to report the extent of the prevalence of child marriages as well as preventive measures taken. I hope that the Supreme Court pursues the matter till the end and uses this opportunity to pass appropriate orders for curbing the practice of child marriage that has been victimizing young girls for a very long time for no fault of theirs. My efforts will be rewarded if arguments in this book could be used in addressing the issues raised in the PIL.

Protecting the girl child has become an issue of major concern for the developing countries, particularly after the Cairo conference on Population and Development; and the Beijing Conference on Women. Even at the regional level, SAARC countries have focused on girl children. SAARC has expressed its concern for the decline in the sex ratio and has showed its commitment to the education of young girls, elimination of the cultural practices of female foeticide, female infanticide and child marriages as well as of girl child labour, trafficking and forced prostitution of young girls. These issues need to be addressed on a priority basis. The inter linkages of these issues also need to be highlighted.

Reforms in the existing laws addressing directly and indirectly the issue of child marriage and the effective enforcement of these laws are equally important tasks that need to be undertaken. Sensitization of personnel involved in drafting, interpreting and enforcing these laws is needed. Parents, communities, professionals, elected representatives—all need to be made aware about the seriousness of the problems faced by young girls. Elected women representatives in local governments, particularly in panchayati raj would be a great source for lobbying, advocating and helping people internalize the law.

Along with legal measures, it is essential to provide supportive measures for preventing child marriages. For that it is necessary to build pressure on governments to make budgetary commitments. Without financial commitment, it is not possible to realise human rights. Therefore lobbying for the same also becomes essential.

I hope this book will help address the issue of child marriage more effectively, efficiently and practically.

Pune
January 2005

JAYA SAGADE

Acknowledgements

This book has come out of the thesis that I did for S.J.D. in the Department of Law of the University of Toronto. It was a wonderful opportunity for me to work with Professor Rebecca Cook, my Supervisor. It is difficult to express my heartfelt appreciation for her invaluable guidance, comments and suggestions while I was working on the thesis and her perseverance in making me convert the thesis into a book. I have no words to express my deep gratitude towards her.

I thank Professor Bernard Dickens, Professor Brenda Cossman and Professor Andrew Byrnes for their to-the-point questions and valuable comments. They helped me formulate my thoughts in an unambiguous way. I am indebted to all of them. Another person who has contributed tremendously in developing my social science understating of the subject is Dr Shireen Jejeebhoy from the World Health Organisation, Geneva. I am extremely grateful to her.

While I was working on this book, I participated in a project sponsored by the British Council on 'Gender and Development'. The project partners were ILS Law College, Pune, MASUM—a Pune based NGO, and School of Oriental and African Studies, London. One of the components of the project was to conduct workshops for selected rural women on women's human rights with special reference to reproductive health. We did focus on and discuss in these workshops, the issue of child marriage. These workshops really enlightened me about the practical aspects of the issue. We also organized a two days seminar for sharing our experiences with law college teachers in the state of Maharashtra as well as NGOs working for children. I got very good feed back. I have attempted to include some of those suggestions in this book. I must thank my friends from villages, all participants and the British Council!

I sincerely acknowledge the cooperation given to me by the library staff of ILS Law College, Pune and Bora Laskin, University of Toronto, Tata Institute of Social Sciences and International Institute of Population Sciences, Mumbai.

I wish to mention the source of my material, moral and emotional strength in Toronto—Mandatai and Dr Keshav Tilak and their extended family! Without their support and encouragement, it would have become difficult for me to complete this task. I must acknowledge my friends from Toronto as well as Pune and my colleagues from the ILS Law College who supported me in times of difficulties and despair. I really appreciate their support and prefer to remain in their debt.

I must pay special tribute to my mother whose eternal support has been my greatest strength. It is what made me complete this book. I have dedicated it to her.

Acronyms

CEDAW	Committee on Elimination of Discrimination Against Women
CESCR	Committee on Economic, Social and Cultural Rights
CMRA	Child Marriage Restraint Act
CPD	Commission for Population and Development
CRC	Committee on the Rights of the Child
CSW	Commission on the Status of Women
DESA	Department of Economic and Social Affairs
ECOSOC	Economic and Social Council
FGM	Female Genital Mutilation
FWCW	Fourth World Conference on Women
HIV/AIDS	Human Immunodeficiency Virus/Acquired Immune Deficiency Syndrome
HMA	Hindu Marriage Act
HMGA	Hindu Minority and Guardianship Act
HRC	Human Rights Committee
ICCPR	International Covenant on Civil and Political Rights
ICDS	Integrated Child Development Schemes
ICESCR	International Covenant on Economic, Social and Cultural Rights
ICMA	Indian Christian Marriage Act
ICPD	International Conference on Population and Development
IPC	Indian Penal Code
IWRAW	International Women's Rights Action Watch
MPL	Muslim Personal Law

NCW	National Commission for Women
NFHS	National Family Health Survey
NGOs	Non-Governmental Organizations
NHRC	National Human Rights Commission
PLA	Beijing Platform of Action
PMDA	Parsi Marriage and Divorce Act
POA	Cairo Programme of Action
Prep Com	Preparatory Committee
SMAM	Singular Mean Age at Marriage
SPMA	Special Marriage Act
STDs	Sexually Transmitted Diseases
UDHR	Universal Declaration of Human Rights
UN	United Nations
UNFPA	United Nations Fund for Population Action
UNICEF	United Nations Children's Fund
VVF	Vesico Vaginal Fistula
WHO	World Health Organization

Tables

A. Minimum Legal Age at Marriage   xl
    by Region and Country

2.1 Age at Marriage   44

2.2 Punishment for Offences   49

Introduction

I am one of those unfortunate Hindu women whose hard lot is to suffer the unnameable miseries entailed by the custom of early marriage. This wicked practice of child marriage has destroyed the happiness of my life. It comes between me and the thing which I prize above all others—study and mental cultivation. Without the least fault of mine I am doomed to seclusion; every aspiration of mine to rise above my ignorant sisters is looked down upon with suspicion and is interpreted in the most uncharitable manner.[*]

Rukhmabai

Throughout the world, girls are married young, sometimes even before they reach the age of puberty and many a time before they reach the age of eighteen years. The practice of marrying girls as children is common in developing countries of Africa, Asia, and Latin America. A survey conducted by UNICEF[1] indicates that in the region of Sub-Saharan Africa, in many countries, a large percentage of girls between the age of fifteen and nineteen years are married. For example, 74 per cent of girls in the Democratic Republic of Congo, 50 per cent in Mali, 57 per cent in Niger and 50 per cent in Uganda are already married in adolescence. In the South Asian

---

[*] Extract from a letter written by Rukhmabai, a victim of child marriage, to *The Times of India* on 26 June 1885 on the adverse consequences of child marriage. It reveals how acutely she felt about the correlation between child marriage and denial of education to women in the days when educating girls was not common. Unfortunately, even after nearly 120 years the scenario has not changed much. She was one of the crusaders fighting for raising the age of marriage. She pleaded for fifteen to be the age of marriage for girls. She was thought to be much ahead of her times! Her case is discussed in Chapter Two.

countries of India, Nepal, and Bangladesh this percentage is 38, 42, and 48 respectively. In the Middle East, it is 28 per cent in Iraq and 24 per cent in Yemen. In Latin America, 29 per cent of girls in Cuba and 24 per cent in Guatemala in the age group of 15–19 years are married.

Anti-Slavery International points out that almost 50 per cent of African girls are married by the time they are eighteen years old.[2] New York-based Alan Guttmacher Institute found that the percentage of women in the age group of 20–24 who are married before eighteen is much higher compared to the women in the age group of 15–19.[3] For example, 78 per cent of women in the age group of 20–24, 84 per cent in Niger, 54 per cent in Uganda, 73 per cent in Bangladesh, 41 per cent in Guatemala are married before the age of eighteen.[4]

The Indian situation if analysed in the global context is not different from that obtaining in these developing countries. More than 34 per cent of girls in the age group of 15–19 years are already married.[5] Such statistics indicates that a large number of girls are married off at an early age.[6] But it does not give the true figures because many marriages are unregistered and are not counted as part of any standard data collection system. National statistics often disguise significant rates of very early marriage. Though the data is not exhaustive, it is an undeniable fact that millions of girls are forced into marriage globally when they are children.

All over the world, attempts have been made to legislate on the age of marriage to control child marriages. A survey of the age of marriage operative in different countries reveals that the minimum age of marriage for girls generally varies between twelve and twenty-one in different countries.[7] In some countries where customary law prevails over legislation, there is no limit put on the minimum age of marriage of girls, for example in Ghana.[8] In Nigeria, the customary law recognises nine years as the minimum age for girls.[9] In most of those countries where there is a statutory law on the age of marriage, legal rules generally provide for the legal age of marriage and the relaxed age of marriage.[10] At the legal age, the person gets freedom to marry without seeking approval from any person. On the contrary, at the relaxed age of marriage one may be allowed to marry, subject to one or the other condition such as consent of parents or in their absence of consent of other guardians and/or special dispensation by the court.

India also has legislation on the age of marriage, namely, the Child Marriage Restraint Act, 1929 (CMRA). It prescribes the minimum age of marriage as eighteen years for girls and twenty-one years for boys. It does not provide for relaxation in the age of marriage. There is no provision to marry either with the consent of parents or with the special dispensation by the court. Under CMRA, child marriage is an offence for which very mild punishment is provided. It is either fine or imprisonment up to a maximum of three months. Child marriage, being a crime, is an illegal act but once performed the marriage is valid. CMRA does not provide for the registration of a marriage. Nor does it require the consent of the parties to the marriage. If a complaint is lodged that a child marriage has been arranged or is about to be solemnized, the court has the power to issue an injunction to prohibit such child marriage. However, before issuing such an injunction against any person, the court is required to give prior notice to such person and has to give him an opportunity to show cause against the issue of such injunction. The offence relating to child marriage is allowed to be investigated only for the period of one year from the date of its commission. The law is secular and is applicable to all citizens of India irrespective of their religion. In spite of having legislative regulation, the practice of child marriage is prevalent on a large scale in India.

Child marriage of girls is a comparatively neglected social problem in India and is seldom given attention by policy makers, law interpreters, law enforcement machinery, and academicians. Recently, a few non-governmental organizations have started addressing the issue more seriously.[11] Some efforts are being made by the National Commission for Women and the National Commission for Human Rights.[12]

Child marriage affects both girls and boys and deprives children of their childhood. However, girls are affected disproportionately. Not only are they far more likely than boys to be married early, but the practice also has more dire consequences for girls than for boys. Often these girls are married to older men. A sexual relationship between the spouses that is inevitable after the marriage affects the health of young girls, particularly their reproductive health as their bodies are not physically mature to accept the burden of child-bearing. Further, they often do not have information about sex and childbirth.

Once married they are responsible for carrying out domestic chores of which they have little knowledge. Often they suffer from domestic violence and sexual abuse. Due to their young age, they are incapable of negotiating with their life partners on all counts including sex. They are likely to become widows at a younger age. Further, as a result of child marriages, girls are deprived of their educational opportunities. Lack of education takes away their future opportunities of gainful employment as well as of personality development and, therefore, the happiness of life. Thus child marriage makes them slaves. In spite of having such severe long-term consequences on the life of young girls, the practice of child marriage is still justified in the name of culture, religion, and morality.

Millions of girls are married off at an early age not only without their consent but also even against their wishes. There is not enough awareness about the adverse impact of child marriage on the lives of young girls. The issue of child marriage is seldom examined from the human rights perspective. Social scientists have by and large addressed this issue from the demographic, population, and health perspectives.[13] It is difficult for the providers of health care to deal with the socially contentious issue of child marriage, as they have not been trained to handle the problem. Legal professionals have not paid enough attention to the issue. Against this background, the problem of child marriage in India is analysed in this book from the human rights perspective and by adopting a feminist method.

Critical analysis of any social problem from a human rights perspective is a challenge, particularly in the developing countries and that too when it is connected to women's human rights. Arguments against universal application of human rights, particularly women's human rights, are raised in the name of religion, culture, social values, and morality. The basis of such arguments lies in the patriarchal social structure and many times it takes the form of paternalistic control over women with an emphasis on the need to provide *protection* to women.

The Term 'Child Marriage'

The term 'child marriage' must be understood in its proper perspective as the two words are quite contradictory. Marriage is a formalized relationship with legal standing between an individual man and woman, in which sexual relations are legitimized. Obviously, one would expect such a relationship only between two consenting adults. How can a child be party to a marriage, when she is unable to understand the nature and consequences of it? How can she comply with the responsibilities that follow such marriage when she is unaware of them? Is it then correct to use the term 'child marriage'?

The term 'child marriage'—that is marriage below the age of eighteen years—is used here for a number of reasons, the first being to emphasize the paradox in the prevalent practice of marrying young girls. Second, in

India legislators, social workers, and law professionals refer to the practice by the term 'child marriage'. Third, a girl below the age of eighteen years is treated as a 'child' for the purpose of marriage according to CMRA. The Indian Majority Act, 1875, also defines the age of majority as eighteen years for the purpose of civil matters.[14] Even the Constitution of India gives the right to vote to a person who is eighteen years of age.[15] So is the case while entering into a valid contract under the Indian Contract Act, 1872.[16] Therefore, in the Indian context 'child marriage' is the proper term. Even the United Nations' Convention on the Right of the Child defines 'child' as a person below the age of eighteen years.

Other terms used by the international community for child marriage are 'early marriage' or 'forced marriage'. These terms have limitations. The term 'early' could be very subjective. Early in comparison to what and for whom are the basic questions that could have different answers in different contexts. Early marriage is also being defined as marriage of a girl before or during adolescence.[17] However, in developing countries like India, rarely is there a stage of carefree adolescence in the life of girls. They are forced to step from childhood into womanhood directly.

All child marriages are forced marriages. But all forced marriages are not necessarily child marriages. The force implies that there is a use of power against the wish of an individual and it is against the person's free consent. In case of a child marriage, there is no question of consent as the girl child is incapable of giving a valid legal consent due to her incomplete physical and mental growth. And even if she is able to express her wish, she is either not allowed to express it or is forced to act against her wishes. On the other hand, even adults could be forced to enter into a marriage in a country like India where marriages are 'arranged' by parents as a norm.

Focus on the Girl Child

Child marriage violates many of the basic rights of children. It involves both girls and boys, but because of the low status of girls, they are usually married off at a much younger age than boys in many countries and to much older men.[18] Child marriage has profound physical, psychological, intellectual, and emotional consequences, particularly on girl children, as it cuts off their educational opportunities and chances for personal development.

Based on the view that 'virginity' is essential in a bride, girls are married off at a young age. As a result, these young girls are traumatized by sex and are forced to bear children before their bodies are fully mature. Parents believe that girls are less valuable than boys. They are viewed as economic burdens because it is costly to raise daughters when the money can be better spent on sons, who will take care of the parents in their old age. Moreover, laws and policies allowing for a lower age of marriage for women stereotype women as child-bearing machines and deny them equal standing with men with respect to their right to consent to marriage. For these reasons, the focus of this book is on the girl children.

Feminist Method

As argued by Ratna Kapur:

> Feminist analysis of law examines the role that law plays in the oppression of women, and the role that law might play in overcoming that oppression. It attempts to go beyond the mere identification of laws that impact on women, to examine the specific conditions of women and analyses the role of law at different points of interaction—conceptual, institutional or community-based. It is an interdisciplinary approach to understand the complex and contradictory nature of the legal regulation of women.[19]

Feminist legal analysis explores the social, economic, political, and cultural factors that cause and reinforce women's oppression. It seeks to reveal social structures, institutions, and relations that have made and continue to make women subordinate to men. It examines the particular ways in which the law has been informed by male norms, male experiences, male values, and male dominance. In doing so, it tries to demonstrate the exclusion of women's experiences from law and the ways in which law serves to reinforce stereotyped and patriarchal assumptions about women.[20] At the same time, it also explores the extent to which law can be used to improve women's position.

Precisely for this reason, the practice of child marriage needs to be challenged within the feminist legal analysis. As against the traditional legal method, Katharine Bartlett's feminist legal method 'Asking the Woman Question'[21] as well as Denise Reaume's conceptual analysis of women's exclusion from law[22] provides the best support for analysing child marriages from the feminist perspective for many reasons.

For the analysis of any socio-legal issue, legal method is important because it shapes one's views of the possibilities for legal practice and reform.

Method 'organises the appreciation of truth, it determines what counts as evidence and defines what it takes as verification'.[23] However, feminist legal method is more relevant than the traditional legal method as it goes into deeper analysis of the issue from feminist perspectives.

Traditional legal method operates within a highly structured framework, which offers little opportunity for fundamental questioning about the process of defining the issues, selecting relevant principles, and excluding irrelevant ideas.[24] It places a high premium on the predictability, certainty, and fixity of rules. On the other hand, feminist legal methods value rules of flexibility and ability to identify missing points of view.

While using traditional legal method, lawyers examine the facts, determine what legal principles are relevant, and then apply those principles to the facts. Facts determine which rules are appropriate, and rules determine which facts are relevant. In doing so, traditional lawyers use a full range of methods of legal reasoning—deduction, induction, analogy—and use hypotheticals, policy, and other general principles.[25] Feminists, in addition, use other methods by which they attempt to reveal those features of the traditional method that are suppressed or overlooked. They unmask the specific assumptions of class, gender, sexuality, and religion on which the law is often premised and confront the assumption of legal neutrality and objectivity, which often serves to mask these underlying assumptions.

The traditional legal method defines its own boundaries. Questions which are inside the defined boundaries are addressed but those outside the boundaries are not 'legal' issues.

It is structured in such a way that it is inaccessible to a feminist perspective and thus women's life experiences are not *relevant* for it.[26] On the other hand, feminist methods expand the traditional notion of legal relevance to be more sensitive to features of a case not reflected in the legal doctrine.[27]

Asking the Woman Question

The feminist legal method, 'Asking the Woman Question' challenges the assumption of gender neutrality of law. The woman question asks about the gender implications of social practice or rule: have women been left out of consideration? If so, in what way and how might that omission be corrected? What difference would it make on corrections? By posing such questions, it challenges those rules and practices that do not take cognizance of women's experiences, which are different from that of men.[28]

Asking the woman question reveals the ways in which political choices and institutional arrangements contribute to women's subordination. Without the woman question, differences associated with women are taken for granted. In exposing the hidden effects of laws that do not explicitly discriminate on the basis of sex, the woman question helps to demonstrate how social structures embody norms that implicitly render women different and thereby subordinate.[29] The woman question reveals how the position of women reflects the organization of society. The difference is located in relationships and social institutions and not in women themselves.

Katherine Bartlett explains:

> In law, asking the woman question means examining how the law fails to take into account the experiences and values that seem more typical of women than of men, for whatever reason, or how existing legal standards and concepts might disadvantage women. The question assumes that some features of the law may not be only non-neutral in a general sense, but also 'male' in a specific sense. The purpose of the woman question is to expose those features and how they operate, and to suggest how they might be corrected.[30]

'Asking the Woman Question' requires a search for gender bias and a decision in the case that is defensible in the light of that bias. It demands, in other words, special attention to a set of interests and concerns that otherwise may be, and historically have been, overlooked. The substance of asking the woman question lies in what it seeks to uncover: disadvantage based upon gender.[31]

In the context of child marriage, asking the woman question requires an examination of the gendered conditions that facilitate or enable child marriage, and the laws intended to regulate it. It requires attention to the ways in which women's experiences and interests have been overlooked. When society approves the practice of child marriage of young girls, it fails to recognize the damaging physical, psychological, social, economic, and developmental repercussions on young women. Or when the law does not declare such practice as illegal or leaves many procedural lacunas, it leaves out women's considerations. Further, an ineffective implementation of CMRA confirms omission of their consideration.

Cultural approval of the practice of child marriage is a clear indication of society's refusal to take cognizance of its adverse effects on women. The practice of child marriage often victimizes girls and they are the ones who suffer the most. They typically face harmful experiences only because of their biological vulnerability. Only women can become pregnant and young girls can suffer because of their immature bodies. The adverse impact of child marriage on women's life is either taken for granted, remains unexamined or is justified under the guise of their need of *protection* from vulnerability and sexual abuse. Similarly, development opportunities, including that of education, are not denied to boys even if they are married off at a young age. Marriage has different meanings for men and women because of women's low social status. An obvious reason behind this is to treat women as subordinate to men.

It is argued that societal pressure and cultural values force parents to marry off their young daughters. Why such values are most vehemently employed when the rights of women are at stake? Why are girls deprived of their rights simply because of their sex, in the guise of culture, tradition, or religion? This certainly is not to suggest that there are no cultural considerations or accommodations to be made while dealing with human rights. However, there is a distinction between considering or accommodating cultural customs, and using culture as a pretext to deny the integrity and dignity of individuals on the basis of sex.[32] The cultural practice that abridges the basic human rights including the right to life, health, education, enjoyment, non-discrimination, and to live with dignity must be condemned at all times.

Social and cultural values have legally reflected men's experiences, and excluded women from participating in the definition of those values. Women also support such values and the customary practices based on those values because they are not being given free choices. Given their economic and political disempowerment, it is not amazing if they support such traditions. To understand the phenomenon of women's support one must probe more deeply.[33] Women are made to believe that it is in their interest as well as in the interest of their families to support such tradition. Women support retrograde traditions, but not on the basis of free will or informed choice. They are compelled by circumstances, lacking as they are in independence and decision making powers. This reflects on how social institutions are built up on patriarchal foundations with a gender bias.

The 'woman question' exposes these assumptions. It challenges social endorsement of child marriages. A feminist methodology strives to ensure that society will no longer ignore women's experiences. Based on women's experiences, society must be made to understand that such harmful, traditional practice of child marriage needs to be condemned.

Conceptual Analysis of Women's Exclusion from Law

The social reality of not providing space to women's experiences or excluding their experiences is also manifested while formulating, applying, or enforcing the law. Denise Reaume's conceptual analysis of women's exclusion from law is of great value in understanding this situation.[34] She argues that legal rules are designed in such a way that they reflect the life experiences, interests, and needs of men, to the exclusion of those of women; that key legal concepts or principles exclude women's values; that legal reasoning excludes women's mode of reasoning.[35] This feminist critique of law can be applied at all levels of legal analysis of child marriage—legislative framework, judicial interpretation, and enforcement of rules regarding child marriages.

As put forward by Reaume, the exclusion of women is sometimes explicit and at other times, implicit. Explicit exclusion clearly excludes women in a very obvious form, on the face of law. The mechanism of exclusion is sometimes legislative, sometimes judicial interpretation. These rules operate explicitly and directly to exclude women. For example, while their husbands are alive women are excluded from the legal guardianship of their children in India.[36] Adultery is an offence under the Indian Penal Code only if committed by a man and allows only the husband of the 'adulteress' to prosecute the man with whom the adultery was committed, but does not allow the wife of that man to prosecute him.[37] Even the judicial decisions have conformed to this legal provision.[38]

Implicit exclusion operates through rules or decisions that are sex-neutral[39] on their face, but which nevertheless assume a male norm. This form of exclusion may be quite deliberate or simply based on unawareness of the different circumstances or conditions of women.[40] I argue in the following pages that enforcement and judicial interpretations of CMRA indicate such implicit exclusion of women's experiences.

An approach that draws attention to the explicit and implicit exclusion of women can be seen as a more specific example of the woman question.[41] The woman question involves identifying and challenging those elements of the existing legal doctrines that exclude or disadvantage women.

Explicit Exclusion

Women's experiences and perspectives have not been taken into account seriously by Indian society.[42] In other words, women's experiences, interests, and needs are excluded or ignored explicitly by the society. Legitimacy accorded to the practice of child marriage through social norms, customs, and laws makes it clear that the patriarchal social order explicitly prefers to exclude those values that women cherish.

The legal provision regarding the age of the parties to a marriage under CMRA reflects the explicit exclusion of women's experiences. CMRA prescribes different ages of marriage for girls and boys. The age disparity at marriage between men and women is rooted in stereotyped gender roles and in a patriarchal presumption that a man needs more time to equip himself to support his life and wife. It underscores the presumption of her economic dependency on the husband. Women are allocated the roles of wives and mothers and their identity is neutralized through a broad range of social, cultural, and religious discourses. It is based on the dominant familial ideology[43] and preconceived notion of presumed inequality between man and woman. The legal provision of age reflects and reinforces this dominant familial ideology and the differences that it assigns.

Certain indefensible factors of sexual bias—culturally created conceptions of the relative places of male and female in society—combined with other less indefensible reasons—more rapid physical development among females than among males—produce different rules for males and females in an otherwise comparable situation. The male perspective is exclusively reflected in this provision. Such differentiation therefore results in the explicit exclusion of women's perspective and thereby discriminates against them.[44]

As Martha Minow argues, there are many unstated assumptions that inform the differences including the assumptions that (a) these are intrinsic, not relational; (b) the perspective of a person seeing is assumed to be objective; (c) the perspective of those being judged is irrelevant; and (d) existing social and economic arrangements are natural and neutral.[45] By applying her argument to the law of age of marriage one finds that the different and lower age prescription for girls is treated by law as intrinsic; the legislators, who are overwhelmingly male, feel that the prescribed age difference is objective; and girls' perspective is treated as irrelevant and the legal acceptance of the lower age for girls is based on social and economic arrangements that are treated as natural. This results in a denial of equality to women and therefore discriminates against them.

Implicit Exclusion

Men and women are exposed to different concrete social conditions and pressures, and consequently they have different life experiences. Women and men's different physical characteristics also sometimes contribute to it. However, the legislative, executive, and judicial personnel attach importance only to men's experiences, either unconsciously or on purpose. CMRA is drafted in such a way that it pays merely lip service to the cause of preventing child marriage. The major substantial and procedural lacunae in CMRA and its weak enforcement implicitly exclude women's experiences.

CMRA is silent about the legal consequence of a child marriage. It declares child marriage as an offence without affecting the validity of marriage. Usually girls are given as children in marriages. Child marriages have more severe and serious effects on girls than boys—on their physical and psychological health, on educational and other opportunities, and on their personality development. These experiences are not valued by the law as child marriage is not declared invalid. The failure to take full account of the devastating effect of child marriage on women results in a situation that meets the needs and interests of women less than those of men. This reflects patriarchal bias and thereby disadvantages girls.

CMRA does not require the consent of the parties nor does it provide for the compulsory registration of the marriage. It does not make offences cognizable nor does it provide severe punishment to the offenders. Had the state agencies taken women's experiences into account, the law might have been different. Inclusion of such provisions would have helped prevent child marriages. It might have also been enforced with more seriousness. Such exclusion of women's experiences takes place because of an indifferent attitude to the conditions of women's lives. Prima facie the absence of such provisions appear gender-neutral. However, it assumes that the experiences of men are universally applicable. Reaume would call this as implicit exclusion of women's experiences.

The judicial interpretation of CMRA so far has also indicated apathy towards the issue of child marriage. So far, it has not looked into the issue of child marriage from the feminist perspective. Neither has it held the government responsible for its failure to prohibit child marriages nor has it inquired into what measures the government has taken for the effective implementation of the law. The judiciary has not questioned the government about what alternatives are made available to girls who are not married off at young age. The judiciary thus excludes women's experiences implicitly. To stop the marriages of young girls in future, inquiry based on the woman question would help bring justice to the doorsteps of adolescent girls.

Human Rights Approach

The practice of child marriage in India can be challenged from the human rights perspective for many reasons. Human rights law establishes a minimal order of forbearance or moral baseline to allow personal development through the pursuance of individual goals.[46] The human rights discourse offers a significant vocabulary to formulate political and social grievances.[47] It lends legitimacy to political demands since it is already accepted by most governments and brings with it established protocols. It is a powerful tool to denounce those acts of omission and commission on the part of the state that transgress against the essence of humanness.[48] Human rights law does have an impact on the behaviour of persons inside and outside of government, as over the last fifty years there has developed an international climate that is less willing to tolerate abuses and more willing to promote and protect human rights.

Individuals expect protection from the state; indeed, one of its fundamental purposes is to provide institutional and other means to ensure the safety and well-being of those within its power.[49] When the state violates human rights, these are the wrongs committed not only against the individual victims but also against the social order and add an element of indignity and frustration.[50] Therefore, the use of human rights arguments along with the constitutional provisions in the national forum can help remedy the injustice. It can have a deterrent effect on those who commit violations and may thereby deter future violations.[51] The compliance with human rights norms by the national judiciary can also help to lead to a positive perception of judicial legitimacy and influence the promotion of the rule of law.[52]

The human rights approach offers a more complete analysis to the issue of child marriage than the demographic, population, and health approaches as they focus more on the social impact of child marriage than on the life of a girl child. A human rights approach requires a holistic analysis of the causes and consequences of child marriage. It requires child marriage to be seen as a part of discrimination against girls. It also requires that family concerns regarded as private matters be understood as public matters. It insists that child marriage must be seen as part of a larger social agenda of any society that is committed to recognizing the full potential of all its members without any discrimination.

I want to illustrate how child marriage violates the standards set out in the major international human rights instruments. International human rights law has not been applied effectively to redress the disadvantages and injustices experienced by women when they are married off as children. The reasons for such failure are complex. They include lack of understanding of systemic nature of the subordination of women, failure to recognize the need to characterize the subordination of women as a human rights violation, and lack of state practice to condemn discrimination against women.[53]

My objective is to argue on behalf of those girls who have become victims of child marriages and whose human rights are violated by reason of the fact that they are girls. The exclusion of women's experiences on the ground of gender becomes the basis upon which violence against them is tolerated. The lack of understanding of women's human rights is reflected in the fact that governments are not fully committed to women's equality as a basic human right. Women's subordination runs so deep that it is still viewed as inevitable or natural rather than as a politically constructed reality maintained by patriarchal interests, ideology, and institutions. The distinction between private and public spheres is often used to justify female subordination and to exclude human rights abuse in the home from public scrutiny.

My arguments rely on expanding the traditional interpretation of public sphere human rights doctrine to prevent the private practice of child marriage.[54] I demonstrate thereby that the Indian state has neglected to comply with its obligations under the major international conventions, viz., the International Covenant on Civil and Political Rights, 1966 (ICCPR), the International Covenant on Economic, Social and Cultural Rights, 1966 (ICESCR),[55] the Convention on the Elimination of All Forms of Discrimination Against Women, 1979 (the Women's Convention),[56] the Convention on the Rights of the Child, 1989 (the Children's Convention),[57] the Convention on the Consent to Marriage, Minimum Age for Marriage and Registration of Marriages, 1962 (the Marriage Convention) and the Supplementary Convention on the Abolition of Slavery, the Slave Trade, and Institutions and Practices Similar to Slavery, 1956 (the Slavery Convention). Various rights recognized under all these conventions that are violated by child marriage are the right to equality on grounds of sex and age, right to marry and found a family, right to life and survival, right to liberty and security, right to the highest attainable standard of health, right to information, right to education and development, and right to be free from slavery.

The Children's Convention, one of the most important international conventions in the context of children's rights, does not specifically prohibit the practice of child marriage. Despite this gap, I argue that the general prohibition against discrimination on the grounds of sex and age can be interpreted to require countries to take appropriate means to eliminate child marriages. Child marriage disproportionately impacts girls because of their sex, and the lack of equal application of the law to girl children. However, violations that primarily affect boys, for example child soldiers, are included in the Children's Convention. The discrimination against girl children is thereby reflected in it. That other treaties contain provisions against child marriage is not a sufficient reason to exclude a provision against child marriage.[58] Though the monitoring bodies are making serious efforts to bring in the gender perspective,[59] I argue that these bodies need to confront the practice of child marriage more seriously and effectively by asking the woman question.

Overview

In this book, the issue of child marriage is explored from a holistic perspective—by examining the social, religious, cultural, and legal barriers in prohibiting the harmful practice of child marriage in India. In the first chapter, I document the incidence of child marriages in India with the help of demographic data. Such documentation is essential as it reflects the gravity of the problem. Analysis of these data also becomes relevant to understand how the situation changes in different settings in the country and how different variables influence patterns of human behaviour. The chapter then proceeds to analyse various social, cultural, and economic reasons behind the practice of child marriages as well as its consequences on the lives of young girls. I argue that for whatever historical reasons a particular social practice was adopted, it must change in the near future. Particularly so, when that practice is violative of the basic rights of a section of the society. Cultural values justified in a patriarchal set-up must be transformed to non-discriminatory, humane values. The patriarchal social order has to face the challenges that are posed by human rights and feminist jurisprudence. Based on this analysis, I suggest the remedial measures that need to be pursued by all those who strive for human rights of young girls.

The second chapter is on the legal discourse on the age of marriage. The chapter focuses on the Indian law. It accounts for the historical developments that led to the enactment of the Child Marriage Restraint

Act in 1929 (CMRA) with a view to restraining marriages below a particular age. A thorough analysis of CMRA along with the judicial treatment of the subject is done in this chapter. To understand the far-reaching consequences of legislation it has to be understood in the broader legal framework. It needs to be connected to other relevant laws.

The discussion in this chapter, therefore, moves on to analyse the other relevant legislation in India including the Constitution and the penal laws. The third chapter analyses the provisions of the various religion-based personal laws of marriage. I argue that the lack of an understanding and a lack of political will on the part of lawmakers about the grave repercussions of the practice of child marriages are some of the reasons for the failure of the law on age of marriage. I argue that the judiciary can play a more constructive role to promote the rights of young girls. I also criticize the judiciary for not playing the educative role of creating public awareness about the harmful consequences of child marriage on girls.

The fourth chapter analyses how international human rights conventions can be used to improve compliance with the human rights of adolescent girls. The role played by the treaty bodies is extremely relevant. I argue that the treaty bodies need to communicate to states parties that child marriage is a form of domestic violence[60] and needs to be dealt with more seriously and holistically. In this discussion references to various United Nations international conferences is inevitable. I analyse how various human rights elaborated in the international instruments are violated by the practice of marrying young girls. In the fifth and sixth chapters there is a detailed discussion on the different kinds of harm that is caused to adolescent girls, particularly in the Indian situation and an analysis of the extent to which India has complied with her international obligations.

Apart from legislative action, I also identify supportive measures taken by the Indian government so as to curb the practice of child marriage and fulfil its responsibilities. My argument is that the Indian government has not paid as much attention as it should have to the issue of marriage of young girls. There is merely tokenism on the part of the Indian government without any serious commitment to resolve the problem of child marriage.

In the last chapter, I discuss various strategies that need to be adopted in future. How can the public be motivated to comply with the minimum age requirement? What alternatives to child marriage are possible? How can the culture of women's economic independence as a value in a family and community be promoted? How can self-enforcement incentives among the citizens—such as the concern for girl children, their status, health, development, and common good—be promoted? I suggest that the inclusion of women's experiences at all levels—amending all relevant laws and applying as well as enforcing those laws with gender sensitivity—would help improve the situation.

Conclusion

My thesis is that law must have a role in effecting social change. If it is not harnessed in support of progress, it obstructs attempts to redress patriarchy. Unless the law articulates and recognizes the rights of people, redressal of violation of human rights is difficult. From this perspective, law must be seen as empowering. However, the programme of using the law in support of a change is a complex process and, in the final analysis, is only one element, though an important one, of a necessarily multi-faceted approach. One needs to adopt more realistic appraisal of the limitations of the law. The myths that presently imbue law with its apparent sanctity must be abandoned. I argue therefore, that along with the reforms in the existing laws, a movement creating a legal culture, making the active agents sensitive to the consequences of child marriage, and furnishing meaningful viable alternatives to young girls, is required to be built up. The responsibility for this lies with civil society.

The effectiveness of law depends upon a number of factors. Commitment of the government by employing effective enforcement machinery to control the mischief that law is trying to correct and legitimacy of the law are the two major factors responsible. In the context of social legislation, the success of the law also depends upon the extent to which the beneficiaries of the law are in a position to make use of that law. However, people's awareness of the law, their access to it and capacity to use it with confidence are essential prerequisites for its effectiveness. For such a law to be effective, it must be backed up by supportive alternatives. And lastly, when the beneficiaries of such a law are children, there is an obligation on the adults to comply with the provisions of that law. Unfortunately, in India, none of the above factors contributes in a significant way in relation to the law that is supposed to prevent child marriages. CMRA is followed more in breach than in compliance. In the following pages, I put forth a deeper, critical analysis of the social reality, different laws at the national and international level, and try to suggest the line of future action for promoting human rights of young girls and thereby improving their status.

Appendix

Minimum Legal Age at Marriage by Region and Country[61]

Africa

Country	Year Reported	Age of Girl	Age of Boy	Country	Year Reported	Age of Girl	Age of Boy
Algeria	1980	16	18	Mauritius	1983	15	18
Cameroon	1980	15	18	Niger	1979	16	18
Egypt	1983	16	18	Nigeria	1979	9–16	9–16
Ghana	1980	None to 21	None to 21	South Africa	1980	16	18
				Uganda	1980	16	18
Mali	1980	15	18	Zambia	1979	16	16

Americas

Country	Year Reported	Age of Girl	Age of Boy	Country	Year Reported	Age of Girl	Age of Boy
Argentina	1984	14	16	Mexico	1983	14	16
Brazil	1984	16	16	Peru	1984	14	16
Canada	1976	12–16	14–16	USA	1979	13–17	14–18
Chile	1984	12	14	Venezuela	1984	12	14
Guatemala	1983	14	16				

Asia

Country	Year Reported	Age of Girl	Age of Boy	Country	Year Reported	Age of Girl	Age of Boy
Bangladesh	1982	18	22	Nepal	1977	16	18
China	1984	20	22	Pakistan	1982	16	21
India	1978	18	21	The Philippines	1983	14	16
Indonesia	1877	16	19	Sri Lanka	1979	12–16	16–18
Malaysia	1983	14	16	Thailand	1977	17	17

End Notes

[1] UNICEF: *Child Marriages Must Stop*, Press Release on 8 March 2001; Web site address www.unicef.org/newsline/01pr21.htm. See also UNICEF, New York, 'Too Many Teen Brides', in *The Progress of Nations 1998*, for global information regarding the extent of child marriage. See also Forum on Early Marriage, *Early Marriage Whose Right to Choose?* (UK: Forum on Marriage, 2000) at 6 [hereinafter *Early Marriage*]; The Alan Guttmacher Institute, *Into A New World, Young Women's Sexual and Reproductive Lives* (New York: The Alan Guttmacher Institute, 1998) [hereinafter *Into A New World*] 15–16; UN, Department of International Economic and Social Affairs, *Adolescent Reproductive Behaviour: Evidence from Developing Countries*, Vol. II (New York, 1989).

[2] Anti-Slavery International, Submission made to the Committee on the Rights of Child, *Role of the Family in the Promotion of the Rights of the Child*, General Discussion Day, 10 October (London: Anti-Slavery International, 1994).

[3] *Into A New World*, supra note 1 at 51.

[4] Ibid.

[5] International Institute of Population Science (IIPS), 'Summary of Findings'—*National Family Health Survey(NFHS)-2, 1998–99, India* (Mumbai: IIPS, 2000) at xx.

[6] I use the term 'married *off*' throughout the book, as my argument is that girls are treated as a burden by their parents and by marrying them, parents are relieved of the burden.

[7] The tables in the appendix show the minimum legal age at marriage by region and country.

[8] See Appendix at xlii.

[9] Ibid.

[10] Tahir Mahmood, 'Marriage-Age in India and Abroad—A Comparative Aspect' (1980) 22 *Journal of Indian Law Institute* 38 at 71–6.

[11] For instance, non-governmental organization VISHAKA is active in Rajasthan.

[12] See Chapter Two for a discussion on NCW at 54 and Chapter Seven on NHRC at 213.

[13] Shireen Jejeebhoy, 'Adolescent Sexual and Reproductive Behaviour: A Review of the evidence from India' in Radhika Ramasubban and Shireen Jejeebhoy (eds), *Women's Reproductive Health in India* (New Delhi: Rawat Publications, 2000) at 40; Sanjeevanee Mulay, 'Demographic Transition in Maharashtra, 1980–93' (1999) 34 *Economic and Political Weekly* 3063; Tara

Kanitkar, 'National Family Health Survey: Some Thoughts' (1999) 34 *Economic and Political Weekly* 3081.

[14] Though the Act is not applicable in the matter of marriage.

Section 3 provides that a person domiciled in India shall be deemed to have attained his majority when he completes his age of eighteen years and not before.

Section 2 provides that nothing in the Act shall affect the capacity of any person to act in the following matters: marriage, divorce, and adoption. Thus the provision is applicable to all civil matters except that of marriage, divorce, and adoption.

[15] Article 328 of the Constitution.

[16] Section 11: Every person is competent to contract who is of the age of majority according to the law which he is subject to and who is of sound mind and is not disqualified from contracting by any law to which he is subject.

[17] *Early Marriage*, supra note 1 at 6.

[18] E.g. Nigeria, Ethiopia, Bangladesh, Nepal, etc.

[19] Ratna Kapur, 'Guest Editorial' (1993) 1 *National Law School Journal*, Special Issue on Feminism and Law viii at viii and ix.

[20] Ibid.

[21] Katharine T. Bartlett, 'Feminist Legal Methods' (1990) 103 *Harv. L. Rev.*, 829–88.

[22] Denise Reaume, 'What is distinctive about feminist analysis of law?: A Conceptual Analysis of Women's Exclusion from Law' (1996) 2 *Legal Theory* 265.

[23] Catherine MacKinnon, 'Feminism, Marxism, Method and the State: An Agenda for Theory' (1987) 7 *SIGNS* 515 at 527.

[24] Mossman Mary Jane, 'Feminism and Legal Method: The Difference it Makes' (1986) 3 *Australian Journal of Law and Society* 30 at 32.

[25] Bartlett, supra note 21 at 836.

[26] Mossman, supra note 24 at 44–5.

[27] Bartlett, supra note 21 at 837.

[28] Ibid.

[29] Ibid. at 843.

[30] Ibid. at 837.

[31] Berta Esperanza Hernandez-Truyol, 'Women's Rights as Human Rights—Rules, Realities and the Role of Culture: A formula for Reform' (1996) 21 *Brooklyn Journal International Law* 605 at 668–71.

[32] Ibid. at 666.

[33] Martha Nussbaum, *Women and Human Development* (New York: Cambridge University, 2000) at 42–3.

[34] Reaume, supra note 22 at 271.

[35] Ibid. at 272.

[36] Section 6 of the Hindu Minority and Guardianship Act states that the father is the natural guardian and only in his absence the mother. Significantly though, in *Geeta Hariharan* v. *RBI & anr.* AIR 2001 SC 123 it has been held that the absence of the father means his physical absence at a specific time and not his death. According to the Muslim personal law, the mother is never a natural and legal guardian of her minor children.

[37] Section 497 of the Indian Penal Code.

[38] *Abdul Aziz* v. *Bombay* AIR 1954 SC 321; *Sowmitri Vishnu* v. *Union of India* AIR 1985 SC 1618. The exclusion of women may not be fully visible on the face of the law in these cases, but it is a crucial and explicit part of its rationale. However, adultery by a spouse is a ground for divorce under the provisions of most of the personal law systems in India.

[39] But not necessarily gender-neutral. See Joan C. Willimas, 'Deconstructing Gender' in Katherine Bartlett & Rosanne Kennedy (eds), *Feminist Legal Theory: Reading in Law and Gender* (1991) 112.

[40] Reaume, supra note 22 at 278.

[41] Ibid. at 294. She mentions that Bartlett covers both explicit and implicit exclusion though without making such distinction.

[42] See Deborah Rhode, 'The "Woman's Point of View"' (1988) 38 *Journal of Legal Education* 39; Sarah Brown, 'Feminism, International Theory, and International Relations of Gender Inequality' (1988) 17 *Millennium* 461 at 472. She argues that women's voice must find a public audience in order to reorient the boundaries of mainstream human rights law so that it incorporates an understanding of the world from the perspective of the socially subjugated. According to her this is the central task of feminist theory.

[43] Ratna Kapur and Brenda Cossman, 'Familial Ideology and the Constitution' in Ratna Kapur (ed.), *Feminist Terrain in Legal Domains* (New Delhi: Kali for Women, 1996) at 68–9.

[44] Leo Karowitz, 'Law and the Single Girl' in *Women and the Law: Unfinished Protection* (1969) at 11.

[45] Martha Minow, 'Forward: Justice Engendered' (1987) 101 *Harvard Law Review* 10 at 34–54.

[46] Dinah Shelton, *Remedies in International Human Rights Law* (New York: Oxford University Press, 1999) at 39.

[47] Rebecca Cook, Bernard Dickens, et al., Advancing *Safe Motherhood through Human Rights* (Geneva: WHO, 2000) at 3.

[48] Elisabeth Friedman, 'Women's Human Rights: The Emergence of a Movement' in Julie Peters and Andrea Wolper (eds), *Women's Rights Human Rights* (New York: Routledge, 1995) at 19.

[49] R. Pound, *Social Control Through Law* (1942) at 25.

[50] Ibid.

[51] Shelton, supra note 46 at 37.

[52] S. Sturm, 'A Normative Theory of Public Law Remedies' (1991) 79 *Georgia Law Journal* 1357 at 1403.

[53] Rebecca Cook, 'Women's International Human Rights Law: The Way Forward', in Rebecca Cook (ed.), *Human Rights of Women* (Philadelphia: University of Pennsylvania, 1994) at 3.

[54] Celina Romany, 'Women as Aliens: A Feminist Critique of the Public/ Private Distinction in International Human Rights Law' (1993) 6 *Harv. Human Rights Journal* 87. See Hope Lewis, 'Between Irua and Female Genital Mutilation: Feminist Human Rights Discourse and the Cultural Divide' (1995) 8 *Harv. Human Rights Journal* 1; Donna Sullivan, 'The Public/Private Distinction in International Human Rights Law' in Julie Peters and Andrea Wolper (eds), supra note 48 at 126; Hilary Charlesworth, et al., 'Feminist Approaches to International Law' (1993) 85 *American Journal of International Law* 613 at 625–40; Charlotte Bunch, 'Women's Rights as Human Rights: Towards a Re-vision of Human Rights' (1990) 12 *Human Rights Quarterly* 486; Rebecca Cook, 'State Responsibility for Violation of Women's Human Rights' (1994) 7 *Harvard Human Rights Journal* 87; Abdullahi A. An-Naím, 'State Responsibility under International Human Rights Law to Change Religious and Customary Law' in Cook (ed.), supra note 53 at 167.

[55] There are also other regional conventions, viz., The European Convention on Human Rights, The American Convention on Human Rights and The African Charter on Human and Peoples' Rights. These are not discussed here as the focus here is on India where no such regional conventions have been formulated.

[56] The Convention on the Elimination of all Forms of Discrimination Against Women, G.A. Res. 34/180, UN GAOR, 34th Session, No. 46 at 193, UN Doc.A/39/45 (1979) (entered into force, 3 September 1981).

[57] The Convention on the Rights of the Child, G.A. Res. 44/25 (XLIV), UN GAOR, 44th Session, Supp. No. 49 at 167, UN Doc. A/44/49 (1989) (entered into force, Sept. 1990).

[58] See Ladan Askari, 'The Convention on the Rights of the Child: The Necessity of Adding a Provision to Ban Child Marriage' (1998) 5 *Journal of International and Comparative Law* 123.

[59] See Human Rights Committee, General Comment 28; See also Jane Connors, 'General Human Rights Instruments and their Relevance to Women', in Andrew Byrnes, et al. (eds), *Advancing the Human Rights of Women* (London: Commonwealth Secretariat, 1997) 27 at 34.

[60] Kirti Singh and Divya Kapur, 'Law, Violence and the Girl Child' (2001) 5 *Health and Human Rights* 8.

[61] *Source*: United Nations, *Adolescent Reproductive Behaviour: Evidence from Developing Countries,* Vol. II (New York: UN, 1989) at 42.

1

Dimensions of the Problem of Child Marriage in India: Causes and Consequences

Introduction

Around the world, there are many adolescents who are sexually active, some within marriage and others outside marriage.[1] In many developing countries sexual relations and pregnancy become socially, culturally, and legally acceptable only if they occur within marriage. Child marriages, i.e. marriages below the age of eighteen years for girls, are part of customary practices and are prevalent since time immemorial. Such marriages are also forced marriages as young girls are not mature enough either to make a choice of a life partner or to understand the meaning and responsibilities of marriage. Parents and family members are responsible for taking such major decisions on behalf of their children affecting their future life.

At the time of marriage, adolescent girls are not even physically mature enough to face the consequences of sexual relations. The major problems of young girls' reproductive health thus result from child marriage. Though these traditional practices of getting children married are giving way and first marriages are taking place at later ages all over the world, including developing countries, the age at which women marry continues to vary widely both across and within countries.[2]

What should be the minimum age of marriage and the age of consent for sex is a widely contested issue all over the world. Attempts have been made to respond to it not only at the national level, but also at the international level. In 1962, the United Nations adopted the Marriage Convention recognizing the importance of raising the age of marriage,[3] the origin of which could be traced back to the Slavery Convention.[4] It was followed by numerous conventions which condemned child marriage and included the right of every person to choose a spouse and to enter into marriage only with his or her free and full consent.[5] However, there is still no international consensus on defining child marriage, as the minimum age of marriage is not stipulated in any of these conventions.[6] The legal minimum age of marriage for girls in various countries, as pointed out in the Introduction, varies.[7] In some there is no such minimum age, in others it varies from age twelve to twenty-one.

This chapter begins with a brief comment on the nature and role of marriage in the life of a woman, which is followed by documenting the incidence of child marriage in India with the help of demographic data. Such documentation is essential to understand the magnitude of the problem that is prevalent in the country. It also explains how people have responded so far to the national and international legal norms regarding the age of marriage. The law is normative and prescriptive; and it describes how people *should* behave. On the other hand, social science is descriptive; it describes how people *do* behave.[8] The use of social science data becomes relevant in judging the impact of law on people's behaviour. I assess with the help of such data[9] whether the normative prescriptions regarding age at marriage have brought any change in marriage patterns in the country.

The chapter discusses causes of child marriage, which are many and common all over the world. But the extent of influence of these causes depends on the culture of each country. I discuss causes that are specific to the Indian culture along with common causes responsible for child marriages of girls.

The chapter proceeds further to analyse the consequences of child marriage, particularly on the reproductive health of young girls, with the help of epidemiological data. Considering the paucity of the research material on young girls' reproductive health generally in India, I refer to data not only from India but also from other regions and countries. Most of the research on young girls' reproductive health problems is hospital-based and is rarely carried out at the community level. Even such hospital-based data reveals the magnitude of the problem prevalent in many developing countries including India.

It will not be out of place to mention here that sexual activity of adolescents outside marriage is increasing in India,[10] a phenomenon already prevalent in the Western world particularly in North America.[11] Early onset of sexual activity has a profound effect on the health of young girls irrespective of whether it occurs within or outside marriage. Early child-bearing puts a woman's health, educational and employment opportunities, and her overall well-being at risk. These consequences then become fresh causes for the onset of early sexual activity also either within or outside marriage. This establishes the mutual relationship between the causes and consequences. These then become the systemic barriers in realizing human rights of adolescents. These rights are denied in the name of culture and tradition including fundamental rights such as the right to live or the right to live with dignity.

A question then is that in spite of such catastrophic results, why are young girls forced to face such situations within the socially approved practice of child marriage? I have made an endeavour to identify barriers faced by young girls in avoiding such marriages. At the end, the chapter summarizes the findings of the discussions. As a student of law, the question which comes to my mind is how law will be able to help solve these problems? Some solutions to these problems are examined in subsequent chapters.

Marriage in India

There are some notable features of marriage in India. Culturally, marriages are universal, arranged by the parents, occur at a young age for the girls and usually with a large age difference between the bride and the groom. Marriage in India is most often arranged between two families instead of between two individuals.[12] Marriage is traditionally a religious ceremony and sacred duty rather than a matter of personal convenience and preference.

In contrast to the North American and European society, where the conjugal family and the individual are at the core, in the traditional family structure in India, every individual is expected to be primarily under the control of the family through its head in particular and elders in general. Major decisions, like marriages in the family, are taken by these elders and are respected by younger individuals. Modern influences have made some impact on the institution of marriage, but the basic values and norms still remain unchanged. On the whole, parents and senior members of the family consider the marriage of a girl child to be a very serious responsibility and they play a key role in arranging the marriage in a traditional manner. Consequently, a large number of families still marry off their girls at an early age.

This custom of solemnizing the marriages of girl children is an entrenched social custom that has prevailed fairly widely, particularly amongst Hindus in India for several centuries.[13] The practice is integrally connected to the cultural heritage and tradition, which has its roots in the patriarchal social structure. It has been contended by legal writers that marriages in the Vedic period were effected when the couples reached a mature age. The girl's consent was always sought. She even had the freedom to choose her life partner.[14] This practice continued until the sixth and seventh centuries. Thereafter, it started to decline under the influence of Brahminic culture. The situation deteriorated further with the advent of Muslim invaders who used to kidnap young girls. In order to protect the women from sexual exploitation and preserve their chastity, pre-puberty marriage began to be considered the best option. With the passage of time it became an institutionalized custom, the violation of which was met with social disapproval and disgrace.[15] It was believed to be a sin to keep a girl in her parental home after she started menstruating.

Child Marriage: The Demographic Context

The timing of the marriage is an important dimension of women's reproductive behaviour with far-reaching consequences, particularly for their reproductive health and social status. Child marriage typically culminates in child-bearing at a young age.[16] Early pregnancy poses great health risks for a young woman and, if she carries the pregnancy to term, for her infant too. These risks are exacerbated by poverty, malnutrition, and inadequate access to maternal and child health care services.

In India the practice of child marriage is giving way to marriage at a later age; nonetheless, child marriages are still not uncommon. The country has one of the lowest median ages at marriage in the world.[17] Rajasthan has the lowest median age of marriage among women currently aged 20–24 years in the country. It is 15.9 years.[18]

According to the National Family Health Survey (NFHS) conducted in 1992–3, though there is some evidence of rise in the average age of marriage, a large percentage of girls are still getting married at a young age. The Singulate Mean Age at Marriage (SMAM) for women has gone up by 3.4 years from 15.9 years in 1961 to 19.3 years in 1991.[19] But still an average of 38.4 per cent girls in the age group of 15–19 years get married.[20] This percentage increases significantly in rural populations, where 44.7 per cent of girls in the age group of 15–19 were married which was more than double the rate of their urban counterparts where the percentage was 21.3.[21] The data also indicate that 11.8 per cent of girls are married by the age of thirteen years, 26.1 per cent by the age of fifteen years, 54.2 per cent by eighteen years and 71.4 per cent by the age of twenty years.[22] The median age at marriage is 17.4 years in the 20–24 age cohort. What is more disturbing is that almost 7 per cent and 17 per cent of girls are married before the age of thirteen and fifteen years respectively in the 15–19 age cohort. Currently, 54.2 per cent of women in the age group of 20–24 years get married before the age of eighteen years and this percentage is much higher in rural (63 per cent) than in urban areas (33 per cent).[23]

The second NFHS (NFHS-2) was conducted in 1998–9. It confirms the further rise in the age of marriage. The Singulate Mean Age at Marriage (SMAM) for women has gone up to 19.7 years[24] in 1998–9 from 19.3 years in 1991. But still an average of 34 per cent of women in the age group of 15–19 years are already married[25] as against 38.4 per cent as per NFHS. These proportions are higher in rural areas.[26] The median age at first marriage[27] has risen in the last six years from 17.4 to eighteen years in the 20–24 age cohort.[28] Marriage at very early ages is becoming less common. As per NFHS-2, 4.7 per cent (as against 7) and 14.3 per cent (as against 17) of girls are married before the age of thirteen and fifteen years respectively in the 15–19 age cohort.[29] The survey also shows that 50 per cent of women currently aged 20–24 years were married before the age of eighteen years as against 54.2 as per NFHS.[30] So, there is a decline by 4 per cent in six years. However, the urban-rural divide continues in the same way. The percentage is much higher in rural (58.6 per cent) than in urban areas (27.9 per cent).[31]

The data also show that 23.5 per cent and 8.9 per cent of women currently aged 20–24 years married before the age of fifteen and thirteen years respectively.[32] Therefore, older women are more likely than younger women to have married at an early age. Although this indicates that the proportion of women who marry young is declining rapidly, half the women even in the age group of 20–24 have married before reaching the legal minimum age of eighteen years.[33] The median age at first marriage for women aged 20–49 in rural areas is only sixteen years, well below the legal minimum.[34] The median age at first marriage is two to three years higher for urban women than for rural women in all age groups. The difference between the median age at first marriage and the median age at first cohabitation is no more than one year among women in any age group, even in rural areas. In addition, the difference between these two medians has been decreasing over time. This suggests that *gauna*[35] or similar cultural practices that introduce a lag between marriage and cohabitation are no longer widely observed in India.[36]

Another significant fact is that performance of child marriages is not uniform in all the states of India. There are stark variations in marriage pattern across the country, from state to state. About half of the women aged 25–49 married before the age of fifteen in Madhya Pradesh (52.6 per cent), Bihar (51.0 per cent), Uttar Pradesh (49.7 per cent), Andhra Pradesh (48.9 per cent), and Rajasthan (47.8 per cent).[37] And about four-fifths of the women of these states—Madhya Pradesh (78.5 per cent), Bihar (83.9 per cent), Uttar Pradesh (79.6 per cent), Andhra Pradesh (79.8 per cent), and Rajasthan (81.5 per cent) were married before reaching the legal minimum age of eighteen years.[38]

By contrast, the median age at first marriage is twenty-two to twenty-three years in Goa, Mizoram, and Manipur, and twenty years in Kerala, Nagaland, Punjab, and Sikkim.[39] Women in these states tend to marry much later: less than 10 per cent of adolescent girls in the corresponding age group in these states are currently married.[40] The level of literacy, socio-economic development, relevance of caste, class, ethnicity as well as religious and cultural hold on the minds of people, and lastly the status of women play a significant role in deciding at what age a woman marries.[41] In the southern states like Goa and Kerala, the high literacy rate has certainly contributed in delaying the marriages of women. In the north-eastern states like Manipur, Mizoram, and Nagaland women's median age at marriage is much higher. The findings of a study show that incidence of child marriage varies inversely with the level of development within the state.[42]

In four states, where more than 50 per cent of women are married before they turn eighteen years of age, religious and cultural hold is very strong. In northern states like Bihar, Madhya Pradesh, and Uttar Pradesh the status of women generally is much lower in comparison with the southern states like, Goa, Kerala, and Tamil Nadu. In the southern states women are more educated and are economically more independent. However, in Maharashtra, which is the most progressive state in the western region of the country and which has a long history of social reform movements and a medium level of educational attainment, 33.5 per cent of girls in the age group of 25–49 years were found to have been already married by fifteen years of age.[43] The median age at first marriage is 16.4, the same as the national average. It is difficult to explain why such a large percentage of child marriages occur in Maharashtra.

Rajasthan, a northern state, is one of the most educationally backward, industrially underdeveloped, and economically poor states in the country.[44] NFHS data show that 38.3 per cent of women aged 15–19 years in Rajasthan are currently married, a percentage that is little better than in other northern states.[45] But the percentages of marriages of girls at ages below thirteen and fifteen years are the highest in the country: 13 and 21 per cent of girls are married before age thirteen and fifteen respectively in the 15–19 age cohort. The percentage of women currently aged 20–24 years and married before the age of eighteen years stands at 70.[46] According to NFHS-2, 30.1 per cent of women in the 25–49 age cohort in Rajasthan and 30.8 per cent in Madhya Pradesh are married before they complete thirteen years of age.[47]

This demographic information indicates that southern states with higher levels of literacy and gender development scores are less likely to report marriage in adolescence than the northern states with educational backwardness, industrial underdevelopment, and economic poverty.

Reasons for Child Marriage

It is difficult to ascertain and determine the origin of the custom of child marriage.[48] But it can be certainly attributed to a patriarchal structure of society. The institution of patriarchy is prevalent not only in India or in developing countries but is universal. Why then it is responsible for the child marriages of girls in developing countries only? The explanation lies probably in the fact that there exists an extensive regional, cultural, and religious variation concerning specific aspects of patriarchy. Marriage has different meanings for men and women in different societies. Culturally, individual liberty is more valued in developed countries. Thus patriarchy does operate in such societies but in different contexts and in different ways. The institution of patriarchy operates in the name of *culture* for justifying child marriage of young girls. The following reasons identify socio-cultural barriers in postponing child marriages of girls.

Institution of Patriarchy

Patriarchy has a strong hold on Indian society. It operates at all levels on the basis of sex, age, and caste and contributes in lowering the status of women in every possible manner. Stratification and differentiation on the basis of gender are an integral feature of patriarchy in India.[49] Gender differences are reflected in the sexual division of labour between the productive and reproductive activities. Productive activities generate income while reproductive activities are usually unpaid work involving childcare, food preparation, health care and collection of fuel and water. Women bear the responsibility of reproductive activities and conduct productive tasks, while men are primarily engaged in productive activities. Thereby women's direct access to key resources is restricted and controlled by men. The rigid system of physical segregation by sex, by restricting women's mobility and activities, effectively prevents their engaging in extra-familial forms of economic activity and income generation outside of the home.

Equally significant is that patriarchy places men in a position to define which resources and contributions are highly valued. Though there is ample evidence that women work longer hours performing laborious tasks, their work is consistently downplayed in importance, which tips the balance of power between men and women with men having greater access to vital productive resources and a higher social status. Such a system of gender stratification also provides the primary justification for excluding or limiting women's participation in the formal education system. These differences in social status and the power imbalance between the sexes heighten young women's vulnerability at all levels.

The collective effect of patriarchy is thus to reinforce subordination of women in the name of care, protection, and welfare, and make them dependent on men throughout their lives. Child marriages for women, comparative seniority of husbands, and patrilocal residence upon marriage are thus the attributes of the patriarchal institution. Besides, patriarchy operates in Indian culture where the role of mother is glorified. In the absence of alternatives to the role of wife and mother from which women's social identity and so-called economic security are chiefly derived, older women have no choice but to support the custom of child marriage. Thereby they also contribute to replication of their subordinate position.[50] Precisely because the practice of child marriage reinforces subordination of women, discriminates against them, and treats them as slaves, I have challenged it by using the feminist method: 'asking the woman question'.

In the patriarchal family structure, the attitude towards women is that they are not to be left independent. So at every stage in their life, they are under the dominion of some male member of the family: father, husband, or son. The purpose of the marriage is transference of the father's dominion over a girl in favour of her husband. Such transfer is then expected to take place before a girl reaches the age when she might question it.[51] Subjugation of women is further achieved through the custom of marrying girls to men who are older by five or more years than they are. The wide age gap assures inequality between them as she has little power and is not included in decision making. Besides the age disparity at marriage between men and women, gender inequality is rooted in stereotyped gender roles which hold that women are to be mothers and wives and men are to be providers for the family unit. Women are therefore deemed to be ready for marriage at an earlier age than men who ought to finish their professional training and ideally be financially secure. Education and career are not perceived as essential for adolescent females.[52] Discrimination against girls in decision making in the family, education, employment, matters of sexuality, etc., is what creates and perpetuates the conditions in which child marriages of women occur.

Control over Sexuality

Another significant implication of patriarchy lies in its control of female sexuality[53] and reproduction, which is at the heart of unequal gender relations and is central to the denial of equality. Through culturally embedded concepts of virginity and chastity, women's sexuality is not only controlled by men but is often a symbol of the honour and status of a family, clan, caste, ethnic group, or race.[54] Since marriage represents an alliance between two families and patrilineages, the honour, reputation, and consequently, power of men is measured in terms of 'purity' of their women.[55] Consequently, there are marked pressures towards performing marriages at early ages of girls in order to minimize the risk of, and attendant dishonour associated with, improper sexual conduct by females.

Society has undue concern about female virginity, and awareness of its absence severely hampers the marriage prospects of young girls. The institution of child marriage reduces possibility of any suspicion regarding the virginity of a young girl. Marriages are arranged therefore, either immediately after or sometimes even before she attains puberty. Such a practice supposedly reinforces the *value* of daughters, but actually only ensures their subordination as women. Otherwise communities talk about the *bad name* which a young girl would bring to a household if she were to become pregnant out of wedlock. To avoid the problem of teenage pregnancy out of wedlock, a solution thought up by parents and society is to marry off the girls at younger ages. Rather than confronting teenage sexuality and encouraging safe and protected sex, child marriage is considered to be the only and proper solution by the parents and the community in the name of culture.

Malleability

Traditionally and culturally marriage in India is arranged by the parents and is looked upon as an alliance between two families more than of two individuals. Parents play a responsible and major role in arranging the marriages of their children, and this practice has acquired a social legitimacy. In an age- and sex-stratified patriarchal society, the choice and preferences of a daughter in selection of her life partner are thought to be irrelevant. It is assumed that parents make decisions in the *best interest* of their daughters. In this background, it is easier to make her, as a young girl, abide by the dictates of the father or senior members of her natal family and get ready for the marriage.

A woman's autonomy, her ability to obtain information and to use it as the basis for making decisions about her private concerns and personal matters, is not recognized or respected culturally in India. In fact it is denied by restricting her movement and refusing her opportunities to interact with the outside world.[56] Her experience has no value and is never reflected in cultural norms. In fact it is seen that her experience is specifically excluded from any norms governing social relations including matrimonial relations. Child marriage ensures her easy submission and acceptance of the traditional gender roles. She herself then becomes the carrier of the patriarchal ideology and unknowingly contributes to the strengthening of patriarchy.

Economic Reasons

The social and economic background of people determines the quantity of resources available for a marriage ceremony, influences marital values and attitudes, affects the cultural milieu in which the need for early or late marriage is felt, and provides the social networks in which spouses are sought. These factors in turn contribute to determine the age at marriage for girls and boys.[57]

In India parents of a girl are required to give gifts, either in cash or in kind, to the bridegroom and/or his family in the form of dowry. The amount of dowry may go on increasing as marriage gets delayed. The reason is that as the girl gets older and older she needs an older bridegroom. An older bridegroom is likely to be more educated. And the more education the more dowry is an established trend. To avoid more expenditure by marrying her at a later age, parents prefer to marry her off at an early age. Thereby the system of dowry perpetuates child marriages.[58] If there are more girls in the family, they are all married off at one time to save expenses on marriage celebrations. Such a situation may involve the child marriage of younger daughters in the family irrespective of their ages.[59]

Child marriage also reduces the economic burdens involved in supporting females as, after marriage, a girl joins the family of her husband. The reason is based on the presumption that women do not contribute monetarily to the income of the family and are therefore burdens to be wiped off as early as possible. In reality, though women contribute substantially, this myth is still accepted in the Indian setting.[60]

Further as women are *out-marriers*[61]—they marry out and go away— parents can expect little help from their daughters after marriage.[62] Culturally, on marriage, the daughters cease to be members of their natal family and there is no responsibility on them to support their parents or siblings. Married daughters are not expected to contribute financially or in any other manner to their natal home. On the other hand, sons remain at home and do contribute financially. Thus it becomes a straight economic, utilitarian calculation of gains and losses in marrying daughters off young.

Lack of Alternatives to Child Marriage

If young girls are not to be married off, alternative opportunities need to be provided to them. The fact is that there are no such constructive opportunities for them.[63] Usually girls are withdrawn from schools because of marriage. Educational opportunities, which could help develop their personality and autonomy or employment skills, are denied to them. Division of labour based on sex identifies a woman with household work for which she is not required to attend a school. Alternatives other than marriage are not provided to adolescent girls. From childhood, daughters are socialized to believe that marriage is the sole goal of their lifes and their own interests are subordinate to those of the family group. Any challenges to this mode of lessons are systematically kept away. It is equally important to note that access to schools in rural areas is not easily available to girls. They are required to travel long distances to reach the school. Parents who are anxious about the possibility of involvement of their daughters in premarital sex do not like to send them a long distance to schools as on their way either they are likely to become the victims of sexual abuse or to get themselves involved with men.

Lack of Awareness about Adverse Health Consequences

All these socio-cultural reasons contribute to child marriages of women on a large scale in India. Child marriages usually have profound adverse effects on the fertility, health, and development of adolescent girls. It is now proved that low age at marriage is one of the important factors responsible for the high rates of maternal and child mortality and morbidity. However, adverse health consequences of early pregnancies or childbirth to a young girl are not well known at the family level.[64] On the contrary, young brides are pressurized to prove their fertility as soon as possible after the marriage and to produce children, especially sons. A young girl with minimal or no education, raised to be submissive and subservient, married to an older man, has little ability to negotiate sexual activity.[65] She has to abide by the dictates of family members. As a result, if and when she suffers from any gynaecological illness or even if she dies due to a too early pregnancy and childbirth, her death is never attributed to her young age.[66] It is accepted as a fact of life or *god's wish* or *fate*.

Lack of Awareness of Law

In India a statute entitled the Child Marriage Restraint Act (CMRA) was enacted in 1929, to curtail the customary practice of child marriage.[67] After the amendments introduced in 1978, CMRA prescribes eighteen and twenty-one years as the age of marriage for a girl and boy respectively. In spite of the fact that this Act has been on the statute book for more than seventy years child marriages are still common and are prevalent on a large scale in certain regions of the country.

One of the reasons for child marriages is that people to a large extent are not aware of the provisions of the law. The finding of NFHS 1992–3, India, is that the CMRA is not widely known among women in India, particularly among women who belong to the disadvantaged sections of Indian society[68]: the illiterate, those from rural areas, and those who belong to a schedule caste or schedule tribe. There are no means of communication available to people to find out about the law. Illiteracy and legal illiteracy are the common features among rural people and more so among women. If people have no knowledge about the law one can hardly expect them to abide by it. Besides, even if people know the law, their attitude is not going to be favourable to such laws that try to bring about change in social values and interfere in intimate, personal relationships. That too if the area is such where cultural and religious influences are strong, people either oppose such laws or just ignore them. Unless people are taken into confidence and explained the need to prevent child marriages, they are unlikely to obey the law.

Lack of Political Commitment

There seems to be no strong political will for amending or enforcing the Indian Act or for creating awareness about it in India. Lastly, women's interests are accorded less weight in the political process thus adversely affecting any further improvement in their status. Over the last two decades, all political parties have stated their commitment to the improvement of women's position. However, no serious efforts have been made either for better implementation of the legislation or for improvement of women's health. The government, in response to the demands of the international community, introduces frequent policy changes regarding the reproductive health of women. But there is enough scope for doubting their commitment, as budgetary provision for implementation of these policies is generally inadequate.

Miscellaneous Causes

The various reasons for child marriage overlap with each other and compound the effects of a cause or causes. The reasons listed in this chapter are also not the only explanations for child marriages in India. There are others also.[69] A tremendous pressure from older members like grandparents and also the community prevails on parents of children to marry off their young daughters. There is also the fear of not getting a suitable match if the marriage is delayed.[70] It is also presumed that it becomes easier for a girl to adapt to her matrimonial home if she is married at a young age. It is interesting to note that child marriage is not looked upon as a problem by the society, as the girl is not sent to her husband's house immediately after the marriage. A ceremony called *gauna* is performed after she gets her menses.[71] Therefore, though the marriage is solemnized before she attains the age of puberty, she starts her married life only after she *grows up*.

Whatever the justifications that may be offered for child marriage, marrying off young girls before they attain maturity—physical, mental, and social, violates the human rights of adolescent girls. Child marriage results in disastrous consequences on the health of girls, particularly on their reproductive health. They lose career and personality-building opportunities in life and overall development. It takes away their right to life, right to live with dignity, and right to personal development, which are integral parts of fundamental human rights. One must, therefore, condemn the practice of child marriage and should not support it in the name of culture or tradition in any society. If the global community is committed to recognition of and respect for the human rights of adolescents, no excuse can be allowed on any ground. The international community has already responded to this issue in various ways. The detailed discussion of this response will appear in a later chapter.

Consequences of Child Marriages: Epidemiological Context

There are multiple consequences of child marriage in terms of the health and the social and economic situation of adolescent girls. Early onset of sexual activity and the pressure on young married women to prove their fertility as soon as possible after marriage results in high rates of fertility.[72] This seriously affects their health as well as that of their children.

These adolescents experience pregnancy and motherhood before they are physically fully developed, and are exposed to particularly acute health risks during pregnancy and childbirth. Therefore, they are more likely to experience adverse pregnancy outcomes than older women. The extra nutritional demands of pregnancy come on the heels of their adolescent growth spurt, a period that itself requires additional nutrient inputs. Any shortfall can result in the further depletion of the already malnourished adolescent. As a consequence of these conditions, pregnancy at an early age, before the adolescent is physically fully developed, can result in elevated risks of maternal mortality, severe damage to the reproductive tract, pregnancy-related complications, perinatal and neonatal mortality, and low birth weight.[73]

Girls below the age of twenty years are likely to suffer from pre-eclampsia and eclampsia, a condition involving high blood pressure, convulsions and which can even result in a person going into coma, iron deficiency anaemia, haemorrhage, toxaemia, and delayed or obstructed labour. Obstructed labour may result in vesico-vaginal or recto-vaginal fistula (VVF), which is a hole between the vagina and bladder or rectum. This results in continuous involuntary leakage of urine or faeces and smells dreadfully.[74] While these risks can be avoided or lessened with or managed through proper nutrition or proper prenatal care, many young women live in poverty and cannot get basic information or access to reproductive health care. In the absence of proper care, treatable conditions can become life-threatening. In addition, as a result of the unpleasant physical consequences of VVF, these young women also have to face the social consequences. Their husbands on whom they are financially dependent are likely to abandon them. Even their parents are not likely to accept them back or support them. They are likely to lead an ostracized life.[75]

Adolescent Fertility

In all countries early onset of child-bearing is associated with high fertility. Early pregnancy therefore has a tendency to lead to larger families, with serious consequences for the health and well-being of the mother as well as her children. In addition to its harmful effects on the health of mothers and children, this phenomenon has universal implications for population growth.[76] Where girls marry at fifteen, the age gap between successive generations may be less than twenty years. Thus future generations of parents would be born more rapidly leading to a higher rate of population growth.

Adolescent fertility in India occurs mainly among married adolescents. As many as 36 per cent of married adolescents aged 13–16 and 64 per cent of those aged 17–19 are already mothers or are pregnant with their first child.[77] This corresponds to 57 per cent of all adolescent females aged 13–19. Moreover, adolescents contribute significantly to the total number of births in the country. A progressively larger share of all births in the country occurs to women aged 15–19: it was 11 per cent in 1971, 13 per cent in 1981, and 17 per cent in 1992–3. The magnitude of teenage fertility in India is thus considerable. About eight million adolescents aged fifteen to nineteen are already mothers and another two million are pregnant with their first child. Worse, about five million have experienced pregnancy by the time they are sixteen years old.[78]

Maternal Mortality

Childbearing at any age involves some risk. Every year worldwide, an estimated 515,000 women die of complications of pregnancy and childbirth,[79] a rate of over 1400 maternal deaths each day. The overwhelming majority of these deaths occur in developing countries.[80] Globally maternal mortality ratios present the largest discrepancy in any public health statistics between developed and developing countries.[81] Young women who have not reached full physical and physiological maturity are almost three times more likely to die from complications in childbirth than older women. Data from studies in several countries consistently show a higher risk of maternal death among teenage girls compared with women aged above twenty years. The risk for very young teenagers (13–14) is much greater than for older teenagers (15–19).[82] Young women between the ages of fifteen and nineteen years are twice as likely as women in their twenties to die in childbirth.[83] According to the World Health Organization, studies in Asia, Africa, and Latin America have shown that adolescent girls under twenty years had higher maternal mortality rates than adult women between twenty and thirty-four years and this was confirmed more recently.[84] In some settings adolescent maternal mortality ratios are almost twice as high as those reported for older women.[85]

The incidence of obstructed and prolonged labour occur much more among adolescents. Obstructed labour often results from disproportion between the pelvic size of the mother and the head and shoulder size of the infant. If the pelvic growth is not completed before child-bearing, obstructed delivery and prolonged labour may result. If emergency medical care including surgical intervention is not made available, these difficult deliveries may result in haemorrhage and even death of both mother and her baby. Worldwide, the potential for such disaster is far too great. Young adolescents, especially those younger than fifteen years of age, experience distressing or even tragic pregnancy outcomes more often than older adolescents or adult women. Young adolescents are more likely to experience premature labour, spontaneous abortion, and stillbirths than older women, and they are up to four times as likely as women older than twenty years to die from pregnancy-related causes.[86]

The consequences of early child-bearing are also acute in India. At the national level, adolescents account for a high proportion of maternal deaths.[87] A study from rural India shows that 45 per cent of all maternal deaths occur among women of age less than twenty-four years and that 15 per cent of these deaths are attributable to complications associated with childbirth and pregnancy.[88] The available evidence suggests that maternal deaths are considerably higher among adolescents than among older women. For example, a hospital-based study in Mumbai indicates that while the maternal mortality ratio among women aged 20–29 years was 138 per 100,000 live births, adolescents experienced considerably higher ratios of

206 per 100,000 live births.[89] A community-based survey, carried out in rural Andhra Pradesh, suggests that adolescent mortality ratios are almost twice as high as those reported for women aged 25–9 years (1484 and 736 per 100,000 live births, respectively).[90] Another study of maternal mortality in rural Maharashtra also pointed out a higher risk of maternal mortality for women below twenty years of age.[91]

Maternal Morbidity

There are very few studies on maternal morbidity suffered by adolescent women in developing countries.[92] But even those few studies point out that levels of maternal morbidity are considerably higher among adolescents than among older women.[93] They suffer from anaemia, high blood pressure, and toxaemia, delayed or obstructed labour, complications in pregnancy, and weight loss during lactation.

Some studies in Africa have also found pregnancy-induced high blood pressure mainly among young women having their first child. Forty per cent of such pregnant women were aged fifteen years or younger.[94] High blood pressure, if uncontrolled, leads to eclampsia, which in turn may lead to congestive heart failure, paralysis, blindness, chronic hypertension, kidney damage, and even death.[95]

Moderate and severe anaemia both present serious risk. It has been proved that severe anaemia can lead to premature delivery or maternal and fetal death.[96] It is one of the most common contributing causes of maternal death and morbidity.

The poor nutritional status of adolescent girls in India is well documented.[97] For example, results of a community-based study of fifty-four pregnant tribal adolescents aged 13–19 years in Rajasthan revealed that 85 per cent weighed less than 42 kg and 94 per cent were anaemic.[98] A south Indian study of forty-seven adolescent girls aged 13–18 years revealed poor growth in all age groups; 73.5 per cent of the girls were classified as anaemic.[99] In yet another study carried out on 105 adolescent girls aged 10–18 years living in the slums of Gujarat, 98 per cent were found to be anaemic.[100] Stunting, as a result of malnutrition, frequently means that girls have a small or deformed pelvis, which may prevent normal delivery. In a study conducted in Karnataka, India, it was found that women below eighteen years at the time of their first pregnancy were one-and-a-half times more anaemic than women in the age group of 18–24 and almost twice as anaemic as women aged twenty-five plus.[101]

Adolescence, malnutrition, anaemia, and the extra nutritional demands thus exacerbate health risks during pregnancy. These risks are further heightened due to the lack of antenatal care. NFHS shows that 35 per cent of pregnant women under twenty years did not receive any antenatal care. Consequently, unlike in other countries, young women in India, particularly in rural areas, experience slightly higher mortality rates than males,[102] largely as a result of a high maternal mortality attributable to their poor reproductive health. In all, 15 per cent of all deaths of rural women aged 15–24 years are attributed to diseases of childbirth and pregnancy—the second largest cause of death following accidents and violence, which account for 34 per cent of all deaths and which may often be associated with child marriage and pregnancy.[103]

Another major problem, which results from early child-bearing that occurs before complete physical maturity, is cephalopelvic disproportion leading to obstructed labour and its *sequelae* including vesico-vaginal fistula (VVF). Other factors contributing to a disproportion between the mother's pelvis and her baby's head include malnutrition from underfeeding girls, material poverty, and inaccessible medical treatment. A number of research studies in African countries have shown that adolescents subjected to child-bearing at an early age suffer from VVF.[104] In India there is no particular research carried out on this problem.[105]

STDs and HIV/AIDS

Adolescents' human rights to life, health, and reproductive health are further compromised when their suffering due to STDs and HIV/AIDS is not comprehensively addressed. Worldwide, STDs account for 16 per cent of the time that women of reproductive age lose to disability—about the same as the time lost as a result of maternal conditions.[106] While people of all ages can be affected by STDs, young women especially are more susceptible to STD transmission. They have fewer antibodies than older women do, and immaturity of their cervix increases the likelihood of such transmission.[107] A young woman's low social status also raises her risk of infection with STD.

In cultures where women have little decision-making power over many aspects of their lives, an adolescent married girl who fears infection from her husband may nonetheless be unable to refuse his sexual advances or insist on use of condoms.[108] They often do not realize that they are infected. Many STDs are initially asymptomatic in women, so they may not seek treatment. Thereby, they frequently bear the most serious consequences of STDs. Untreated STDs can have devastating health effects. Untreated gonorrhea, for example, can lead to ectopic pregnancy, tubal infertility, and chronic pelvic pain. Infection with human papilloma virus is associated with the development of cervical cancer. If adolescents realize that they are suffering from STDs, they may be reluctant to seek help, as STDs are associated with promiscuity.[109] Moreover, infection from STD increases the risk of contracting HIV, which progresses to AIDS and results in death. An STD infection during pregnancy affects the newborn's health as well, potentially resulting in low birth weight, and increased susceptibility to infections and diseases.

There are again few studies of STDs in adolescents in India. NFHS-2 indicates that amongst girls in the age group of 15–24 years, the knowledge of STD and HIV/AIDS is very low.[110] However, epidemiological data on patients with AIDS suggest that in many cases HIV infection was acquired during adolescence and young women appear to be at greater risk of HIV infection than older women.[111]

Unsafe Abortion

A significant portion of maternal morbidity is associated with unsafe abortion and complications arising from it. Abortion contributes to infection, infertility, and mortality among young women in developing countries primarily because the medical services are not easily available, especially to adolescents.[112]

In India, according to NFHS, the percentage of spontaneous abortions among adolescents belonging to the age group 15–19 is almost double that in those belonging to the age group 20–49, particularly in urban areas. It also reports that 10 per cent of all adolescent pregnancies end in miscarriage or stillbirth compared to 7 per cent among older women.[113]

A hospital-based study in Mumbai has reiterated these findings.[114] In that study spontaneous abortion rates were as high as 158 per 1000 pregnant women among adolescents, compared to seventy-seven among women aged 20–29 years, and comparative stillbirth rates in these two age groups were 35 and 29 per 1000 pregnant women respectively. Another hospital-based study has similar findings.[115] It also adds a note that the actual incidence of abortion is underestimated.

Overall, adolescent girls appear to suffer a disproportionate share of unwanted pregnancies in India though a population-based estimate suggests that induced abortion among married adolescents aged 15–19 years is just slightly higher than among all women—1.7 per cent versus 1.3 per cent of all pregnancies respectively. But hospital-based studies suggest that adolescents constitute a significant proportion of abortion seekers: 27 per cent of all abortions conducted in the period 1976–87 in a rural setting and 30 per cent of the 1684 abortions conducted in an urban hospital setting.[116]

Abortion in India was made legal in 1972 by the enactment of the Medical Termination of Pregnancy Act. But limited availability, poor quality, and the cost have kept safe abortion out of reach of the most poor women. Health consequences of unsafe abortions are acute, ranging from complications such as a perforated uterus, cervical lacerations, or haemorrhage in the short term to an increased risk of ectopic pregnancy, chronic pelvic infection, and possible infertility in the long run. The problems are further exacerbated by the fact that the existing health services are ill-equipped to address the needs of these adolescent girls, including timely evacuations and post-abortion care, counselling, and contraceptive services.[117]

Infant Mortality

Infants who are born to young mothers also suffer a great health risk. Infants born to mothers who are below the age of twenty years at the time of the birth are more likely to experience higher perinatal and neonatal mortality than infants of older women.[118] Their risk of death during the first year of life is 30 per cent higher than the risk faced by the infants of adult mothers. According to NFHS, the neonatal mortality rate was 70.8 per 1000 live births among the infants of adolescent mothers compared to 44.8 among those of mothers aged 20–29 years.[119] They are more likely to be of low birth weight. Among younger mothers there is a higher incidence of poor child health care, poor child-feeding behaviour, and inevitably child mortality.

Impact on Mental Health

Another severe consequence of child marriage on young girls is that their mental health is seriously affected. The relationship between gender inequalities and negative mental health consequences—particularly depression and anxiety—has been documented by health research.[120] Child marriage along with low levels of education or no education, economic dependence, denial of decision-making power, inequality in the home, and sexual exploitation, has a negative impact on mental health.[121] Recent WHO statistics show that mental health problems account for 11.5 per cent of disability-adjusted life years[122] lost compared to 10.7 per cent for infectious and non-infectious respiratory diseases, 10.3 per cent for cardiovascular diseases, 8.1 per cent for maternal and perinatal conditions, 6.1 per cent for STDs/HIV, and 5.8 per cent for cancer.[123] Depression, in particular, ranks as the fourth most serious disease worldwide.[124] In India, child marriage, and cultural constraints on female roles have been associated with depression.[125] In Pakistan young age at marriage, illiteracy, low income, and severity of physical abuse have been found to be significant predictors of anxiety and depression in women.[126]

Other Consequences of Child Marriage

Apart from affecting reproductive health, child marriage has other consequences too.[127] It usually takes away educational opportunities of adolescent girls. As a consequence, it limits their opportunities for employment and income generation, sowing the seeds for a lifetime of dependency.[128] It also takes away their personality development opportunities as they get hardly any exposure to the outside world. It thereby limits their career options.[129] The resulting lack of education limits women's ability to make informed choices.[130] In terms of development, child marriage prevents women from participating fully in the life of the family, the community, and society. Energies, which might be directed towards social good and development, are curtailed. Women's potential and their contribution towards development and growth are important aspects of the development process. Child marriage prevents women as well as society from realizing their full potential.

Their opportunities for socio-economic advancement in later life are considerably reduced.[131] A young girl's potential for acquiring skills to deal with a wide range of experiences in the outside world, her socialization, is severely limited. This ends up in creating lower self-esteem in her own eyes and lower status in the eyes of other. Finally, it also makes her pass on the age-old patriarchal values to future generations, thereby contributing to the vicious circle of women's subordination and dependency.[132] This in turn may have a negative impact on their position in and potential contribution to society. Adolescent wives are also observed to have little autonomy and decision-making authority in their homes, exposing them to additional health and other risks, including violence.[133]

In a study carried out in Latin America and the Caribbean it was found that early child-bearing reinforces the poverty of women with low incomes. Poor mothers work more and earn less than other mothers do, and the timing of their child-bearing is directly related to their nutritional status.[134]

Society bears a phenomenal cost by allowing the continuation of the practice of child marriage. Much of the cost is hidden since statistics on this issue are rare. The material cost of the consequences of child marriage is exceeded by the more intangible costs relating to the quality of life, the suppression of human rights and the denial of women's potential to participate fully in the development of society.

Despite this frightening scenario, both married and unmarried adolescents continue to be vulnerable to early and often unprotected sexual activity. Why is this happening? What are the barriers in overcoming these problems?

Barriers Faced by Adolescents

Marital status legitimates sexual activity and fertility. In fact a young bride is forced to prove her fertility as soon as possible after marriage, since this is the only means of establishing her position in terms of social acceptance and economic security in her marital home. Findings from a study carried out in rural Maharashtra show that where both adolescent wife and husband would have liked to delay their marriage and first pregnancy, the decision was usually taken by the mother-in-law.[135] Adolescents' reproductive health is affected not only due to biological and physiological reasons. A number of other reasons have been pointed out ranging from illiteracy, ignorance, lack of proper personal hygiene, pregnancies in quick succession, non-utilization of health care facilities, and so on.[136]

Gender Norms

The institution of patriarchy, which is mainly responsible for creating cultural values in favour of child marriages, is equally accountable for promoting gender norms supporting male dominance in sexual relations.[137] Young and newly married women are powerless, secluded, and voiceless. Once married, they have little choice whether or not to have sex. The marriage institution itself does not recognize forced sex as an offence. There is no legal right available to wives to say no to sex. The position of young wives is more vulnerable compared to that of older adult wives. The prevailing gender ideology, as reinforced by the media, parents, educators, religious leaders, family planning professionals, policy makers, and politicians, profoundly influences views on sexuality affecting the reproductive health of adolescents.

Ignorance

Adolescents are often ignorant about their own sexuality and physical well-being, their health, and their bodies. The knowledge they have is incomplete and inaccurate. Low levels of education, limited sex education, and inhibited attitudes towards sex compound this ignorance. Adolescents are generally ignorant about menstruation and other physiological changes until they occur. They are unaware about the connection between these changes and their relationship to sex and reproduction.[138] Results of a hospital-based study show that 88 per cent of the 100 unmarried rural girls, who came seeking abortions, did not know that sexual intercourse could lead to pregnancy or STDs and 90 per cent did not know about contraception.[139] A retrospective investigation of poor women residing in Mumbai corroborates the finding of general ignorance.[140] Ignorance of contraceptives was found to be equally prevalent even among married adolescents. More than 90 per cent knew only about sterilization, which is unsuitable for them.[141] They were equally ignorant about STDs or HIV/AIDS, its mode of transmission, and how to have safe sex.

Lack of Access to Information

The situation is further aggravated by the fact that parents and teachers are reluctant to impart relevant information to them. Sex and puberty are considered to be embarrassing, distasteful, and dirty subjects, not to be discussed. The educational system is also ambivalent about imparting sex education. Teachers by and large find the topic embarrassing and they avoid teaching/discussing it in the class-rooms.[142]

Newly married adolescents too face sexual vulnerability, as they are uninformed and therefore, are totally unprepared for sexual intercourse and its consequences. Overall, the fear of adult recrimination frequently prevents adolescents from asking any questions or seeking help from their parents or adults. Information on sexual matters comes either from peer groups, which is usually incorrect or from the media which tends to portray both sexual and gender roles as stereotyped extremes.

Lack of Access to Services

Despite the special needs of adolescents in matters of reproductive health and information, there are hardly any such services available. Public sector services are not planned for adolescents, married or unmarried. Contraceptive information is not provided and the needs of even married adolescents are not met as the focus of the family planning programme has been, until recently, on married adult women. In short, neither the government health care providers nor NGOs have so far seriously considered the reproductive health needs of adolescents. Even men in the family do not feel that they need to share the responsibility for adolescent wives' reproductive health problems.

For all these reasons, as well as the socio-cultural inhibitions surrounding sexuality and reproductive health, hardly any reproductive health information, services or counselling have reached adolescents.

Summary and Conclusions

The above discussion can be summarized as follows:

— Although marriage in adolescence has been declining in India, a significant proportion (of those currently aged 20–24) marry by age eighteen and even by age fifteen. There are wide disparities from region to region within the country.

— Urban women with higher education marry late as compared to women from rural areas with little or no education.

— There is a great paucity of well-conducted, community-based studies on sexual activity among adolescents, married or unmarried. Whatever information is available is similar to that of the findings from other countries.

— Among adverse consequences of child marriage, the most life-threatening is the increased risk of maternal mortality and obstetric complications, some of which, if survived, have far-reaching adverse consequences.

— Awareness among adolescents about sexuality, contraceptive, and overall reproductive health is extremely poor. The low social status of girls and the traditional dominance of males in sexual matters lead to their inability to use family planning and health care services and thus puts them at a high risk of experiencing the detrimental consequences of STDs, HIV/AIDS.

— Infants of adolescent mothers are also at more risk, particularly when compared to those of older mothers in the age group of 20–29.

— Adequate and accurate information about sexual and reproductive health is not available to adolescents. Accessible and affordable reproductive health services are also not provided to adolescents by parents, schools teachers, government health care providers, or the community at large.

— While data are sparse, the evidence in general suggests that child marriage has other consequences too: it deprives females of a supportive social environment; it limits their decision-making roles, their education, career, and income-earning options.

— Marriage and family institutions based on patriarchy have the worst impact on the lives of adolescents, as they are forced to undergo child marriages and then to face its lifelong consequences.

It is universal that marital status legitimates sexual activity and fertility. But since information and access to reproductive health issues and services are not easily available to married adolescents, one can imagine the pathetic situation of those adolescents who are sexually active outside marriage. Of late, concern has been expressed about increasing sexual activity among unmarried adolescents in developing countries.[143] India is no exception.[144] Thus even if we succeed in postponing marriages, it would expose young people to the risks of premarital sexual activity for longer periods of time and thereby place them at greater risk of unintended pregnancies, unsafe abortions, and STDs. Thus child-bearing, whether within marriage or outside, does create potential risk for adolescents. How these challenges of early sexuality and child-bearing will be met in the near future will depend upon the response of communities, the nations, and civil society to the demand of adolescents in connection with their sexuality. If we do not prepare ourselves for it, we shall be risking the lives of future generations to an unimaginable extent.

End Notes

[1] Forum on Early Marriage, *Early Marriage Whose Right to Choose?* (UK: Forum on Marriage, 2000) at 9 [hereinafter *Early Marriage*].

[2] UNICEF, *Early Marriage: Child Spouses*, 2001, www.unicef.org/ programme/gpp/profiles/earlymg.htm. In Ethiopia, Israel, and Palestine, girls are often married before puberty or in their early teens. See Hail Gabriel Dagne, 'Early Marriage in Northern Ethiopia', (1994) 4 *Reproductive Health Matters*

35; Andrew Treitel, 'Conflicting Traditions: Muslim Sharia Courts and Marriage Age Regulation in Israel' (1995) 26 *Columbia Human Rights Law Review* 403.

[3] The Convention on Consent to Marriage, Minimum Age for Marriage and Registration of Marriages, 1962 (Marriage Convention).

[4] The Supplementary Convention on the Abolition of Slavery, the Slave Trade, and Institutions and Practices Similar to Slavery, 1956.

[5] Convention on the Elimination of All Forms of Discrimination against Women (Women's Convention); Convention on the Rights of the Child (Children's Convention); International Covenant on Civil and Political Rights.

[6] Art. 16 (2) of the Women's Convention, CEDAW has recommended it to be 18 years.

[7] See Appendix to Introduction at xlii; see also Tahir Mahmood, 'Marriage-Age in India and Abroad—A Comparative Aspect' (1980) 22 *Journal of Indian Law Institute* 38.

[8] Erikson Rosemary and Simpson Rites, *Use of Social Science Data in Supreme Court Decisions* (Chicago: University of Illinois, 1998) at 6.

[9] The next chapter discusses the legal framework relating to child marriage in India. The legal framework refers not only to the legislation in the context but also the judicial interpretation and administrative actions.

[10] Till recently a myth was prevalent in India that sexual activity occurs only within marriage. Consequently no data at national level is collected on this issue. Shireen Jejeebhoy, 'Adolescent Sexual and Reproductive Behaviour: A Review of the Evidence from India' in Radhika Ramasubban and Shireen Jejeebhoy, *Women's Reproductive Health in India* (New Delhi: Rawat Publications, 2000) 40 at 47–58.

[11] The Alan Guttmacher Institute, *Into A New World, Young Women's Sexual and Reproductive Lives*, (New York: The Alan Guttmacher Institute, 1998) [hereinafter *Into A New World*]; UN, Department of International Economic and Social Affairs, *Adolescent Reproductive Behaviour: Evidence from Developing Countries*, Vol. II (New York, 1989) at 1 [hereinafter *Evidence from Developing Countries*].

[12] A.G. Sathe, 'The Adolescent in India: A Status Report' (1987) 34 *Journal of Family Welfare* 11.

[13] M.K. Jabbi 'Child Marriages in Rajasthan' (1986) 16 *Social Change* 3 at 6; see also Gooroo Dass Banerjee, *Hindu Law of Marriage and Stridhan*, (Calcutta, 1879) at 45–6 He states: '... a woman is not regarded in Hindu law as an active party in a marriage. In fact, she is hardly regarded as a party at all. Marriage is viewed as a gift of the bride by her father to another guardian, the bridegroom: the bride, therefore, is regarded more as the subject of the gift than as a party to

a transaction. The early age at which the girl is enjoined to be married, makes her unfit to act as a party to the nuptial contract, and throws upon her guardian the sole responsibility of negotiating a proper match for her .... Minors are not only eligible for marriage, but are the fittest to be taken in marriage.' *Also see,* Werner F. Menski, *Hindu Law: Beyond Tradition and Modernity* (New Delhi: Oxford University Press, 2003) at 326–34 where he discusses child marriage in traditional Hindu Law.

[14] Werner F. Menski.

[15] See generally, K.M. Kapadia, *Marriage and Family in India,* 3rd ed. (New Delhi: Oxford University Press, 1992); S. N. Agarwala, *Age at Marriage in India* (Bombay: Kitab Mahal Publishing Ltd., 1962).

[16] Singh Susheela et al., 'Early Marriage Among Women in Developing Countries' (1996) 22 *International Family Planning Perspectives* 148 at 157, 175.

[17] Department of Women and Child Development, Ministry of Human Resource Development, Government of India, 'Demographic Profile and Future Strategies for Development of the Girl Child in India' (1995) 25 *Social Change* 24 at 29.

[18] International Institute for Population Sciences (IIPS), *National Family Health Survey (NFHS)* 1992–93 *Rajasthan* (Mumbai: IIPS, 1995) at 49.

[19] Census Report of India 1991. Census-based estimates of mean age at marriage is known as Singulate Mean Age at Marriage.

[20] International Institute for Population Sciences (IIPS), *National Family Health Survey (NFHS)* 1992–93 *India* (Mumbai: IIPS, 1995) [hereinafter cited as NFHS] at 76.

[21] Masuma Mamdani, 'Adolescent Reproductive Health: Experience of Community-Based Programmes', in Saroj Pachuri, *Implementing Adolescent Reproductive Health Agenda for India: The Beginning* (New Delhi: Population Council, 1998) 263 at 266.

[22] *NFHS,* supra note 20 at 77, 79.

[23] Ibid.

[24] International Institute for Population Sciences (IIPS) and ORC Macro., *National Family Health Survey (NFHS-2)* 1998–99 *India* (Mumbai: IIPS, 2000) [hereinafter cited as NFHS-2] at 22.

[25] International Institute for Population Sciences (IIPS) and ORC Macro., *National Family Health Survey (NFHS-2)* 1998–99 *India,* 'Summary of Findings' (Mumbai: IIPS, 2000) at xx.

[26] Ibid. at xx.

[27] The median age at marriage is the age by which 50 per cent of the cohort marries.

[28] NFHS-2, supra note 24 at 56.

[29] Ibid.

[30] Ibid.

[31] Ibid.

[32] Ibid.

[33] NFHS-2, Summary of Findings, supra note 25 at xx.

[34] NFHS-2, supra note 24 at 55.

[35] A bride is not sent to her husband's home immediately after the marriage. A ceremony known as *Gauna* or *Garbhadhan* is performed after the first menstruation and then the cohabitation begins.

[36] NFHS-2 supra note 24 at 56.

[37] Ibid.

[38] Ibid.

[39] Ibid. at 57.

[40] Ibid.

[41] N.J. Kurian, 'Widening Regional Disparities in India: Some Indicators' (2000) 35 *Economic and Political Weekly* 538.

[42] See K. Srivastava, 'Socio Economic Determinants of Child Marriage in Uttar Pradesh' 12 *Demography India* 59–73 (1983); Ashok Mitra, 'Levels of Regional Developments in India' *Census of India Part I* (New Delhi: Govt of India, 1961); see also Kurian, supra note 41; Ashish Bose, 'North-South Divide in India's Demographic Scene' (2000) 35 *Economic and Political Weekly* 1698; Preet Rustagi, 'Identifying Gender Backward Districts Using Selected Indicators' (2000) 35 *Economic and Political Weekly* 4276.

[43] NFHS-2, supra note 24 at 57; see also Alka Barua and Kathleen Kurz, 'Reproductive Health-seeking by Married Adolescent Girls in Maharashtra, India' (2001) 9 *Reproductive Health Matters* 53 at 54.

[44] See Vinaya Pendse, 'Maternal Deaths in an Indian Hospital: A Decade of (No) Change', in Berer Marge and Ravindran Sundari (eds), *Safe Motherhood Initiatives: Critical Issues* (New York: Reproductive Health Matters, 1999) 119 at 121.

[45] NFHS, supra note 20 at 77.

[46] Mamdani, supra note 21.

[47] NFHS-2, supra note 24 at 57.

[48] C. Rajyalakshmi, 'Socio-cultural Roots of Child Marriages' (1990) 20 *Social Change* 38; Mita Bhadra, 'Changing Age at Marriage of Girls in India', in Mita Bhadra (ed.) *Girl Child in Indian Society* (New Delhi: Rawat Publication, 1999) at 120.

[49] See generally, Michael Koeing and Gillian Foo, 'Patriarchy, Women's Status and Reproductive Behaviour in Rural North India' (1992) 21 *Demography India* 145.

[50] Ibid. at 147.

[51] Malini Karkal and Irudaya Rajan, 'Age at Marriage: How Much Change' (1989) 24 *Economic and Political Weekly* 505.

[52] Sanjay Das and Prasamita Mohanty, 'Adolescent Girl and Education' in Sunil Mehra (ed.), *Adolescent Girl: An Indian Perspective* (New Delhi: Mamta Publication, 1995) at 85.

[53] Koeing, supra note 49 at 147.

[54] See Purnima Mane, 'Socialisation of Indian Women in their Childhood: An Analysis of Literature' (1991) 52 *Indian Journal of Social Work* 81.

[55] Tim Dyson and Mick Moore, 'On Kinship Structure, Female Autonomy, and Demographic Behaviour in India' (1983) 9 *Population and Development Review* 35.

[56] Ibid. at 44; Barbara Mensch et al., *The Uncharted Passage* (New York: Population Council, 1998) at 19–21.

[57] However, the relationship between socio-economic status and age at marriage is complicated. What is true at one place for one group may not be so for the other group at other place.

[58] Though the Dowry Prohibition Act, 1961, has been in existence for more than last forty years, it is followed more in the breach. The social sanction of the practice does not allow parents of daughters to condemn it publicly.

[59] In Rajasthan child marriages take place on a mass scale in thousands, on a special, auspicious day '*Akha Tij*' (in the month of April–May). Mass-scale marriages save lots on marriage expenses, as villagers are distributed among relatives, and thereby reduces the number of guests who attend the marriage and marriage feast. Additionally, on this day it is not necessary to consult a pandit for *Muhurtam* (auspicious time for the wedding). The harvest is just over and the farmer has enough grains for marriage and also has money after selling the surplus grains. The farmers have relatively more free time as the next crop is to be sown only after the rains come. See Jabbi, supra note 13 at 6.

[60] Rajyalakshmi, supra note 48 at 38.

[61] Out-marriers means women leave their parent's house and join the husband at his house.

[62] Dyson, supra note 55.

[63] Mahmood, supra note 7.

[64] Shireen Jejeebhoy, 'Reproductive Health Information in India: What are the Gaps?' (1999) 34 *Economic and Political Weekly* 3075.

[65] M.E. Khan, et al., 'Sexual Violence within Marriage' (1996) 447 *SEMINAR* 32 at 33.

[66] Mass child marriages are still common in Rajasthan under the banner of social custom. See Pendse, supra note 44.

[67] For discussion on CMRA, see Chapter Two.

[68] NFHS, supra note 20 at 83.

[69] Kapadia, supra note 15 at 146.

[70] Jabbi, supra, note 13.

[71] Ibid.; Rajyalakshmi, supra note 48; *gauna* is a ritual performed after a girl begins menstruating. This is a ceremony performed through which it is made clear to the public that the girl is physically capable enough to have sexual intercourse with her husband. It is presumed that the age of menarche qualifies a girl to have relation with her husband.

[72] WHO, *Safe Motherhood: Health Day 1998: Delay Childbearing* from Annie Bunting, *Particularity of Rights, Diversity of Contexts: Women, International Human Rights and the Case of Early Marriage* (unpublished Doctoral Thesis, 1999) at 117.

[73] Jejeebhoy, supra note 10 at 40.

[74] Pramilla Senanayake, 'Adolescent Fertility and Teenage Pregnancy', in Helen M. Wallace et al. (eds), *Health Care of Women and Children in Developing Countries* 651 at 653; K. Srinivasan, 'Fertility Proximate Determinants' in J.K. Satia and Shireen Jejeebhoy (eds), *The Demographic Challenge* (New Delhi: Oxford University Press, 1991) 36 at 61; B.P. Singh, *Women, Birth Control and the Law* (New Delhi: Deep and Deep Publisher, 1993) 24–36.

[75] WHO, *Obstetric Fistulae: A Review of Available Information* WHO/ MCH.MSM/91.5 (Geneva: WHO, 1991).

[76] World Health Organization, *The Health of Young People: A challenge and a promise* (Geneva: WHO, 1993) 23–4 [Hereinafter *Young People*].

[77] Shireen Jejeebhoy, 'Adolescent Sexuality and Fertility' (1996) 447 *SEMINAR* 16 at 18.

[78] Jejeebhoy, supra note 10 at 62–3.

[79] World Health Organization, United Nations Children's Fund, and United Nations Population Fund, *Maternal Mortality in 1995. Estimates developed by WHO, UNICEF and UNFPA.* WHO/RHR/01.9. (Geneva: WHO, 2001).

[80] Rebecca Cook, *Advancing Safe Motherhood through Human Rights* (Geneva: WHO, 2001) at 3.

[81] A. Starrs, *The Safe Motherhood Action Agenda: Priorities for the Next Decade. Report on the Safe Motherhood Technical Consultation* (New York: Family Care International, 1998).

[82] *Young People*, supra note 76 at 23–4.

[83] See John Hobcraft, 'Delay Marriage and First Birth', Background Paper for the WHO Technical Consultation on Safe Motherhood, 1997.

[84] Mamdani, supra note 21.

[85] L. Liskin et al., 'Youth in the 1980s: Social and Health Concerns' (1985) 13 *Population Report* (M9) 349.

[86] *Into A New World*, supra note 11 at 32.

[87] Shireen Jejeebhoy, 'Safe Motherhood in India: Priorities for Social Science Research' in Ramasubban, supra note 10 at 134, 150–2.

[88] Barua, supra note 43 at 54.

[89] Saroj Pachauri and A. Jamshedji, 'Risks of Teenage Pregnancy' (1983) 37 *Journal of Obstetrics and Gynaecology* 477.

[90] There are other studies carried out in rural West Bengal, rural Maharashtra, and urban Uttar Pradesh, which also confirm the above finding. See Mamdani, supra note 21 at 270.

[91] B.R. Ganatra et al., 'Too far, too little, too late: a community-based case-control study of maternal mortality in rural west Maharashtra, India' (1998) 76 *Bulletin of the World Health Organization* at 591. This study did not focus on adolescents but covered the cases of women under 20 and over 35. It identified, apart from age, other causative factors such as multiparity, anaemia, home delivery, untrained delivery attendant, and absence of transport and absence of auxiliary nurse, midwife for maternal mortality.

[92] Jejeebhoy, supra note 10.

[93] K.B. Pathak and F. Ram, 'Adolescent Motherhood: Problems and Consequences' (1993) 39 *Journal of Family Welfare* 17 at 18–21; Stephen J. Atwood and Julia Hussein, 'Adolescent Motherhood: Priorities and Next Steps' (1997) 43 *Journal of Family Welfare* 8 at 10–12.

[94] NHFS, supra note 20; see also Efiong and Banjoko, 1975 'The Obstetric performance of Nigerian primigravidae aged 15 and under' (1975) 82 *British Journal of Obstetric and Gynaecology* at 228.

[95] Lettenmaier et al., 'Mothers' lives matter: Maternal Health in the community' *Population Report Series L*, No 7 (Baltimore: Johns Hopkins University, 1988); Liskin et al., 'Youth in the 1980s: Social and Health concerns' (1985) *Population Report Series M*, No. 9 (Baltimore: Johns Hopkins University 1990); World Health Organization, *Maternal Mortality: A Global Fact Book* (Geneva: WHO, 1991).

[96] National Academy of Science, *In Her Lifetime: Female Morbidity and Mortality in Sub-Saharan Africa*, (Washington DC: National Academy of Science, 1996); Zabin Laurie and Kiraguk K., 'The Health Consequences of Adolescent Sexual and Reproductive Behaviour in Sub-Saharan Africa' (1998) 29 *Studies in Family Planning* 216; P. Ramchandran, 'Nutrition in Pregnancy' in C. Gopalan and S. Kaur (eds), *Women and Nutrition in India* (New Delhi: Nutrition Foundation of India, 1989) at 93.

[97] Gopalan, C., 'Women and Nutrition in Developing Countries: Considerations', in H.M. Wallace and K. Giri (eds), *Health Care of Women and Children in Developing Countries* (1990) 252–63; Ramchandran, supra note 96.

[98] Mamdani, supra note 21 at 271.

[99] Ibid.

[100] Ibid.

[101] J. Bhatia and John Cleland, 'Self reported Symptoms of Gynaecological Morbidity and their treatment in South India' (1995) 26 *Studies in Family Planning* 208 at 203–16.

[102] Mamdani, supra note 21 at 273.

[103] Ibid.

[104] Mensch, supra note 56 at 94–5.

[105] But that does not mean that the problem is not there.

[106] *Into A New World*, supra note 11 at 34.

[107] Ibid.

[108] Ibid. at 35.

[109] Ibid.

[110] NFHS-2, supra note 24 at 231. Sixty-four per cent have never heard about HIV/AIDS.

[111] India, Country Paper, South Asia Conference on Adolescents, July 1998, at 9–10; see also Geeta Sethi, 'AIDS and the Adolescent Girl' in Mehra, supra note 52 at 53.

[112] *Into a New World*, supra note 11 at 33–4.

[113] NFHS, supra note 20 at 102.

[114] Pendse, supra note 44.

[115] P. Reddi et al., 'Adolescent Pregnancy' (1993) 43 *Journal of Obstetrics and Gynaecology of India* 764.

[116] Jejeebhoy, supra note 77 at 19–20.

[117] Mamdani, supra note 21 at 274.

[118] Anne Tinker, 'Making Newborn Lives a Priority' (2001) Issue 3 *FIGO* (The International Federation of Gynaecology and Obstetrics) no page reference; also see www.savethechildren.org.

[119] NFHS, supra note 20 at 180.

[120] *See*, for example, L. Dennerstein, J. Astbury, and C. Morse, *Psychological and Mental Health Aspects of Women's Health* (Geneva: WHO, 1993).

[121] Leyla Gúlcúr, 'Evaluating the Role of Gender Inequalities and Rights Violations in Women's Mental Health' (2000) 5 *Health and Human Rights Journal* at 46.

[122] Disability-adjusted life years are a quantified measure of the global burden of disease-assessing years of life lost to premature death and recently revised to include years lived with a disability of specified severity and duration. Ibid. at 61 reference 11.

[123] World Health Organization, *World Health Report* (Geneva: WHO, 1999).

[124] C.J.L. Murray and A.D. Lopez, *The Global Burden of Disease* (Cambridge: Harvard Uni. Press, 1996).

[125] J. Jambunathan, 'Socio-cultural Factors in Depression in Asian Indian Women' (1992) 49 *Social Science and Medicine* at 1461 from Gúlcúr, supra note 121 at 55 reference 40.

[126] F. Fikree and L.I. Bhatti, 'Domestic Violence and Health of Pakistani Women' (1999) 65 *Gynaecology and Obstetrics* 195.

[127] However, literature in this area has been largely confined to health effects only. The broader consequences of early child-bearing in developing countries have been largely neglected as research and policy subject. See Mensch, supra note 56 at 72, 73; see also Susheela Singh, 'Adolescent Childbearing in Developing Countries: A Global Review' (1998) 29 *Studies in Family Planning* 118 at 117–36; Leo Karowitz, 'Law and the Single Girl' in *Women and the Law: The Unfinished Protection* (1969) at 11.

[128] Studies carried out in Mexico, Chile, Guatemala, and Barbados confirmed these observations. See Mensch, supra note 56 at 75.

[129] Ranjana Kumari, 'Rural Female Adolescence: Indian Scenario' (1995) 25 *Social Change* 177 at 183.

[130] *Young People*, supra note 76 at 22.

[131] K.D. Gangrade, 'Social Development and the Girl Child' (1995) 25 *Social Change* 70 at 76.

[132] Sarah Lai and Regan Ralph, 'Female Sexual Autonomy and Human Rights' (1995) 8 *Harvard Human Rights Journal* 201 at 222–3; Berta E. Hernandez, 'To Bear or Not Bear: Reproductive Freedom as an International Human Right' (1991) 17 *Brooklyn Journal of International Law* 309 at 335.

[133] Barua, supra note 43 at 54.

[134] M. Buvinic, 'The Cost of Adolescent Childbearing: Evidence from Chile, Barbados, Guatemala and Mexico' (1998) 29 *Studies in Family Planning* 201 at 208.

[135] Barua, supra note 43 at 55.

[136] V. Sharma et al., 'Can Married Women Say No to Sex?' (1998) 44 *Journal of Family Welfare* 1 at 6.

[137] Adarsh Sharma, 'Socio-Cultural Practices Threatening the Girl Child' (1995) 25 *Social Change* 94.

[138] Asha Bhende, 'A Study of Sexuality among Adolescent Girls and Boys in Underprivileged Groups in Bombay' (1994) 55 *Indian Journal of Social Work* 557.

[139] S. Chhabra, 'A Step towards helping mothers with unwanted pregnancies' (1992) 3 *Indian Journal of Maternal and Child Health* 41.

[140] A. George, 'Understanding sexuality from the perspective of poor women of Bombay', 1993. Paper presented at workshop on Sexual Aspects of AIDS/ STD Prevention in India.

[141] NFHS, supra note 20 at 230.

[142] Bhende, supra note 138 at 559.

[143] *Evidence from Developing Countries*, supra note 11 at 1.

[144] Jejeebhoy, supra note 10.

2

Legal Discourse on Age of Marriage

Introduction

The previous chapter explored how child marriage in India is controlled by age-old socio-cultural and religious practices. A young girl does not have much understanding of what is happening in her life when she is married off. A major decision about her life is taken by the older members in the family on her behalf. Neither is she able to express her wishes nor is her opinion asked for. Her *free and informed consent* has little place in the scheme of traditional arranged Indian marriages. And none other than her own parents are responsible for it. It may be that they themselves are victims of societal pressure to marry her off at a young age. But the fact remains that as a corollary to it she has to face a number of adverse consequences—physical, psychological, financial, and developmental. These consequences were discussed at length in the previous chapter.

In this chapter, I focus on how the Indian legal framework has addressed the issue of child marriage. I begin the discussion with the historical developments that took place prior to the enactment of the Child Marriage Restraint Act, (CMRA) 1929, for controlling child marriages. Efforts for the legal prevention of child marriages began in 1880 with the change in the *age of consent* for the offence of rape. Instead of laying down the minimum age of marriage, social reformers of that time thought of punishing those men who had sexual intercourse with their wives below a particular age. The change was intended to give protection to young girls from sexual abuse within the institution of marriage.

The debate on raising the *age of consent* resulted in the establishment of two committees to examine the issue of child marriage.[1] The reports of these two committees ultimately led to an enactment of a separate, secular, and uniform statute entitled the Child Marriage Restraint Act. I review the provisions of this statute and critically analyse the substantive as well as procedural lacunae in it. My concern is to find the extent to which the laws and policies relevant to the age of marriage and reproductive health have promoted the rights of young girls. My analysis discloses that the enactment of this statute was merely tokenism without serious commitment to prohibiting child marriages. My argument is that the policy makers have not addressed the question from women's perspective. They have not taken into account *the woman question* that exposes their patriarchal bias while legislating. There has been no change in the approach since the law came into force in 1929 and the same perspective continues even today.

I then analyse the judicial interpretation of CMRA and try to demonstrate how an otherwise active judiciary has not taken much of a lead in delivering justice to young girls. I argue that it could have played a more effective role in preventing child marriage in India had it interpreted the practice of child marriage from women's perspective and with a human rights approach. By analysing laws and judicial decisions, I argue that neither the policy makers nor the judges have been seriously committed to solving the problem of child marriage right from the inception of CMRA. Nor were there any consistent and holistic efforts on the part of the government to enforce CMRA, primarily for the reason that young girls are the real victims of child marriages.

I further focus on how and to what extent other legislation, including the Indian Penal Code, 1860 (IPC), have tried to *respect* and *promote* the dignity of a girl child. I have commented on the offence of rape within marriage which is dealt with in a limited manner in the Indian Penal Code. Here I highlight particularly the *age of consent* controversy from the feminist perspective. I argue that the Indian legislators of the late twentieth century still share the notion of Victorian morality and uphold the dominant familial ideology by recognizing the authority of the husband over his wife.[2] In the next chapter I propose to discuss the religion-based personal laws and guardianship laws, pointing out the contradictions and lacunae in the laws and suggesting reforms.

Law Relating to Child Marriages

The law relating to the age of marriage, namely the Child Marriage Restraint Act (CMRA) enacted in 1929 was subsequently amended in 1949 and 1978 to raise the age of marriage. However, each time the objects of the amendments were different. Societal need at a given point of time was reflected in bringing the changes in the provisions of CMRA. But at the same time the objects did not cross the boundaries of sexual considerations. It merely focused on what is the appropriate age for a husband to have sexual relations with his wife. There was no reference to negative effects on the development of a girl child or to her free consent. Her consent was immaterial since parents were thought to be better equipped than an immature girl to handle the vital question of her security.

History of Legislation in India

Efforts to prohibit child marriage through legislation began in India in the latter half of the nineteenth century. It became one of the most burning topics of public debate during the early decades of the twentieth century. But it is unfortunate that even at the beginning of the present millennium, the situation has not improved substantially. Child marriages are still taking place in the country and are rampant in many parts, especially in the rural areas of the four major northern states—Uttar Pradesh, Bihar, Madhya Pradesh, and Rajasthan—and in one southern state, Andhra Pradesh.[3]

In the latter half of the nineteenth century, social reformers were trying to build up public opinion in favour of the legal sanctions against child marriage. The major reason to prevent child marriages was to give protection to young wives who suffered enormously due to forcible sexual intercourse with them by their husbands. They had to face their husbands sometimes even before they reached the age of puberty or immediately after reaching menarche. Another reason for demanding legal sanctions against child marriage was to control a large population of young widows. Very young girls were given in marriage to men who were in their thirties or even forties. Life expectancy in those days being quite low, young brides used to become widows on a large scale during the first few years of their married life. Remarriage of a widow, particularly of a Hindu widow, was not allowed by law, religion, and society.[4] The living conditions of such widows were very pathetic.

Age of Consent Controversy

The issue of child marriage was initially dealt with by the offence of rape under the IPC. The offence is defined in the IPC as follows:

> A man is said to commit 'rape' who, except in the cases hereinafter excepted, has sexual intercourse with a woman under circumstances falling under any of the six following descriptions:

Firstly: Against her will.

Secondly: Without her consent.

Thirdly: ...

Fourthly: ...

Fifthly: ...

Sixthly: With or without her consent, when she is under sixteen years of age.

Explanation: Sexual intercourse by a man with his own wife, the wife not being under fifteen years of age, is not rape.[5]

Rape is an act of sexual intercourse by a man with a woman against her will and without her consent. Sexual intercourse even with the consent of a woman is rape if she is below the age of consent. In 1860, the age of consent was ten years. It was raised to sixteen years in 1949. However, as per the explanation to Section 375 of IPC, sexual intercourse without the consent or against the will of a woman is not rape when committed by a man with his wife provided she is not below the age prescribed by the section. This was ten years in 1860 and was raised to fifteen years in 1949.

In the 1880s, when a serious campaign was launched to raise the age of consent, a man was not held guilty of the offence of rape even if he had forcible sexual intercourse with his wife who was above ten years of age. When the campaign was launched to raise the age of consent from ten to twelve years, a heated controversy emerged. A strong political view from the nationalists echoed the opposition of public at large. Bal Gangadhar Tilak, a staunch nationalist and the editor of a newspaper, severely criticized, through his editorials, the legitimacy of the power of the colonial government to legislate on the intimate domestic matters of the Hindus. He opposed the use of law to bring about change in the behaviour of people. But other social reformers like Malbari, Phule, and Agarkar were in favour of using the law to prevent child marriages.[6]

Rukhmabai's Case

At this juncture, it is important to note the two cases that came before the courts for hearing. One was the case of Rukhmabai[7] and another was of Phulmonee.[8] Rukhmabai was married in 1874 when she was just eleven years old. She did not live with her husband till 1884. In 1884 Dadaji, her husband, asked Rukhmabai to come and stay with him. But she refused to go and stay with him. Dadaji then filed a petition against her for the restitution of conjugal rights. Rukhmabai pleaded in her answer to the petition that Dadaji was not entitled to the decree of restitution of conjugal rights on the ground of social, economic, and personal incompatibility. Rukhmabai averred that she had not 'arrived at the years of discretion' at the time of her marriage. So she could not be forced to cohabit with her husband. This entailed a fundamental proposition that a marriage ought not to be binding on a spouse who had *not consented* to it.[9]

In the trial court, Justice Pinhey dismissed Dadaji's petition. He observed:

> It is a misnomer to call this a suit for the restitution of conjugal rights. The parties to the present suit went through a religious ceremony of marriage eleven years ago when the defendant was a child of eleven years of age. They never cohabited. And now that the defendant is a woman of twenty-two, the plaintiff asks the court to compel her to go to his house, that he may complete his contract with her by consummating the marriage. It seems to me that it would be a barbarous, cruel, revolting thing to do to compel a young lady under these circumstances to go to *a man whom she dislikes* in order that he may cohabit with her *against her will* ...[10]

Justice Pinhey looked at the marriage from purely a contractual basis. In his view the explicit consent of the parties was required for the marriage to be valid. However, it was argued that Hindu marriage was a sacrament, and hence an indissoluble, divinely ordained union to which the consent of the parties was irrelevant. Indeed to introduce the requirement of consent would render almost all current Hindu marriages invalid, and the children of such union illegitimate, besides opening the door to improper alliances and the ultimate breakdown of the social order of castes.

The decision provoked immediate public uproar. For some, it was a bold declaration of the rights of Indian women to personal freedom and dignity. For others, it was an assault on the sanctity of Hindu marriage and family. Dadaji appealed to the division bench of the Bombay High Court, which overruled Justice Pinhey's decision and sent the matter back for reconsideration. By then Justice Pinhey had retired. The matter was heard by Justice Farren. The then existing law did not allow a defence of incompatibility for the petition of the restitution of conjugal rights. The court therefore, ordered Rukhmabai to join Dadaji within a month, failing which she was to be imprisoned for six months. A compromise was reached out of court between Rukhmabai and Dadaji. She paid him Rs 2,000. In return he agreed not to press for the execution of the decree for the restitution of conjugal rights.[11] She was saved from having to go to prison.[12]

Rukhmabai's case received attention because at the time when child marriages were common and supported by law, religion, culture, and society, a woman who was given in marriage when she was a child had refused to accept the marriage and a husband whom she did not like. This was the first case of its kind. Rukhmabai's defiance was disturbing, as it not only threatened the sanctity of child marriage but also because it posed a risk to male domination, since she had rejected *the idea of woman's inferiority*.[13] Questioning what was assumed to be natural, she offered a subversive model of assertion by women of their desire, as individuals, in a society dominated by the family, community, and men.[14]

Phulmonee's Case

The second case[15] was tragic and galvanized public support for the Age of Consent Bill, and, in many ways, silenced the opposition.[16] Phulmonee, a girl aged eleven years and three months, had died because of haemorrhage from a rupture of the vagina caused by her husband who had forcible sexual intercourse with her. He was charged with the offence of murder. But the court exonerated him of the charge of murder as the girl was above ten years.

The event added enormous weight and urgency to Malbari's campaign for raising the age of consent from ten to twelve. The reformists began to collect and publish accounts of similar incidents from all over the country systematically. Forty-four women doctors brought out long lists of cases where child wives had been maimed or killed because of rape. From the possible effects of child marriage on the health of future generations, the debate shifted to the life and safety of Hindu wives.[17]

Phulmonee's case was by no means an isolated case. Dr McLeod's report on child marriage amply made clear the serious consequences of pre-menstrual cohabitation.[18] Again, only those cases that needed urgent medical attention or police intervention were entered into the records. These were then the cases of serious damage that resulted from premature sexual activity. An Indian doctor reported in court that 13 per cent of the maternity cases that he had handled involved mothers below the age of thirteen.[19] The defence lawyer threw a challenge at the court: cohabiting with a pre-pubescent wife might not have religious sanction, yet so deep-rooted was the custom that they wondered how many men present in the court were not in some way complicit with the practice.[20]

Efforts were made to distinguish between the two distinct stages in marriage; the wedding ceremony was treated as a sort of betrothal, after which girls remained in their parents' homes. It was only after the onset of puberty that they went through a *second marriage*[21] and went off to live with their husbands. A group of medical reformers supported legislation to ban marital cohabitation before the performance of the second marriage.

While there was widespread recognition that girls should begin regular cohabitation only after they attained puberty, the custom was commonly violated. Once the marriage was performed, a lot of domestic pressure pulled the wife into the husband's family. Further there was a problem in defining the age of puberty. According to the custom that was supported by the nationalists, it was equated with the onset of regular menstruation. They insisted that it occurred between the ages ten and twelve.[22] However, reformists argued that puberty was a prolonged process, and menarche was the sign of its commencement, not of its culmination. The beginning of menstruation did not indicate the girl's sexual maturity to sustain sexual penetration without serious pain or damage.[23]

It was unfortunate that all opinions agreed on a definition of consent that was nailed to a purely physical capability, entirely dissociated from free issues like choice of partner, sexual, emotional, or mental compatibility or other social considerations such as a girl's personal development.[24] Consent was made into a biological category, a stage when the female body was ready to accept sexual penetration without serious harm. The only difference lay in assessing when this stage was reached.[25] However, reformers could not be completely equated with nationalists. Reformers always had to struggle with a minimal programme to get some social support. On the other hand, nationalists were staunch supporters of patriarchal absolutism. Their insistence on self-rule in the domestic sphere coincided with their insistence that the girl should sacrifice her physical safety and even her life to defend the community's claim to autonomy.[26]

Phulmonee's case highlighted the then existing inadequacies of law and ultimately led to an amendment in the law of rape. The age of consent in section 375 of the IPC, which initially was ten years in 1860, was raised to twelve years in 1891. It was subsequently raised to thirteen years in 1925 and later on to fifteen years in 1949 for legal consummation of marriage. After 1949, the age of consent for sexual intercourse within marriage with or without consent has not been raised further though the age of marriage for a girl has been raised by CMRA to eighteen years in 1978.

These changes were aimed at treating women more humanely and were basically informed by a form of protectionism.[27] Social reformers, barring a few exceptions such as Phule and Agarkar who struggled for amendments in the age of consent, were not women's rights advocates or advocates of women's equality.[28] They belonged to the socio-economic elite and were conscious of women's oppression. Their attitude was patronizing. They were seeking to protect young girls from vulnerability at the hands of men through exclusion of women's experience. They never truly asked what impact the patriarchal social institutions had on women.[29] As Sathe argues: 'There was no consciousness about the oppressive character of the patriarchal system.'[30] Women were not assumed to be equal to men. They were assumed naturally to be wives and mothers. The social reform movement at that time was merely animated by the oppressive cultural and traditional practices, which were offensive to women. The concern was not to recognize the equal rights of women. Unfortunately, the same attitude continues even today.[31]

The Sarda Bill

Many social reformers started campaigning for raising the age at marriage after Phulmonee's case.[32] In February 1927, Rai Saheb Harbilas Sarda introduced a bill to restrain the solemnization of child marriages. The bill was popularly known as the 'Sarda Bill'. It was applicable only to Hindus, and other religious communities were not within the purview of the Bill. The Bill declared child marriage invalid. It was circulated throughout the nation to gauge public opinion. A large number of people opposed the provision of the Bill that declared child marriage to be invalid. The Bill was then referred to a Select Committee. The Select Committee submitted its report in 1928, and made it applicable to all irrespective of their religion, and not only to Hindus. It recommended that the validity of a minor's marriage be kept out of the scope of the proposed Act and should exclusively lay down the penalties for such marriage.[33]

Along with the Sarda Bill, there was another bill pending for raising further the age of consent under Section 375 of the Indian Penal Code. In June 1928, the Government of India appointed the Age of Consent Committee (henceforth the Committee) to examine the issue under the chairmanship of Mr M.V. Joshi. The terms of reference did not directly include the question of the appropriate age at marriage. But the Committee found it impossible to delink that question from the age of consent for marital and non-marital sexual intercourse. The Committee collected evidence extensively by interviewing people throughout the country. There were mixed responses. One of the objections raised to the Bill was that the delaying of marriages would lead to immoral sexual practices.[34] Another objection was that the law should not touch upon the matters of domestic nature and reform should be left to be achieved by an educative process.

The Committee submitted its report in 1929. It opined that in every civilized society, legislation had been used as a remedy to remove social injustice. It quoted the examples of Egypt and Turkey and some native Indian states[35] that had already passed legislation restraining marriage below a particular age. The Committee observed: 'There is an ample justification for legislation to prevent early maternity, both on the grounds of humanity and in furtherance of social justice.'[36]

The Committee recommended that the age of consent under section 375 of the IPC be raised to fifteen and a law penalizing marriages below the age of fourteen years be enacted. It strongly recommended that no exemptions should be granted on any grounds for performing a marriage below this age.[37] At the same time the Committee was of the strong opinion that the validity of a marriage should be left unaffected.[38] After prolonged debates on the report, the Sarda Bill was finally given the shape of legislation in 1929. It was entitled the Child Marriage Restraint Act.

Child Marriage Restraint Act, 1929

The Child Marriage Restraint Act, popularly known as the 'Sarda Act' received the Governor-General's assent on 1 October 1929. It came into force on 1 April 1930. The object of CMRA is to prevent child marriages. It is applicable to all citizens of the country irrespective of their religion.[39] In 1929, CMRA defined 'child' as 'a person who, if a female, has not completed fourteen years of age and if a male, has not completed eighteen years of age'. 'Every person, of either sex, who is under eighteen years of age' was described as 'minor'. 'Child Marriage' was defined as a marriage 'to which either of the contracting parties is a child'. And the term 'contracting parties to a marriage' was explained as 'either of the parties whose marriage is or is about to be solemnized'.

Age at Marriage

Initially in 1929, CMRA prescribed, as mentioned above, the age of marriage as fourteen years for girls and eighteen years for boys. In 1949, the age of marriage for girls was raised by one more year and was prescribed as fifteen years. In 1978, it was raised further to eighteen years for girls and to twenty-one years for boys. CMRA has not been amended since then. So today the age of marriage is the one that was prescribed in 1978. Table 2.1 below helps understand the amendments that took place in the age of marriage from 1929 to 1978.

TABLE 2.1 Age at marriage

Law in the Year	Age at Marriage in years	
	Bride	Bridegroom
1929	14	18
1949	15	18
1978	18	21

After 1978, the age prescribed for women by CMRA is in conformity with the international norms that are found in the two major conventions: The Convention on the Consent to Marriage, Minimum Age for Marriage and Registration of Marriage (the Marriage Convention) of 1962, and the Convention on the Elimination of all Forms of Discrimination Against Women (the Women's Convention) of 1979 both refer to the age at marriage.[40] Both these conventions have not prescribed the minimum age of marriage. However, the Committee on the Elimination of Discrimination Against Women, a treaty body, has recently recommended eighteen years as the minimum age of marriage.[41]

Different Age Prescription

Right from its inception, CMRA did not prescribe the same age at marriage for girls and boys. Culturally, in India, a bride is always expected to be younger than the groom. It is presumed to be natural and thus essential. The same principle seems reflected in CMRA. The age disparity at marriage between men and women is rooted in stereotyped gender roles and in a patriarchal presumption that a man needs more time to equip himself to support his life and wife. It underscores the presumption of her economic dependency. Justification for child marriage in the name of culture thus clearly exposes the patriarchal ideology behind it.[42] Certain indefensible factors of sexual bias—culturally created conceptions of the relative places of male and female in society—combined with other less indefensible reasons—the more rapid physical development among females than among males—produce different rules for males and females in an otherwise comparable situation.

The different age prescription at marriage thus explicitly excludes women's experience and their perspective. Given a choice, women would also prefer to have better education and would like to equip themselves in a manner that would contribute to the enjoyment of their lives and make them more meaningful. Besides, they could also acquire skills for employment, with which they would be able to contribute not only to the household but also to the nation's development. Had the method of asking the woman question been applied at the time of prescribing the minimum age for marriage, the present disparity in the age of a girl and a boy would not have remained in CMRA.

No one has challenged so far the constitutional validity of the different prescriptions of the age at marriage for a girl and a boy. Article 14 of the Constitution of India states explicitly that all are equal before the law. It reads:

> Equality before law: The State shall not deny to any person equality before the law or equal protection of the laws within the territory of India.

Article 15 (1) prohibits the state from discriminating against any citizen on the grounds of sex, caste, and religion. However, Article 15 (3) provides for differential treatment to women and children and allows the state to make special provisions for them. Article 15 reads:

> Prohibition on the ground of religion, race, caste, sex, or place of birth:
> (1) The State shall not discriminate against any citizen on grounds only of religion, race, caste, sex, or place of birth or any of them.
> (2) ...
> (3) Nothing in this article shall prevent the State from making any special provision for women and children.

Article 15(3) has been widely resorted to and the courts have upheld the validity of the special measures through legislations and executive orders favouring women.[43] But prescribing a lower age of marriage for women than for men is certainly not a favour to women. Therefore, the disparity in the minimum age prescription for men and women is violative of equality guaranteed in Articles 14 and 15 of the Constitution of India. But even without regard to the constitutionality of such differentiation, the intelligent, humanitarian urge and the realistic social and legal policies would require their elimination.[44]

Concern for Reproductive Health

CMRA was amended in 1978 to raise the age of marriage for a girl from fifteen to eighteen years and for a boy from eighteen to twenty-one years. The statement of objects and reasons for the amendment expressed in clear terms the concern for the need to control the growth of population as well as the health of young mothers. It stated:

> The question of increasing the minimum age of marriage for males and females has been considered in the present context when there is an urgent need to check the growth of population in the country. Such increase in the minimum age of marriage will result in lowering the total fertility rate on account of later span of married life. It will also result in more responsible parenthood and in better health of the mother and child.[45]

One would expect serious efforts on the part of the government to implement CMRA keeping in mind these objects behind raising the age of marriage, particularly when the control of population growth was the concern of the government. However, the discussion in the previous chapter has made it clear that due to ineffective implementation of CMRA even today, a large population is getting married at an age lower than the legal prescription.

The issue of child marriage continued to be linked with the sexuality of women. Even in 1978, the major concern for raising the age of marriage was to control their fertility. The legislators did not give much importance to the social consequences of child marriage. In fact, the Joshi Committee's concern for promoting social justice as one of the reasons behind preventing child marriages expressed in the formative stage of CMRA was not taken seriously by the government. A child marriage denies the right to education and development. It denies the right to develop the skills useful to gain better employment, and thereby forces women to depend economically on men. It makes them subordinate to men due to lack of gainful employment.

Nobody even thought that education makes life more enjoyable. And lastly, the question of her selection, self-choice, and consent for marriage were the most irrelevant. On the whole, women's experiences had no space in the area of law-making.

Women's education and their development were not the priority matters on the agenda of any government. The widespread prevalence of child marriages could be attributed to this attitude of the legislators. Had education, employment, and personality development of young girls been the objects behind prohibiting child marriages along with the concern for their reproductive health, instead of fertility control, the percentage of child marriages probably could have been reduced substantially. Adoption of such a perspective could have helped in handling the problem holistically. Even a wider awareness of these issues would have played some reformative role. Education of girls could have then become the top priority. Formal, informal, and sex education could have given better opportunities to young girls. Alternatives could have been evolved for them, which could have helped to postpone marriages to a later age. But women's holistic development not being the priority and women being always looked upon as daughter, wife, or mother, legislators did not address women's issues seriously. Discrimination against women on the basis of gender being treated as *natural*, no thought is given to the concept of women's equality in the private sphere of matrimonial relations. The result has been the ineffective enforcement of CMRA.

Punishment

CMRA provides punishments for violations of its provisions. The main purpose behind prescribing punishments for contracting child marriages is to deter people from arranging child marriages. CMRA declares child marriage to be an offence and punishes those who arrange and abet them. In 1929, punishments prescribed by the law was very mild. The law was changed in 1949, and since then there has been no change with respect to punishment. A few cases of punishment under the original Act and its amended versions are discussed here:

(a) A bridegroom above eighteen years of age but below twenty-one years who contracts a child marriage is held liable. As per the original Act, he would have been punished only with fine up to Rs 1,000 and there was no provision for imprisonment.[46] If he was above twenty-one years, the punishment for him was simple imprisonment up to one month and/or fine up to Rs 1,000.[47] In 1949, the amended CMRA enhanced the penalties. The bridegroom between eighteen and twenty-one years is now punished with simple imprisonment up to fifteen days and/or fine up to Rs 1,000. If he is above twenty-one years of age, the punishment is simple imprisonment up to three months and/or fine. CMRA does not prescribe any punishment for a bride.

(b) One who, having lawful or unlawful charge of a minor person as guardian or otherwise, promotes or permits that person's marriage or negligently fails to prevent it, is held liable. Initially, parents or guardians, relatives who promoted or failed to prevent child marriage, were punishable with simple imprisonment up to one month and/or fine up to Rs 1,000. In 1949, CMRA enhanced the punishment. Since then it provides for punishment of such people with up to three months simple imprisonment and/or fine.[48] CMRA provides that a woman guardian found guilty of the offence is not to be punished with imprisonment.[49]

(c) One who knowingly performs, conducts, or directs a child marriage is also liable. Therefore, a priest or *purohit* who solemnizes a child marriage can be held guilty of the offence.[50] Initially, he was punished with simple imprisonment up to one month and/or fine up to Rs 1,000. Since 1949 it has been enhanced to three months and/or fine.

How the law was changed from 1929 to 1949 in terms of punishment is explained in a tabular form. Table 2.2 describes different punishments for various offenders under the law. Though the law was amended to raise the age of marriage only in 1978, the punishment that could be awarded was increased in 1949.

As seen from Table 2.2, CMRA always provided for a mild punishment or penalty. This fact obviously reflects the legislators' view that the offences under CMRA are of non-serious nature. This is also one of the major factors responsible for limited success in restraining the solemnization of child marriages. Further, very few cases ever reach the court of law and even fewer result in conviction. So one could doubt the success of the changed law in achieving the object of preventing child marriages through deterrence, even though it has increased the punishment that may be awarded.

TABLE 2.2 Punishment for offences

Offender	Punishment in the year	
	1929	*1949*
Bridegroom in the age group of 18–21 years.	Fine up to Rs 1,000.	Simple imprisonment up to 3 months and/or Fine (amount not mentioned).
Bridegroom above 21 years.	Simple imprisonment up to one month or/and fine up to Rs 1,000.	Simple imprisonment up to three months and/or fine (amount not mentioned).
One who performs, conducts or directs a child marriage.	Simple imprisonment up to three months and/or fine up to Rs 1,000.	Simple imprisonment up to three months and/or fine (amount not mentioned).
Guardian or a person in charge of a minor, who promotes, permits, or negligently fails to prevent child marriage.	Simple imprisonment up to one month or/and fine up to Rs 1,000.	Simple imprisonment up to three months and/or fine (amount not mentioned).
One who violates an injunction issued to prohibit a proposed child marriage.	Simple imprisonment up to three months or/and fine (amount not mentioned).	Simple imprisonment up to three months and/or fine (amount not mentioned). No change.

Cognizance of Offences

In the beginning and also after the substantial amendments introduced in 1938 and 1949, the offences under CMRA were not declared cognizable.[51] The law enforcement machinery—the police—were not allowed to arrest those persons who were involved in organizing and solemnizing child marriages without a warrant of arrest. The reason often given was that the police would unnecessarily harass the parties if the offences were declared as cognizable. Another reason was the belief that the state should be restrained from interfering in the *private* and *personal* matters of the people. Even the offence of bigamy under Section 494 of the Indian Penal Code is not a cognizable offence on the same grounds. Offences against matrimony, particularly involving women, are not treated as serious offences under one pretext or the other. Instead of adopting the policy of making the offences non-cognizable, the situation should have been handled in a different way. The police should have been given gender sensitization training with special focus on the issue of child marriage or bigamy.

Even accepting that the police might misuse their power, the question is, as rightly pointed out by B. Sivaramayya,[52] whether by making an offence cognizable under CMRA, its object of restraining child marriages would be promoted. In his opinion, police harassment is a lesser evil than the monstrous evil of child marriage. To support his argument he has quoted the report of the committee appointed by the Government of Gujarat in 1962.[54] The committee was asked to investigate the high rate of suicide among young married girls. The committee found that child marriage was an important cause for the high rate of suicides.[54] The government of Gujarat in a bid to curb child marriages declared all the offences under CMRA cognizable by amending its Section 7.[55]

The central government's Committee on the Status of Women (CSW) in its report drew attention to the findings of the Gujarat committee's report and recommended that all offences under CMRA be made cognizable and special officers be appointed to enforce the law.[56] In pursuance of the recommendations of CSW, since 1978, all the offences under CMRA have been declared cognizable but only for certain purposes. Section 7 provides that for the purpose of investigation and for all matters other than (i) those referred to in Section 42 of the Code of Criminal Procedure and (ii) arrest of an accused without a warrant or magisterial order, the offences under the Act are cognizable.[57]

By this provision, any person is now allowed to lodge a complaint with the police, if a child marriage is about to take place or has already taken place. The police are empowered to investigate such complaints. But the police have neither the authority to arrest the offender nor the power to stop the solemnization of the child marriage. The reason is that the offence is cognizable only for the purpose of investigation. After investigation the police have to report to the magistrate and obtain a warrant of arrest from him. And before issuing a warrant, the magistrate has to give notice to the person/s concerned and a hearing. By the time this procedure is completed, the marriage is usually solemnized.

One would rather be interested in preventing the solemnization of child marriage rather than seeing that a person involved is sent to jail or is required to pay the fine. Making the offences cognizable only for the purpose of investigation does not help prevent child marriages. Making offences cognizable only for the purpose of investigation also gives an impression to the enforcing authorities that the offences under CMRA are less serious. Thus declaring these offences cognizable only for the purpose of investigation has not really served the purpose of preventing child marriages. Such a halfway approach has undermined the seriousness of a qualitatively grave offence.

Furthermore, CMRA provides that the cognizance of an offence could be taken only within one year from the date of the solemnization of the marriage.[58] After one year the law itself decriminalizes the solemnization of the child marriage. Punishment prescribed for a crime is generally a parameter for deciding the gravity of the crime. And the gravity of the crime decides how long a file is to be kept open for the investigation and prosecution. The lighter the punishment, the shorter is the duration for taking action against the offender. This is the general principle of procedural law.[59] The maximum punishment provided under CMRA is only simple imprisonment for three months. Therefore, to initiate an action within one year against any offence under CMRA from the date of the solemnization of the marriage is proportionately enough time as per the general principles of criminal procedure. The question is, is it necessary to apply this general principle in all situations? Or should one make an exception on the basis of the seriousness of the mischief that the law has selected to correct?

Decriminalization of the offences after one year from the date of the solemnization of the marriage does not promote the policy and purpose of CMRA. Sivaramayya rightly points out that given the weak monitoring system and the influence-peddling that ignores the threat integral to the violation of CMRA by the powerful sections of society, it is better if the Damocles sword of prosecution hangs for a longer duration on the heads of those who solemnize child marriages.[60]

CMRA should be amended to make child marriage a serious crime by increasing imprisonment to more than one year.[61] However, unless serious efforts for effective enforcement are initiated, mere amendments in the law to enhance the punishment would not bring about the desired change. Equally important is to keep in mind a commonly held view that the certainty of the punishment has a greater deterrent effect on the crime rate. If people know that they would certainly be prosecuted and punished for contracting child marriages, they would think twice before engaging in such an offence.

Injunction—Preventive Action

At its inception, CMRA did not make a provision for issuing an injunction for prohibiting a proposed child marriage. However, nine years later when it was amended in 1938, the provision for an injunction was introduced.[62] Accordingly CMRA now gives power to the courts to issue an injunction prohibiting a child marriage from being arranged or solemnized. The courts can issue such an injunction on receiving a complaint or even otherwise regarding the proposed child marriage against any of those persons responsible for arranging or solemnizing a child marriage or contracting such a marriage. If a marriage is solemnized in contravention of an injunction issued by the magistrate, the person disobeying the order of the court is liable to be punished with imprisonment up to three months, or fine up to Rs 1,000 or both. But this provision has serious limitation as the magistrate is allowed to issue the injunction only after giving notice to the persons concerned and only after giving an opportunity of hearing to the suspects. By the time this procedure is completed, the child marriage has usually taken place.

Legal Effect of Child Marriage

CMRA does not provide either for the validity or invalidity of an under-age marriage.[63] It is silent about the legal effect of child marriage. The issue of the validity of child marriage was kept out of the scope when CMRA was drafted according to the suggestions of the Joshi Committee.[64] The same policy continues even today.

Reasons in the Past for Not Addressing the Question of the Validity of Child Marriage

One could think of a number of reasons for not touching upon the issue of the validity of child marriages in the 1920s. Once a girl underwent a marriage ceremony, it would have almost become impossible for her to marry subsequently if her marriage were declared void. Particularly, if she had cohabited with her husband, the presumption would have been the loss of her virginity, which would have been a great barrier to her subsequent marriage. As a single person without sufficient skills to earn for survival, it would have become difficult for her to lead a life with dignity. Thus it would have given her an additional blow, further lowered her status and increased her sufferings. Instead of helping her, the law declaring child marriage void would have further victimized the young bride. Besides, she would not have got any inheritance or maintenance from the man to whom she had been married. Children born of such void marriage would have suffered the same deprivation of legal and social status as children born out of wedlock. The denial of legal status would have resulted in the denial of the right of inheritance of the father's property. In the absence of social status the life of both the mother and her children would have become miserable as the family and the community would not have accepted them.

All these arguments might have been plausible justifications for keeping child marriages valid in the beginning of the last century. But the question is whether these arguments are valid in today's context. The issue of the validity of child marriages was discussed by the Committee on the Status of Women in India (CSW)[65] appointed by the Government of India in 1974. CSW discussed three alternatives.[66]

— The first option was to maintain the status quo, that is, to treat child marriage as valid and legal and at the same time as an offence.

— The second was to declare it void.

— The third was to give the victim girl an option to obtain the dissolution of the marriage, which obviously would incorporate the first option also.

CSW recommended the third one.[67] It observed 'In the present social and economic conditions, such a rigorous measure (declaring child marriage void) may create more problems than it seeks to solve.'[68]

The issue of the validity of child marriage has also been raised many times before the court. But even the judiciary followed the policy of the legislators and declared it as valid.[69] Thus, jurisprudentially it creates a paradoxical situation. An act of contracting child marriage is an offence. It is a criminal act, but if successfully carried out it is valid and legal. The question that requires consideration is whether the time has now arrived, at the beginning of the new millennium, to change the law and to declare child marriage void.

Why Child Marriage Should Be Declared Void

One cannot continue to raise the twentieth century objections in the twenty-first century for not declaring child marriage void. It is necessary that to create a jurisprudentially sound situation; an act which is an offence should be illegal. If the law declares child marriages void, the parents would be compelled to think twice before arranging the marriage of their daughter who has not reached the legal age of marriage. It would become one of the important strategies to help prevent child marriages. Declaration of child marriage void would indicate that the state considers it as a serious matrimonial wrong.[70] Moreover, it would send a strong message that the state is committed to prevent it in the interest of girls who are the principal sufferers.

One may argue that instead of declaring child marriage void it is better to take preventive measures. However, so long as the marriage remains valid the parents would continue to arrange marriage of their young daughter while she is a child. The most suitable step would be to take both steps simultaneously—to declare it as void and at the same time to adopt various measures to prevent it.

The National Commission for Women (NCW), a body established for the improvement of the status of women prepared a draft bill providing for a uniform law of marriage entitled the Indian Marriage Bill.[71] It submitted the draft bill to the government in 1994. A provision was included in the draft for declaring child marriage void[72] and for compulsory registration of marriages to avoid child marriages.[73] The National Human Rights Commission also supported these suggestions of the National Commission for Women though it commented that there should be a greater emphasis on the prevention of child marriages rather than on their annulment.[74]

However, the government responded with the view that only through social and economic uplift of certain sections of society could the practice be better eradicated and stated that no further legislative measures were contemplated.[75] The government further argued that it would be inappropriate to introduce any form of legislation requiring the compulsory registration of marriages since this would impinge on personal laws.[76]

Considering the opinion of the government on the draft marriage bill, to prevent child marriages, an immediate step that could be taken is to prosecute more and more people involved in child marriages. The maximum publicity should be given to the judicial decisions convicting the wrongdoers so as to make people aware of the law and consequence that follows if it is not complied with. Simultaneously, intensive lobbying should be done to convince the government about why there is a need to amend the law to declare child marriage void.

Anticipating some opposition to declare child marriage void from certain sections of society and the government, it is submitted that initially for a specific period, for example ten years, child marriage should be declared as voidable at the option of women. Voidable marriage would allow the wife to go to the court to annul her marriage. Such a provision would give a choice to the wife of either continuing or discontinuing with the marriage. But then it should be an interim step. Any child marriage solemnized after the passage of these ten years should be void. People should be made aware during these ten years that an under-age marriage solemnized after a particular date would become void.[77] Such change in the law would provide an opportunity to all those who are likely to be party to a child marriage to give serious thought before they decide to act.

It is recommended that child marriage should be declared as voidable only for ten years. The reason being that if it is made voidable and not void for all time to come, though the girl would in reality be entitled to get the decree of annulment, she would rarely exercise this option. As a result, it would not help prevent child marriages.

Measures to Avoid Victimization of Girl Children

It is not denied that the custom of solemnizing child marriages would continue even if the law were to declare them void. One needs to take care of the consequences of void child marriage on the lives of young girls. The victimization of such girl children could be avoided by taking legal as well as other supportive measures.

Legal Measures

Marriage laws generally do not entitle the parties to a void marriage to claim maintenance against each other. However, the girl child should be given the right to claim maintenance from the man to whom she was married. Such a right should be created in the personal marriage laws.[78] If the man himself is dependent on his parents or guardians for his maintenance, the parents or guardians who were responsible for such marriage should be made liable to pay maintenance to her.[79]

If there are any children born of such a marriage, the law should confer legal status on them. There is already such a provision under the Hindu Marriage Act that treats children born of void marriages as legitimate.[80] The concept of 'illegitimate' child born out of wedlock must undergo a change. Such change is overdue. A newborn child cannot be illegitimate. At the most it is the relationship between the two adults that could be labelled as illegitimate. However, when a child is born in child marriage, this question becomes redundant, because the relationship is not between two consenting adults. The consciousness of society, community, parents, and men and women must be raised about this issue.

Supportive Measures

To minimize the harsh consequences of void child marriages, the government should take responsibility of providing education and vocational skills to girl children who were given in marriages below the legal age. The government otherwise is also under the constitutional obligation to provide compulsory primary education to all.[81] There is a special responsibility on the government for these victims of child marriages because of its failure to prevent such marriages. Education and job skills would help these girls become economically independent in future.

To avoid further victimization of child brides, the parents, community, and society need to be informed that virginity of a girl need not be *the* sacrosanct value. They need to be told how women are culturally discriminated against because of unnecessary and undue emphasis on their virginity. No one raises similar issue about men's chastity. The parents, community, and society need to be convinced that giving young girls in marriages so as to prevent the community from raising doubts about their virginity is a very short-sighted, harmful remedy. People need to be informed about adverse physical, social, and economic consequences of child marriages. Women's virginity need not be treated as a virtue at the cost of their lives, health, and development. Virginity need not be the criterion of their status. On the contrary, their status could be improved by adopting more affirmative measures such as providing an opportunity for education and employment than by giving them in marriage as children.

It is reiterated that the legality of child marriage could no longer be justified on the basis of circumstances that were prevalent a hundred years ago. Social progress and development over the period of almost a century, founded on respect for the dignity and value of the human person should take care of many of these mentioned arguments. It should ensure the promotion of human rights and social justice.

Social progress and development require the full utilization of human resources including the encouragement of creative initiative under conditions of enlightened public opinion; the dissemination of national and international information for the purpose of making individuals aware of changes occurring in society as a whole; the active participation of all elements of society in defining and in achieving the common goals of development; and lastly, the assurance to disadvantaged sectors of the population of equal opportunities for social, educational, and economic advancement in order to achieve an effectively integrated society.[82] Child marriage denies all such opportunities. To help women contribute to the economy and social development, they need to be properly equipped with education, which could happen if their marriages are delayed and they are allowed to go school and are retained there. At the beginning of the new millennium, the existing legality of child marriages needs to be challenged from women's perspective. Women's experiences, their needs, informed opinions, and values should be reflected in policies and laws.

In the long run, therefore, the declaration of child marriage as void would prove to be more beneficial to young girls as well as to society. For a short while, social and cultural forces might victimize child brides on declaration of child marriage void. Efforts could be made to reduce such victimization. But keeping in mind the long-term gains, during the interim period, a few would have to face the hardship of the law declaring child marriage void.

Other Lacunae in CMRA

CMRA merely attempted to restrain child marriage by providing penal sanctions for contracting such marriage. A number of important provisions that could have helped to prevent child marriage are missing from CMRA. Consent of the parties to a marriage and compulsory registration of a marriage, are some important provisions that should have been incorporated in CMRA. There are a number of reasons for including such provisions in CMRA. Registration of marriages is the best method to control child marriages effectively. Mandatory requirement of consent would automatically reinforce the condition relating to the age at marriage, as a person would be capable of giving legal and valid consent only at the age of maturity. Such amendments should be brought into the personal laws of marriage prevalent in India. However, it would be more difficult to amend these religion-based laws for the reasons discussed in the following pages. It would be comparatively easy to amend CMRA.

Consent of Parties

All over the world, the law of marriage generally prescribes a certain age for parties to a marriage and provides for their free consent so that both can meet their responsibilities with physical and mental maturity. A matrimonial relationship which comes into existence on the basis of affinity cannot and should not be a forced relationship. Therefore, free and informed consent of the parties is and should be an essential prerequisite for marriage.

The competence of a person to enter into a matrimonial relationship is an important aspect of matrimony. Such competence is judged on the basis of physical and mental maturity of an individual. The person entering into a new relationship has to be in a position to understand the additional responsibilities emerging from that relationship. At a young age, physical and mental faculties of an individual are not developed enough to help a person to distinguish between good and bad, beneficial and hurtful. In the absence of sufficient experience and exposure to the external world, a person is not in a position to determine preferences and inclinations. As a child, a girl is not capable of making a choice of a life partner. When she is married off at a young age, freedom of choice regarding whom to marry and when to marry is denied to her. Child marriage does not allow her to give her free and informed consent. On the contrary, she is forced and pressurized to enter into marriage.

CMRA presumes that a girl attains the age of responsibility at the age of eighteen years to enter into a marriage. But it does not prescribe that such relationship should be based on the mutual consent of the parties.[83] There is no specific provision in CMRA regarding the free consent of the marrying parties.[84] This is a serious lacuna in CMRA and it needs to be rectified. The National Commission for Women in its draft on the Indian Marriage Bill in 1994 did provide for the free consent of the parties to a marriage as an essential prerequisite and proposed that any marriage be void in the absence of it.[85]

As a ratifying country to the Women's Convention, India is under an obligation to make a provision in the relevant statutes for the free consent of the parties to a marriage.[86] In the absence of free consent of the parties, such marriage should be declared as void. By not providing so in CMRA, or under the existing personal laws,[87] India has violated her obligation. To comply with the obligation under the Women's Convention therefore, CMRA as well as the other marriage laws should be amended to provide for the free consent of both the parties as an essential prerequisite for a marriage to be legal and valid.

Registration of Marriage

Registration of a marriage is a prima facie proof of the marriage. A certificate of registration of marriage gives the relevant details about the parties to a marriage. To prevent under-age marriages, the best practice could be to provide for their compulsory registration. Unfortunately, CMRA has not provided for the registration of marriages. Since this essential procedural detail is not covered in CMRA, it is very difficult to keep a track of under-age marriages.

The Marriage Convention[88] and the Women's Convention[89] require state parties to make laws for compulsory registration of marriages. India has accepted in principle the need to adopt a law for compulsory registration of marriages under the Women's Convention.

However, India has filed a declaration to Article 16(2):

> With regard to Article 16 (2) of the Convention on the Elimination of All Forms of Discrimination against Women, the Government of the Republic of India declares that though in principle it fully supports the principle of compulsory registration of marriages, it is not practical in a vast country like India with its variety of customs, religions, and level of literacy.[90]

If the Government of India is seriously committed to the eradication of child marriages, it should create awareness about the need for registration of marriages and develop an infrastructure for making it possible for people to register marriages. The National Commission for Women has already suggested in the draft on the Indian Marriage Bill that to prevent child marriages, all marriages must be registered compulsorily.[91]

Registration of marriage falls under the Concurrent list of the Seventh Schedule to the Constitution of India[92] and therefore Parliament as well as the state legislatures are entitled to legislate on the subject. CMRA being an Act of Parliament, the Parliament has power to amend it. However, as the responsibility for enforcing CMRA lies with the states, they would be required to do the budgeting for creating the infrastructure for the registration of marriages.[93] To begin with, the states could use the existing infrastructure for the registration of births and deaths for the registration of marriages. A step toward implementation could be to establish a pilot project for registration of marriage in one state. For example, the State of Rajasthan, where child marriages are even now taking place on a large scale, could be selected for such a pilot project. Analysis could be done of the situation whether the registration of marriages makes any difference in reducing the number of child marriages. Based on that experience, the governments of other states could be convinced to introduce the compulsory registration of marriages.

Age Difference between the Parties

It was very common in India to give young girls in marriage to older men. Sometimes, there used to be a large age difference between the bride and the bridegroom, even more than twenty to thirty years. Prior to enactment of the Sarda Act, some states had enacted a provision restraining marriages of minor girls with old men.[94] However, CMRA never had any such provision. Even today marriages do take place where there is a large age difference between the girl and the man.[95] This difference further contributes to the inequality of the relationship. A wife who is younger than her husband is compelled to *obey* the dictates of her husband. Such a relationship does not promote mutual respect and an equal relationship between the spouses. On the contrary it reinforces women's subordination.

Judicial Approach

The judicial approach to CMRA has not been very favourable to young girls. The Indian judiciary, which is otherwise very active, has not interpreted CMRA so as to do real justice to the victims of child marriages. There are many reasons for the court's ineffective role to date. So far, the judiciary has interpreted the words of the statute very technically without focussing on the purpose behind it. It has not attempted to respond to women's voices and their experiences. It has expressed little concern about the serious repercussions of child marriage. It seems that the judiciary has ignored the repercussions of child marriages in the wider context affecting the whole of society and not only the young girls who are the victims of such marriages. Equally responsible is the legal community that has not brought the severe consequences of child marriage on a girl child's reproductive health and development to the notice of the judiciary. The combined result is the denial of justice to the young child brides.

Soon after the enactment of CMRA, attempts were made to challenge the validity of child marriages. For instance the validity of a marriage was challenged before the Patna High Court in 1933. A widowed mother gave her daughter of seven years to a man whose age was more than twenty-four years. But the court held that the marriage was valid and supported its decision by quoting the recommendation of the Select Committee.[96] Similar decisions were given by several high courts.[97] The Orissa[98] and Madras[99] High Courts too have upheld the validity of child marriages. However, there was an exceptional decision of the division bench of the Andhra Pradesh High Court. It declared in *Panchireddi* v. *Gadela Ganapatlu*[100] an under-age marriage to be void ab initio. The court held that if child marriage was not to be treated either as void or voidable 'it will throw open once again the floodgate of child marriages'.[101] However, the full bench of the same high court in *Vankataramana* v. *State*[102] overruled this decision on the ground that it was erroneous to regard an under-age marriage as void or invalid, since Parliament did not intend to do so. It is interesting to note that though the high courts, in pursuance of the object of the Act, refrained from declaring child marriages invalid, the Allahabad High Court in one case went so far as to not allow a husband to take possession of his minor wife.[103]

Another important issue brought before the judiciary was to decide the guilt of those individuals who were responsible for offences under CMRA. The courts have examined the responsibility of persons involved in child marriages, namely, parents, guardians, priests, mediators, creditors, etc. The approach of the courts appears to be very compassionate towards the parents. Negotiating, preparing, or doing any other preliminary acts in connection with the child marriages by parents were not treated as an offence by the courts.[104]

The court demanded that a prima facie case must be established that the marriage had duly been performed in accordance with the essential religious rites and the said marriage must be valid according to law applicable to the parties. Thus, when the prosecution could not prove the performance of *kanyadan*[105] by the bride's parents, they were not held guilty.[106] But in another case participation by a parent in *Kanyadan* ceremony was proved. Even then the court did not hold him guilty.[107] Similarly, the mother of a child bride was declared to be out of the purview of CMRA as she was neither in charge of the child nor could she prevent the marriage.[108] In the same case the court held that the parents of the bridegroom could not be convicted merely because the bride was below the age of fourteen years.[109] The grandfather of a minor daughter was not held guilty though he was attending the marriage. Only the father, as her guardian was held guilty.[110]

In a few cases the priests responsible for performing the ceremonies of marriage were punished for not making reasonable inquiries as to the age of the bride and groom. The Madras[111] and Allahabad[112] High Courts have held that a priest invited to perform the marriage ceremony was legally bound to make an inquiry about the age of the parties. The Madras[113] and Bombay[114] High Courts have held that relatives and invitees attending a child marriage, who did nothing that could amount to 'performing', 'conducting', or 'directing' the marriage, could not be held guilty of any offence under CMRA. Sometimes there are also conflicting decisions which create confusion about the scope of CMRA. A person who advanced money for marriage expenditure of an infant was held not guilty under the Act by the Calcutta High Court.[115] But the Bombay[116] and Punjab[117] High Courts held the creditors guilty for advancing money to a guardian for the marriage expenses of a child under CMRA. Later, even the Calcutta High Court changed its decision[118] and the purpose for lending the money was held unlawful and against public policy.

Analysis of these cases indicates a contradictory and very technical approach of the judiciary while dealing with the problem of child marriage. It also indicates that the judiciary did try to promote, though in an inadequate way, the object of CMRA by punishing persons involved in the commission of a crime. But on the whole, the courts were more inclined to punish those outside the family (the moneylender or the priest) than the family members themselves (parents, guardians).

One of the explanations for such decisions could be that the judicial attitude continues to be shaped by the prevailing assumptions about child marriage. The society at large seems not to have internalized the law. Deeply rooted traditional practice of child marriage continues to preclude more positive social change. At the same time the judiciary has not taken cognizance of women's experiences and has not asked the woman question to analyse the practice of child marriage. The practice of child marriage is not questioned within the framework of constitutional rights. Nor it has been tested from the feminist perspective. It is equally disappointing to note that lawyers have never raised arguments before the courts about the adverse consequences of early marriages. They have never presented the social science data before the courts to indicate the harsh realities about socio-cultural and economic repercussions of child marriages on young girls and most importantly the severe effects on their reproductive health.

The Indian Penal Code and the Minimum Age for Consensual Sexual Intercourse

Before enacting CMRA, efforts were made to raise the age of consent in the offence of rape.[119] The reason was to give protection to young brides from their husbands. As mentioned earlier, the age of consent was raised from twelve years to thirteen in 1925. In 1949, it was further raised to fifteen years if the victim was the wife. It was done in pursuance of CMRA, which had increased the minimum age of marriage from fourteen years to fifteen for girls. In 1978, the age of marriage for girls was raised to eighteen years. But the minimum age of consent was not raised correspondingly, in spite of the demands made by women's organizations. Later on, in 1983 substantial changes were introduced in Section 375 of the IPC.[120] However, these did not touch upon the age of consent. This legislative policy was indicative of inconsistent lawmaking. It must also be mentioned here that the age of consent for rape today is sixteen years where a woman is not the man's wife. If she is his wife, the age of consent is fifteen years. Even this anomaly was not corrected in 1983.

The presumption behind laying down the minimum age as *age of consent* is that young people lack the maturity to comprehend fully the nature and long-term consequences of sexual intercourse. However, this presumption is negated within the marital relationship. Forcible intercourse by the husband with his own wife, the wife not being under fifteen years of age is not rape in India.[121] There is little protection provided against marital rape. Probably the reason lies in the presumption that a woman unconditionally surrenders her right to withhold consent to sexual intercourse on entering into a marriage. This obviously sustains the dominant familial ideology and control over female sexuality, which treats a woman as the property of her husband.[122] This ideology is supported even by the latest amendments introduced to the Indian Penal Code in 1983.[123]

Another anomaly that needs to be highlighted is, regarding the punishment provided for the offence of rape. The minimum punishment for the offence of rape is seven years imprisonment and the maximum is life imprisonment.[124] But in case of a rape by a man of his own wife, who is above twelve years but below fifteen years of age, the husband is liable to be punished only with two years' imprisonment.[125] Once the child marriage is prohibited by the law, why should there be a less severe punishment for rape of the wife who is above twelve years but below fifteen years of age? The provision thus reflects the Victorian notions of morality of the lawmakers of India.[126]

End Notes

[1] The Age of Consent Committee (also known as Joshi Committee) and the Select Committee. For details see note 35 infra and the accompanied text.

[2] See Ratna Kapur and Brenda Cossman, *Subversive Sites: Feminist Engagements with Law in India* (New Delhi: Sage Publications, 1996).

[3] Department of Women and Child Development, Ministry of Human Resource Development, Government of India, 'Demographic Profile and Future Strategies for Development of the Girl Child in India' (1995) 25 *Social Change* 24 at 29; See also International Institute for Population Sciences (IIPS), *National Family Health Survey, NFHS-2 1998–99 India* (Mumbai: IIPS, 2000) at 54–6.

[4] Tahir Mahmood, 'Marriage-Age in India and Abroad—A Comparative Aspect' (1980) 22 *Journal of Indian Law Institute* 38 at 39.

[5] Section 375 of the Indian Penal Code.

[6] S.P. Sathe, *Towards Gender Justice* (Bombay: S.N.D.T. Women's University, 1993) at 25.

[7] *Dadaji Bhikaji* v. *Rukhmabai* IX Indian Law Reporter (Bombay Series) 529 (1885).

[8] *Queen Empress* v. *Huree Mohan Mythee* XVIII Indian Law Reporter (Calcutta) 49 (1891).

[9] Emphasis is mine. This was the threat to the then existing notion of a marriage for Hindus who considered marriage as a *samskar* (religious ceremony) and was generally believed not to require the bride's consent as she was to be the subject of a gift in marriage. See Sudhir Chandra, *Enslaved Daughters Colonialism, Law and Women's Rights* (New Delhi: Oxford University Press, 1998) at 2. In the domestic social order this notion still prevails to a large extent. This book is a wonderful exposition on colonialism, law and women's rights in the context of unique events that occurred in the life of Rukhmabai.

[10] Supra note 7 (emphasis added).

[11] See Y.D. Phadke, *Shodh Bal Gopalancha* (in Marathi, Pune: Sri Vidya Prakashan, 1993) at 119.

[12] Later on, Rukhmabai went to UK to do her medicine. After becoming a doctor she came back and practised in Gujarat.

[13] Patricia Uberoi, 'Hindu Marriage Law and the Judicial Construction of Sexuality' in Ratna Kapur (ed.), *Feminist Terrains in Legal Domains* (New Delhi: Kali, 1996) at 184.

[14] Chandra, supra note 9 at 2. It is interesting to note that Rukhmabai wrote a letter to *The Times of India* (9 April 1887) on the ills of child marriage. She emphatically expressed her views about the correlation between early marriage and denial of education to women. I have quoted a para from it at the beginning of the introduction.

[15] *Queens Empress* v. *Huree Mohan Mythee* XVIII Indian Law Reporter (Calcutta) 49 (1891).

[16] Kapur, supra note 2 at 50.

[17] Tanika Sarkar, 'Colonial Lawmaking and Lives/Deaths of Indian Women: Different Readings of Law and Community' in Kapur, supra note 13 at 210 (225).

[18] Bengal Government Judicial, McLeod's Medical Report on Child Wives NF J C/17Proceedings 104–17, June 1893.

[19] Ibid.

[20] Ibid.

[21] Other regional terms for which are *Garbhadhan* or *Gauna*.

[22] See Rajat Ray, '*Social Conflict and Political Unrest in Bengal: 1875–1927*' (New Delhi: Oxford University Press, 1984) Chapter 2.

[23] Ibid.

[24] Sarkar, supra note 17 at 231.

[25] Ibid.

[26] Ibid. at 232.

[27] Kapur, Supra note 2 at 52.

[28] See Kosambi Meera, 'Girl Brides and Socio-legal Changes, Age of Consent Bill (1891) Controversy' (1991) 26 *Economic and Political Weekly* at 1857; *also* 'Women's Emancipation and Equality—Pandita Ramabai's Contribution to Women's Cause' (1998) *Economic and Political Weekly* WS-38.

[29] Rebecca Cook, 'State Accountability under the Convention on the Elimination of Discrimination against Women', in Rebecca Cook (ed.), *Human Rights of Women* (Philadelphia: University of Pennsylvania Press, 1994) 228 at 242.

[30] Sathe, supra note 6 at 25.

[31] It will not be out of place to mention a story of Phoolan Devi at this stage. In 1994, a Hindi film titled *Bandit Queen* was released in India, which is

based on the 'true life history' of Phoolan Devi, the woman outlaw who went on to become a celebrity. Phoolan, a low-caste girl, was married *at eleven against her will to a thirty-year-old man.* She was raped and was beaten by him. She was also made to work hard in his house. As a result she ran away to her parents' house. She was thrown out of the village after she rejected advances made by the upper-caste village head's son. Later on she joined a gang of bandits and became the bandit queen. She committed many murders in revenge for atrocities that she had to face in her life. But ultimately she surrendered to the police. She was tried and convicted but was released later on. She became a political leader and was elected to the Parliament. Recently in 2002, she was murdered. Though it is a unique case, it is worth understanding that the root cause of the mysterious life that she had to live lies in the fact of her child marriage against her wish. For an analysis of the film from a feminist perspective, see Shohini Ghosh, 'Deviant Pleasures and Disorderly Women', in Kapur, supra note 13 at 150.

[32] For this part I have extensively relied on Mahmood, supra note 4.

[33] See *The Gazette of India*, part V at 111,165 (1928).

[34] Government of India, *Report of the Age of Consent Committee* (1929) at 99–100.

[35] E.g. Baroda, Indore, Kashmir, Kota, Mysore, and Rajkot.

[36] Supra note 34 at 102.

[37] Ibid. at 179–80.

[38] Ibid. at 180–1.

[39] This is significant because when the Bill was discussed, one objection raised was that the Bill would interfere with the religious laws of the natives and thus would violate Queen Victoria's Proclamation of 1858, under which the British were committed not to interfere in religion and its affairs.

[40] These are discussed in detail in a later chapter.

[41] CEDAW, *General Recommendation 21*, UN GAOR, 1994, Doc. No. A/47/38 para 36.

[42] Sarkar, supra note 17 at 220–4.

[43] *Yusuf* v. *State of Bombay* AIR 1954 S.C. 321; *Sagar* v. *State* AIR 1968 A.P. 165.

[44] Leo Karowitz, 'Law and the Single Girl' in *Women and the Law: Unfinished Protection* (1969) at 11.

[45] See *The Gazette of India*, 15 December 1977, Part II, S.2, Extra., at 882.

[46] Section 3: *Punishment for male adult below 21 years of age marrying a child*: A bridegroom who is above 18 but is below 21 years of age if contracts a

marriage, is punishable with simple imprisonment up to 15 days or with fine up to one thousand rupees.

[47] Section 4: *Punishment for male adult above 21 years of age marrying a child:* A bridegroom who is above 21 years of age, if marries a girl below 18 years, is punishable with simple imprisonment up to three months and also fine.

[48] Section 6: Any person having charge of the child, whether as parent or guardian or in any other capacity, lawful or unlawful, who does any act to promote the marriage or permits it to be solemnized, is punishable with simple imprisonment up to three months and fine. However, a female guardian is not to be sent to imprisonment.

[49] Ibid.

[50] Section 5: *For the one who solemnizes the marriage:* A person, who solemnizes, performs, conducts, or directs any child marriage, is punishable with simple imprisonment up to three months and fine.

[51] Offences are classified as cognizable and non-cognizable under the Criminal Procedure Code. In case of cognizable offences the police are allowed to initiate an action against an accused on their own. The police are not required to wait for the filing of a formal complaint by the victim. The police are authorized to arrest an accused person without a warrant of arrest from the Magistrate. Serious offences involving danger to the society at large are categorized as cognizable offences. Secondly, to prevent repetition of such crimes, the accused is allowed to be taken into custody by the police. And thirdly, to avoid repeated occurrence of an offence, it is declared to be cognizable.

[52] B. Sivaramayya, 'Towards Equality: The Long Road Ahead', in A. Dhanda (ed.), *Essays in Honour of Lotika Sarkar* (Bombay: Tripathi, 1999) 387 at 389.

[53] Popularly known as the Pushpaben Committee.

[54] Government of Gujarat, *Report of the Suicide Inquiry Committee,* 1964, at 63.

[55] See the Gujarat Act XI of 1964. The Child Marriage Act is a central legislation and is applicable to all states. But the subject of marriage, divorce, and maintenance is included in the Concurrent List of the seventh schedule to the Constitution, which enumerates the subjects in respect of which the centre, as well as, the states have the legislative power. The centre as well as the states can pass legislation relating to the subjects mentioned in the Concurrent List. That is why the Gujarat government could make an amendment to CMRA.

[56] Government of India, *Towards Equality*, Report of the Committee on the Status of Women in India, 1974 at 113; for detail discussion see note 65 infra.

[57] Section 7: *Offences to be cognizable for certain purposes*: The Code of Criminal Procedure, 1973 shall apply to offences under the Act as if they were cognizable offences:

(a) for the purpose of investigation of such offences; and

(b) for the purposes of matters other than (i) those referred to in Sec. 42 of that Code, and (ii) arrest of an accused without a warrant or without an order of a magistrate.

[58] Section 9: *Mode of taking cognizance of offences*: No court shall take cognizance of any offence under this Act after the expiry of one year from the date on which the offence is alleged to have been committed.

[59] And it is also reflected in Section 468 of the Criminal Procedure Code. It states:

(1) ... no court shall take cognizance of an offence after the expiry of the period of limitation.

(2) The period of limitation shall be—

(a) six months, if the offence is punishable with fine only;

(b) one year, if the offence is punishable with imprisonment for a term not exceeding one year.

[60] Sivaramayya, supra note 52 at 390.

[61] A justification to raise it to more than one year is based on Section 468 of the Criminal Procedure Code. There is no limitation for the purpose of investigation of crimes punishable with more than one year imprisonment. Such crimes are treated as of serious nature by the law. See Section 468, supra note 59.

[62] Section 12: Power to issue injunction prohibiting marriage in contravention of this Act:

(1) Notwithstanding anything to the contrary contained in this Act, the Court may, if satisfied that information laid before it through a complaint or otherwise that a child marriage in contravention of this Act has been arranged or is about to be solemnized, issue an injunction against any of the persons mentioned in sections 3, 4, 5 and 6 of this Act prohibiting such marriage.

(2) No injunction under sub-section (1) shall be issued against any person unless the Court has previously given notice to such person, and has afforded him an opportunity to show cause against the issue of the injunction.

(3) The Court may either on its own motion or on the application of any person aggrieved rescind or alter any order made under sub-section (1).

(4) Where such an application is received, the Court shall afford the applicant an early opportunity of appearing before it either in person or by pleader; and if

the Court rejects the application wholly or in part, it shall record in writing its reasons for so doing.

(5) Whoever knowing that an injunction has been issued against him under sub-section (1) of this section disobeys such injunction shall be punished with imprisonment of either description for a term which may extend to three months, or with fine which may extend to one thousand rupees, or with both:

Provided that no woman shall be punishable with imprisonment.

[63] See Sara Hossain, 'Women's Rights and Personal Laws in South Asia' in Cook, supra note 30 at 465 (476); See also Ladan Askari, 'The Convention on the Rights of the Child: The Necessity of Adding a Provision to Ban Child Marriage' (1998) 5 *Journal of International and Comparative Law* (1998) 123.

[64] The Age of Consent Committee, supra note 34.

[65] CSW was appointed by the Government of India to judge the status of women. CSW submitted its report, *Towards Equality* in 1974.

[66] Ibid. at 135–6.

[67] The recommendation was accepted by the Central legislature for Hindus and accordingly changes were introduced in the Hindu Marriage Act in 1976. Section 13 (2) (iv) was added to the Hindu Marriage Act by which it granted a special ground of divorce to a wife.

[68] CSW, supra note 65 at 113.

[69] A detailed discussion follows.

[70] In 1955 the Hindu Marriage Act declared bigamous marriage as void. Similar objections were raised at the time of drafting the law. Still the Parliament did declare it void. The same analogy needs to be applied to the provision regarding the age of the parties to a marriage.

[71] The National Commission for Women (NCW) was established in 1990 by the National Commission for Women Act. One of its functions is to suggest amendments in the existing law, and new laws. The Commission submitted its report to the government on Uniform Law of Marriage and Divorce in 1994.

[72] Section 8 of the bill declares that all marriages in contravention of any of the conditions laid down in Section 3 shall be void. Section 3 of the bill lays down the condition for a marriage. Section 3 (1) states that the groom should have completed the age of twenty-one and the bride eighteen years at the time of marriage.

[73] Section 7 of the bill. It is interesting to note that CEDAW referred to the legislative reforms suggested by NCW in its concluding observation on the report of India and called upon the government to reform the laws as proposed by the NCW. CEDAW/C/2000/1/CRP.3/Add.4/Rev.1, 1 Feb 2000, Para 30.

[74] It has not opposed declaration of child marriage void. But the Women's Convention in Article 16(2) declares that 'the marriage of a child shall have no legal effect'.

[75] Memorandum of Action taken on the Annual Report of NHRC for 1995–96. The government filed the same declaration on Article 16 of the Women's Convention. See NHRC Annual Report, 1996–97.

[76] Ibid.

[77] One can learn from the experiences of other countries, particularly from Asia, which have declared over the period child marriage void. For example, in Indonesia, the marriage law declares child marriage void. It was so done in 1991. Similar is the situation in Sri Lanka. It is interesting to note that in both these countries the prescribed age of marriage for a girl is much lower than the Indian law. But in reality percentage of girls marrying below eighteen years is much less than in India. See Savitri Goonesekere, *Child, Law and Justice* (New Delhi: Sage, 1996).

[78] For example, Sections 24 and 25 of the Hindu Marriage Act provide for right to maintenance. These sections could be amended to give the right to maintenance to a woman whose marriage was void on the ground of the breach of the condition regarding the minimum age of marriage prescribed by the law.

[79] In case of Hindus amongst whom the concept of the joint family property is recognized by the law, her right could be enforced against such property also.

[80] Section 16 of HMA.

[81] Article 21A and Article 45 of the Constitution of India as amended by the eighty-sixth amendment in 2003.

[82] Article 5 of the Declaration on Social Progress and Development Proclaimed by General Assembly Resolution 2542 (XXIV) of 11 December 1969.

[83] There is a provision under the personal laws of marriage. See below at 77.

[84] See Paras Diwan, *Law of Marriage and Divorce* (New Delhi: Wadhwa Publication, 1996) at 60–7.

[85] See Sections 3 and 8 of the Bill, supra note 72.

[86] Article 16 (1) (b).

[87] Except for Muslim personal law.

[88] See Article 3.

[89] See Article 16.

[90] Declaration of India to Article 16.

[91] Bill, supra note 72.

[92] See item 5—marriage and item 6—registration of documents.

[93] See Section 14 of CMRA as introduced by Gujarat in 1962.

[94] E.g. the erstwhile state of Mysore had enacted a law in 1894, which disallowed marriage of a girl below the age of fourteen years with a man above fifty. See The Mysore Infant Marriage Prevention Act, 1894. The state of Kota provided punishment for marriage of a girl below eighteen with a man of more than double her age. See Kota State Law of 1927.

[95] Ravi Dugal, *Population and Family Planning Policy: A Critique and a Perspective* (Bombay: CEHAT, 1994) at 4.

[96] *Mt. Jalsi Kaur* v. *Emperor* AIR 1933 Patna 471.

[97] *Munshi Ram* v. *Emperor* AIR 1936 All 11; AIR 1936 All 852; *Ram Baran* v. *Sital Pathak* AIR 1939 All 34.

[98] *Birupakshya Das* v. *Kunju Behari* AIR 1961 Orissa 104.

[99] *Sivanandy* v. *Bhagavathyamma* AIR 1962 Mad 400.

[100] AIR 1975 AP 193.

[101] Ibid. at 195.

[102] AIR 1977 AP 43. This and the above case was decided under the Hindu Marriage Act.

[103] AIR 1935 All 916.

[104] AIR 1938 Nagpur 235.

[105] *Kanyadan* means gift of a daughter. It is one of the religious ceremony performed while solemnizing a Hindu marriage, though it is not an essential ritual under the Hindu Marriage Act.

[106] AIR 1963 MP 126.

[107] AIR 1940 Bom 363.

[108] *Public Prosecutor* v. *Thammanna Rattayya* AIR 1937 Madras 490.

[109] Ibid.

[110] *Bhagwat Sarup* v. *Emperor* AIR 1945 All 306.

[111] *Ayyah Pillai* v. *Manikk Pillai* (1965) 1 Madras Law Journal 172.

[112] *Jwala Prasad* v. *Emperor* AIR 1934 All 331.

[113] *Ayyah Pillai* v. *Manik Pillai* (1965) 1 Madras Law Journal 172.

[114] *Emperor* v. *Fulbhai Bhulbai* AIR 1940 Bom 363.

[115] ILR (1937) 2 Cal 764.

[116] *Rambhau* v. *Rajaram* AIR 1956 Bom 250.

[117] *Ghulam Bhik* v. *Rustom* Ali AIR 1949 East Punjab 354.

[118] AIR 1941 Cal 244.

[119] Note 6 supra and accompanying text.

[120] The burden of proof was shifted on the accused in case of custodial rape. These changes were brought in response to strong pressures created by women's movement.

[121] As mentioned in note 6 supra, the minimum age for statutory rape is sixteen but in case of a married woman it is fifteen. And as discussed earlier, the minimum age for marriage is eighteen for a girl. Unfortunately, the Indian legislators have not taken cognizance of these contradictions.

[122] Ratna Kapur and Brenda Cossman, 'Women, Familial Ideology and the Constitution: Challenging Equality Rights' in Kapur, supra note 13 at 61 (80).

[123] The amendment added s. 376A—Sexual assault on judicially separated wife. The section provides for just two years imprisonment and fine for non-consensual intercourse with such wife and does not treat it as rape.

[124] Section 376 (1).

[125] Ibid.

[126] Vasudha Dhagamwar, *Law, Power and Justice* (Bombay: Tripathi, 1974) at 145.

3

Personal Laws, Legal Reform, and the Judiciary

Introduction

In this chapter I proceed to discuss the different religion-based personal laws of marriage prevalent in India. Hindus, Muslims, Christians, Jews, and Parsis in India have their own, separate marriage laws that prescribe the age of marriage for the bride and the bridegroom. I examine the relevant provisions of these laws and compare them with CMRA. My argument is that the personal laws practically nullify the effect and authority of the uniformly applicable secular CMRA. In spite of the constitutional mandate of a uniform civil code,[1] the discriminatory religion-based marriage laws continue to remain in force in India, again for the reason that by and large it is women who are victims of these laws; and women's issues have a low priority on the political agenda. Women's experiences and views are not considered to be worth accommodating in policy formulation even if they are the direct object of the legislation.

I then analyse the relevant provisions of the law relating to guardianship, as these provisions declare a husband to be the guardian of his *minor wife*. I argue that the guardianship law, in its present form, fosters social legitimacy for the legally prohibited practice of child marriage. I conclude with the observation that by not amending the guardianship law in conformity with CMRA, the legislators have reconfirmed the patriarchal nature of the law and have also reflected their piecemeal approach towards the issue of child marriage. A reading of CMRA, marriage laws, guardianship law, and criminal law together clearly indicates the indiscriminate approach of the policy makers.

At the end, I suggest a series of reforms to the existing laws, namely CMRA, the marriage laws of Hindus, Parsis, Christians, and Muslims, guardianship law, and rape law with a view to making CMRA more effective. These recommendations are based on the method of 'Asking the Women Question'. My argument is that women's experience must be the foundation of laws to promote their human rights and achieve social justice.

The chapter ends with a brief comment on the role of law in bringing about change in human behaviour. A detailed discussion of the sociology of law and feminist theories on the role of law has been purposely avoided so as not to lose focus. Any social legislation that tries to bring about a change in society faces resistance from within the society, the more so in the field of personal relations. However, one has to appreciate that the law has a definite role to play in bringing about social reforms. No one can guarantee, particularly in the area of personal relations, that legislation will succeed in changing the behaviour of people. But social behaviour needs specific directions for bringing reforms in itself. Law certainly plays and has to play a role to give such direction.

The success of socially reformist piece of legislation then depends upon an active judiciary, deployment of effective implementation machinery, and other supportive measures. Attainment of social justice rests upon the extent to which these agencies are prepared to understand the patriarchal nature of the system and to address injustice done to women on the basis of 'asking the woman question'. Unless such holistic efforts are made, any social legislation just has a symbolic standing and makes no effective impact on social behaviour. Continuation of the practice of child marriages on a large scale in India needs to be evaluated from this perspective.

Personal Laws

In addition to CMRA, there are religion-based personal laws in the matters of marriage and divorce. Hindus, Muslims, Christians, and Parsis have their different marriage laws. These laws prescribe conditions for performing a valid, legal marriage. One of the conditions is regarding the age of the parties to the marriage. The other conditions are monogamy, for women only in the case of Muslim law, soundness of mind, prohibition against consanguinity, and the mode of solemnization of marriage for Hindus, Christians, and Parsis. The Muslim law of marriage permits polygamy for men and soundness of mind is not an essential prerequisite.

Hindu Marriage Act

The Hindu Marriage Act (HMA), 1955, is applicable to Hindus, Buddhists, Sikhs, Jains, and to those who are not Muslims, Christians, Parsis, or Jews.[2] In 1955 it laid down fifteen years as the age of marriage for girls and eighteen years for boys.[3] It required girls in the age group of 15–18 years to obtain guardian's consent for the marriage.[4] HMA prescribes penalties for non-compliance with the condition of the age of marriage.[5] A bridegroom as well as the bride is liable to be punished with a fine or imprisonment for up to fifteen days. However, HMA does not specify a failure to comply with minimum age as a ground that could make the marriage either void or voidable. Sections 11[6] and 12[7] of HMA deal with the grounds that declare the marriage void and voidable respectively. Neither section covers contravention of the condition regarding the age of the parties. Reading Sections 5, 11, and 12 together the Supreme Court declared in *Lila Gupta* v. *Laxmi Narain*[8] that a marriage contracted in contravention of the condition of age was not void. It stated:

> The Child Marriage Restraint Act was enacted to carry forward the reformist movement of prohibiting child marriages and while it made marriage in contravention of the provisions of the Child Marriage Restraint Act punishable, simultaneously it did not render the marriage void. It would thus appear that voidness of marriage unless statutorily provided for is not to be readily inferred.[9]

The Punjab and Haryana High Court also mentioned in *Nasib Chand* v. *Surinder Kaur*:[10]

> The only consequence of the solemnization of the marriage with one of the spouses being of less than the prescribed age was the punishment of the guilty party under Section 18 of HMA, but all the time the validity of the marriage remains intact.[11]

In 1976, when substantial amendments were introduced to HMA, a new ground for divorce was made available only to a wife. It states as follows:

> A wife may also present a petition for the dissolution of her marriage by a decree of divorce on the ground,
>
> (i) ...
>
> (ii) ...
>
> (iii) ...

(iv) that her marriage was solemnized (whether consummated or not) before she attained the age of fifteen years and she has repudiated the marriage after attaining that age but before attaining the age of eighteen years.[12]

Thus a girl who was married before the age of fifteen years is entitled to seek divorce on the ground that she has refuted the said marriage after attaining the age of fifteen and before completing the age of eighteen years.[13] She is entitled to file a petition for divorce after attaining the age of eighteen years. This provision was adopted from the Dissolution of Muslim Women's Marriage Act, 1939.[14] However, it is more liberal than the corresponding law applicable to Muslim girls. In case of a Muslim girl, she can repudiate her marriage and apply for its dissolution only if the marriage is not consummated. But in case of a Hindu wife even the consummation of marriage does not defeat her right to have the marriage dissolved. While drafting this amendment, the lawmakers probably might have thought of giving recognition to the choice of a girl in not accepting the marriage arranged by her parents without her consent in her childhood. In fact, in *Batoolan* v. *Zahoor Shah Roshan*[15] Justice Abdul Hakim Khan explained the importance of the option of repudiation of marriage:

> On one hand, it encouraged the principle of mutual liking, which is regarded as a sure foundation of a happy married life, and on the other hand it put a curb on the tendency prevalent in ancient society to perpetuate child marriage, for fear of its repudiation by either party on attaining the age of majority.[16]

As mentioned earlier, at the time of the 1976 amendments introduced in HMA, the minimum age for the marriage of a Hindu girl was fifteen years. CMRA raised the age to eighteen years in 1978 and its application was specifically extended to HMA. Requirement of the age as per the amended CMRA in 1978 and the new ground of divorce for wives introduced in 1976 created another anomalous situation under HMA. The 1976 amended clause recognized the right of a Hindu wife to repudiate her marriage only if she was below the age of fifteen years when her marriage was performed. The right was not available if her marriage was performed after attaining the age of fifteen years. Thus the situation today is that HMA does not provide any remedy to a girl whose marriage was performed by her guardians after she attains the age of fifteen years. Such anomaly highlights the inconsistent legislative policy. Unless an amendment is introduced to the newly added ground of divorce, the present anomalous position of girls married between fifteen and eighteen years will continue.[17]

To conclude, the position under HMA is that a Hindu girl above eighteen years of age can marry on her own, without obtaining the consent of her guardians. But if she is below eighteen years of age she cannot marry even with the consent of her guardians. HMA does not recognize the right of guardians to marry off their children below the prescribed age limit and provides punishment to the bride and groom if marriage is performed in contravention of the age provision.[18] However, such a marriage is valid in the eyes of law and produces all legal effects as HMA is silent regarding the legal effect of an under-age marriage.[19] A minor wife has a choice to seek divorce on the ground of under-age marriage on attaining the age of eighteen years. But she can obtain divorce only if the marriage was performed when she was below the age of fifteen.

Consent of Parties under HMA

There are two provisions of HMA that involve *consent* of the parties to a marriage. A marriage between two Hindus may be solemnized provided that among other criteria, 'at the time of marriage, neither party is incapable of giving consent because of unsound mind or even if capable of giving a valid consent is not suffering from mental disorder, or insanity'.[20] If either party to a marriage is of unsound mind the marriage does not become void but is voidable at the option of the other party.[21]

The other condition about consent provides that if the consent of either party to a marriage was obtained by force or fraud, the marriage would be voidable at the option of the party whose consent was so obtained.[22] A petition has to be filed within one year from the date on which either the force ceased to operate or fraud was discovered.[23] However it is repeatedly emphasized in the case law that the meaning of fraud is not to be defined as in Section 17 of the Indian Contract Act. But it to be so modified on the understanding that 'it is undisputed that a Hindu marriage is a sacrament and not a contract'. Certainly, fraud must be more substantial than the petty misrepresentations of the qualities of the bride and groom that are common features of every marriage negotiations, it being conceded that 'in negotiations and courtship parties are bound to exaggerate'.[24] In a well-known case *Harbhajan Singh* v. *Brij Balab Kaur*,[25] the judge noted:

> If the term fraud is to be interpreted according to the definition given in the Indian Contract Act, then it would become impossible to maintain

the sanctity of the marriage. All sorts of misrepresentations will be alleged in order to break the marriage tie. This obviously could not have been the intention of the legislature.

In *Alka Sharma* v. *Abhinesh Chandra Sharma*[26] it was reiterated that consent in the context of Hindu marriage includes consent to marriage given by a spouse through his/her parents, friends or relatives. Making rather a virtue of social necessity on behalf of the stability of marriage, Justice D.M. Dharmadhikari said that when the son authorized his father to settle his marriage, the disclosure to the father about the bride was disclosure to the son also.[27] The father's consent was the consent of the son. Sometimes it is also asserted that when the parties to a marriage participate in the religious rituals performed by the priest it amounts to their consent[28] or that consent must be implied in a person's going through with the marriage ceremony.

A marriage, therefore, is valid even in the absence of free consent or for that matter even if the consent is obtained by force or fraud. In such a situation the marriage remains valid if either party does not take action within the stipulated time. And in case if the party fails to take such action within one year, she has no choice but to continue in the relationship. The provision makes it clear that the presence of consent or *free consent* is not an essential prerequisite for a marriage to be valid.

There is a subtle distinction between free consent and consent without force. Consent obtained without force need not necessarily be free consent. For consent to be free it needs to be an informed consent. A person must understand the meaning, nature, and consequences of the event or action or contract to which she is giving consent. And she must also have freedom and choice to say either yes or no to that event, action, or contract. It may be argued that her consent can be presumed when she participates in marriage ceremonies. But the point is that consent, if given, would never have been given on the basis of free will and nor would it have been an informed one. This is a substantial lacuna in HMA. In 1978, though the age of the bride and the bridegroom was raised to eighteen and twenty-one respectively, HMA did not provide explicitly that for the marriage to be valid and legal, the consent of the parties to a marriage is a mandatory prerequisite. Under the Indian law, the age of majority is eighteen years and at eighteen a person is treated as competent and capable of giving legal consent.[29]

It is further important to note that according to Section 5 (vi) of HMA, as it stood before 1978, it was necessary that the guardian should give consent to the marriage where the bride was below the age of eighteen years. When the age of the bride was raised to eighteen years in 1978, this provision regarding the guardian's consent to a marriage was deleted.[30] Section 6 of HMA provided a list of persons entitled to act as guardians in marriage. That list too was deleted in 1978. A presumption behind the amendment was that since the girl herself could give consent to the marriage, there would be no need to have the guardian's consent. However, the fact remains that HMA did not mention in specific terms that the consent of the parties to a marriage is an essential condition. Nor did it provide for invalidation of the marriage in the absence of such consent.

The Women's Convention puts a strong emphasis on free consent of the parties to a marriage.[31] As India has ratified the Women's Convention, the government is bound to comply with its obligations. A detailed discussion follows in a subsequent chapter.

Muslim Law of Marriage

The Muslim Personal Law (MPL) of marriage is not codified in India.[32] It is customary and is based on the Sharia. It lays down the age of puberty as the age of marriage. Unless the contrary is proved, the age of puberty is presumed to be fifteen years for both girls and boys.[33]

Girls who have attained the age of puberty are competent to marry freely, without obtaining the consent of parents. Boys and girls, who have not reached the age of puberty, can be lawfully contracted into marriage by their marriage guardians.[34] A pre-puberty marriage contact entered into by guardians on behalf their children is valid. A husband or wife can avoid such marriage on attaining the age of puberty. This is known as *option of puberty* and is available if a guardian other than the father or father's father had contracted the marriage.[35] This option is available to a wife if her marriage is not consummated. She has to exercise the option of puberty within three years following completion of the fifteenth year of age.[36] Her decision needs to be confirmed by the court.[37] These provisos are not applicable to a husband.

As mentioned earlier, CMRA is applicable to all citizens of India irrespective of their religion. So CMRA is applicable to Muslims also. But still MPL maintains its distinctiveness. Guardians are allowed to enter into a contract of marriage *on behalf* of their pre-puberty age children. The rules of Muslim law relating to a minor's marriage do, therefore, conflict with the provisions of CMRA. As CMRA made changes in HMA in 1978, it did not incorporate such changes in MPL. So, on one hand, the Muslim guardians in India are entitled to marry off their daughters under the age of fifteen years according to their personal law. On the other hand, for entering into such marriage on behalf of their daughters they could be held criminally liable under the secular law of the country.[38]

Contrary to HMA, MPL provides in clear terms for the consent of the parties to a marriage. According to MPL, a marriage is a contract. It requires free consent of the parties to enter into a valid contract of marriage.[39] The law presumes that parties are capable of giving consent at the age of puberty, i.e. fifteen years.[40] Marriage performed without the consent of the parties who have reached the age of puberty is treated as illegal and thus void under MPL. When HMA was amended in 1976, it did take into account the provision of MPL regarding the *option of puberty*. But the provision regarding the consent of the parties to the marriage was not brought into HMA. There was no reason for not incorporating this positive aspect of MPL.

Christian Law of Marriage

The Indian Christian Marriage Act (ICMA), 1872, applicable to Christians, initially prescribed thirteen and sixteen years of age for girls and boys respectively. If parties were below the age of eighteen years, consent of the guardians was required.[41] This provision relating to the age of the parties continued till 1952 even though the age at marriage was changed through CMRA in 1929 and 1938. ICMA was brought on parity with CMRA in 1952 and the age of marriage was raised to fifteen and eighteen years for girls and boys respectively. However, the provision relating to the consent of guardians, if parties were below the age of eighteen years, was not changed though it had become redundant with reference to boys and remained relevant and applicable only to the girls.

In 1978, when CMRA raised the age of marriage to eighteen and twenty-one years for girls and boys respectively, it was made applicable to Christians who marry according to Section 60 of ICMA. The provision relating to the consent of guardians in case the parties were below the age of fifteen and eighteen (the bride and the bridegroom respectively) under Section 60 of ICMA was deleted. However, if either the bride or the bridegroom or both are below the prescribed age, the marriage is still valid under ICMA as is under HMA.[42] Further, ICMA, like HMA, does not require consent of the parties as an essential condition for a valid marriage.

Parsi Law of Marriage

For Parsis in India, there was no statutory law of marriage until 1865. They were governed by custom and usage. Customary law did permit child marriages. The Parsi Marriage and Divorce Act (PMDA), enacted in the year 1865 did not prescribe explicitly the condition relating to the age of parties to a marriage. But it required that persons of either sex below the age of twenty-one years could marry only with the consent of parents. The marriage without such consent was invalid. The 1865 Act was replaced in 1936 by a new Parsi Marriage and Divorce Act, and was further amended in 1989. PMDA did make changes regarding the age of the parties to a marriage in 1989. It was brought in parity with CMRA. According to PMDA, a marriage is invalid if the condition of age is not complied with. It states as follows:

> *No marriage shall be valid* if—
>
> (a) ...
>
> (b) ...
>
> (c) in the case of any Parsi who, if a male, has not completed 21 years of age, and if a female, has not completed 18 years of age.[43]

PMDA mentions that such marriage is invalid.[44] Invalid means without legal effect or consequences. The effect of void marriage is practically the same. However, PMDA does not make under-age marriage a ground to declare the marriage void.[45] Therefore, it can be argued that under-age marriage is not void under PMDA. The situation under PMDA therefore, is similar to ICMA. PMDA not being specific about the effect of under-age marriage, it creates a confusing situation. Regarding the consent of the parties to a marriage, PDMA is silent in the same way as HMA and ICMA.

Jews in India have no statutory law of marriage and are governed by their religion-based personal law. It prescribes the age of puberty as the minimum age for marriage. And it is presumed to be twelve for girls and thirteen years for boys. Pre-puberty marriages are strictly prohibited. Thus the situation of Jews is similar to that of Muslims. CMRA is applicable to Jews. But the resultant effect of the two conflicting laws is that the marriage of a girl above twelve years is valid and legal according to the Jewish personal law but is an offence under CMRA.

The de facto effect of these provisions under different personal laws of marriage is that practically there is no uniform law regarding age at marriage. Though CMRA prescribes the age of marriage for all persons irrespective of their religion, in practical terms, the other existing personal laws of marriage nullify the effect of CMRA. The tolerance of legal pluralism creates a situation of conflict of laws. On the one hand law restrains child marriage and on the other the personal laws give it validity. Besides this conflict of laws situation, due to its other lacuna discussed earlier, the CMRA has remained merely a paper tiger.

Civil Law of Marriage

In addition to these personal laws conflicting with CMRA, there is also a civil law of marriage in India. In 1872 the first civil law of marriage, the Special Marriage Act, was enacted in British India. It prescribed the age of marriage for a girl as fourteen years and for a boy eighteen years. This law was substantially amended in 1954. The Special Marriage Act (SPMA) recognizes a marriage to be valid and legal only if it is registered according to specified conditions. One of the conditions for marriage is the age of the parties. It prescribes twenty-one years for a boy and eighteen years for a girl. Non-compliance with the condition of age at marriage makes the marriage null and void.[46]

SPMA is the only legislation in India, which in clear term mentions that the condition relating to the age of marriage must be complied with. It is a mandatory condition. If the parties are not of the age as required by the Act, then it is not possible to solemnize the marriage as a civil marriage. The ages prescribed under SPMA as well as under CMRA for the bride and the bridegroom are the same. But the effect of non-fulfilment of this condition is not the same. Under the civil law it becomes void, but under the special legislation enacted with the object of restraining the marriages below a particular age, it remains a perfectly valid marriage.

It is also interesting to note that even the civil law of marriage is silent about the consent of the parties to a marriage. SPMA does not prescribe free consent of the parties to a marriage as an essential condition for a valid marriage. It seems legislators in their wisdom never thought of giving importance to the concept of the consent of the parties to marriage.

Registration of Marriage

Some of the personal marriage laws do make provision for registration of a marriage. For example, HMA provides for registration of marriages.[47] However, non-registration of the marriage does not affect its validity.[48] It merely imposes fines on the parties to the marriage. Under the personal laws of the Muslims, the Kazis who solemnize the marriage do keep the register with them. The same is the case with the Christians and the Parsis. The register of marriage is kept in the Church and Agyari. The purpose behind registration is merely to provide a mode of evidence and not a conclusive proof of the marriage. Non-registration does not invalidate the marriage under any of these personal laws. The Women's Convention does subscribe to the view that child marriage or polygamous marriage could be avoided if registration of marriage were made compulsory.[49] India has ratified this Convention but with a declaration regarding this provision. In principle India subscribes to the view that marriages shall be registered but has expressed inability in making a law to this effect due to the vastness of the country and the extent of illiteracy.[50]

Law of Guardianship

In India, matters relating to guardianship are governed by personal laws. For Hindus much of the law, including the law of guardianship has been codified. In 1956, the Hindu Minority and Guardianship Act (HMGA) was enacted. The *welfare of the minor* is the *paramount consideration* under this law. HMGA defines minor as 'a person who has not completed the age of 18 years'.[51] The law presumes that a person who is below the age of majority needs to be looked after in respect of her/his person and property. HMGA recognizes the rights of persons who could look after the interest of a minor as guardians. Section 6 of HMGA explains who are the natural guardians of a Hindu minor. It states:

> The natural guardians of a Hindu minor, in respect of the minor's person as well as in respect of the minor's property are—
> (a) in the case of a boy or an unmarried girl—the father, and after him, the mother ....
> (b) ...
> (c) in case of a married girl—the husband.

This provision of HMGA when read with CMRA and HMA, creates an anomalous situation. On one hand CMRA provides that the marriage of a girl should not take place unless she is eighteen years of age. HMA also reiterates the same age for a girl who is marrying according to its provisions. But it seems that HMGA does not share this principle. Section 6 (c) of HMGA mentions that the husband is a natural guardian of his minor Hindu wife. If there is a prohibition on marrying at a minor age, there was no need of providing for guardianship of a minor wife. HMGA has implicitly supported a child marriage by making such a provision.

In addition to HMGA, there is another statute entitled the Guardians and Wards Act, 1890 that is applicable to non-Hindus and non-Muslims. The provisions of the Guardian and Wards Act that are not in conflict with HMGA are applicable to Hindus.[52] This law also incorporates the principle of the 'welfare of the minor' as the 'paramount consideration'.[53] However, it too contains a provision similar to that of HMGA regarding the vesting of guardianship of a minor wife in her husband.[54] Thus the Guardians and Wards Act also tacitly accepts child marriage.

There is another provision of HMGA that incapacitates a minor from becoming a guardian of the property of another minor. It states:

> A minor shall be incompetent to act as the guardian of the property of any minor.[55]

A reading of Section 10 with Section 6 of HMGA indicates that a minor cannot act as a guardian of the *property*[56] of another minor. But it does not prohibit, in explicit terms, a minor from acting as a guardian of another minor's person. So a minor can be a guardian of the *person* of another minor. Thus a minor husband can be a natural guardian of his minor wife. A person, who himself is a minor and is under the guardianship of somebody else for his own welfare, is entitled to act as a guardian of another minor just because she is a woman. By retaining such a provision after 1978, HMGA is upholding child marriage and discriminating against women where both parties may be younger than the age prescribed by the law relating to marriage. Man's supremacy over woman irrespective of age—his image as her protector—is reflected in this provision. To avoid such an anomalous situation, care should have been taken to scrutinize all relevant laws while amending CMRA and to introduce the necessary changes. By not doing so, it shows the callousness and negligent attitude of the legislators towards the problem of child marriage.[57]

The Guardians and Wards Act is applicable to Christians and Parsis. Christians and Parsis do not have their separate laws for guardianship as Hindus have. Therefore, a Parsi or a Christian minor husband is eligible to act as a guardian of his minor wife though PMDA and ICMA both provide that the bride should be of eighteen years and the bridegroom should be of twenty-one years of age at the time of marriage. Such provision is particularly contradictory to PMDA as it invalidates the marriage when parties to the marriage are below the prescribed age. Utmost care is expected to be taken by the legislators when they introduce any change in any law so as to avoid conflicting situations. But in the case of child marriages it has been proven time and again that such care has not been taken.

The Muslim personal law has its own principles regarding guardianship. Besides general principles of guardianship, it recognizes the concept of *marriage guardianship* and allows guardians to enter into a contract of marriage on behalf of the minor children.[58] It is interesting to note that under the Muslim law, a mother of a child, who otherwise is never the guardian of her minor children, is entitled to be a *marriage guardian*. She can enter into a valid contract of marriage on behalf of her minor child in the absence of the father or grandfather of the child. Similar to the provisions of the Hindu law, under the Muslim personal law also, the guardianship of a minor wife passes to her husband irrespective of whether he himself is a minor or not.[59]

Despite the focus on the child's best interest and the welfare principle in the guardianship laws, colonial and post-independence policies in India have failed to take cognizance of the traditional practice of child marriage. Child marriage, which is clearly against the interest of a girl child and is an offence under CMRA, is still supported and approved by the Guardians and Wards Act and HMGA. These guardianship statutes continue to recognize the 'husband's guardianship over his minor wife'. The Guardians and Wards Act and HMGA have not taken into account the developments in the law preventing child marriages in India. These statutes should have deleted the respective provisions conferring guardianship of a minor wife on her husband. The recognition of the status of a husband as a guardian of his child wife affords legal and social legitimacy to the legally prohibited practice of child marriage. It reflects a patriarchal bias of legislators.

Absence of a consistent policy with regard to marriage, guardianship, and minority undermines the object of CMRA of prohibiting child marriages. As marriage does not terminate the girl's status as a minor, inevitably the alternative legal value system allows the concept of the *natural guardianship of a husband* over his *minor wife*. This concept of a *minor wife* is particularly anomalous where values of gender equity demand that the law should recognize the full legal status of women.[60]

Lacunae and Contradictions in Laws

So far, I have analysed the provisions of CMRA and the relevant provisions of the Indian Penal Code, personal laws of marriage and guardianship. This analysis points out that though the age of marriage for girls was raised to eighteen years under CMRA in 1978, there are still many lacunae in the Act. Besides, other legislation connected directly or indirectly with the question of age at marriage was not amended to conform to CMRA. The result—a number of anomalies. At the cost of repetition, it is worthwhile briefly noting these lacunae in CMRA and the contradictions between it and marriage laws, guardianship laws, and the penal laws. This method would help to understand the desired reforms that need to be introduced in the immediate future.

— CMRA prescribes *different minimum ages* for the bride and the groom.

— An underage marriage, once solemnized, becomes *legal* and CMRA merely *penalizes* such marriage. It does not touch upon the validity of child marriage.

— CMRA does not require *free consent* of the parties for a marriage.

— CMRA does not make provision for *registration* of marriages.

— CMRA declares offences to be *cognizable* only for the purpose of *investigation*.

— There is no provision in CMRA for *ex-parte injunction to prevent* solemnization of child marriages.

— There are *contradictions* between CMRA and the *personal laws of marriage*.

— There are *contradictions* between CMRA and the *personal laws of guardianship*.

— There are *contradictions* in respect of the age of consent between CMRA and law regarding the offence of *rape* under the *Indian Penal Code*.

Reforms in Law

If early marriage of girls is to be discouraged in the interest of the health and development of girl children, the law must reflect a consistent value system. Raising the age of marriage is a vital reform that has social and economic consequences. Therefore, to achieve these objectives, all other relevant laws need to have consistent provisions. All the existing relevant laws including CMRA, civil law of marriage, personal laws of marriage and guardianship, and the penal code, therefore, need to be changed. In the following sections the desired changes in these laws regarding the age of marriage are discussed.

Same Age for Bride and Bridegroom

CMRA, civil law of marriage as well as all the religion-based marriage laws of Hindus, Christians, Parsis (eighteen years for a woman and twenty-one years for a man), and Jews (twelve years for a girl and thirteen years for a boy) prescribe a lower age of marriage for women as compared to men. Such different prescription of age at marriage discriminates against women on the basis of sex and thereby violates the principle of equality. CMRA as well as all the marriage laws, viz., SPMA, HMA, ICMA, PMDA, and Jewish law (personal marriage laws) should be amended so as to provide the same minimum age of marriage for both men and woman.

The Muslim personal law prescribes the age of puberty, which is presumed to be fifteen years, unless the contrary is proved, as the age of marriage for a girl and a boy. Additionally, guardians are also allowed to enter into a valid contract of marriage on behalf of their children who are below the age of fifteen years. Thus, there is no sex-based discrimination regarding the condition as to the age of marriage but it is lower and is contradictory to CMRA. Therefore, the Muslim personal law also needs to be amended accordingly.

Legal Effect of Child Marriage

CMRA is silent about the legal effect of a child marriage. It does not mention whether child marriage is valid, void, or voidable. Under all the religion-based personal laws of marriage a child marriage is a valid marriage. Only the civil law of marriage, SPMA, declares it to be void. As discussed earlier, it is one of the reasons for the failure of CMRA. For eradication of the evil of child marriage, it is necessary that CMRA should be amended so as to make compliance with the prescribed age at marriage as an essential mandatory condition.[61] In case of breach of this condition, the marriage should be declared null and void having no legal effect.[62]

Such a declaration would, however, have adverse consequences for married adolescent girls. To avoid such an outcome, it would be helpful to stipulate a specific initial period, say ten years, when a child marriage, could be made voidable at the option of the child bride. After that period any child marriage carried out could be made void at initio, that is to say, from its very inception.[63] To avoid inconsistency between CMRA and the religion-based personal laws of marriage, child marriage should be declared void under the personal laws too. As an additional precaution, an independent section, with a non-obstantee clause, defining the scope of CMRA, should be added to CMRA giving it overriding effect over the personal laws. Such a section should expressly oust the application of other marriage laws.[64] To protect further the interests of the young girl whose marriage would become void on the ground of age, the personal laws of marriage should recognize her right to claim maintenance from the man. to whom she was married and from his parents.

Free Consent

CMRA lays down what should be the age of the parties at the time of marriage. It does not provide for their free consent for the marriage. Except for the Muslim personal law of marriage, no other personal law of marriage, including the civil marriage law, SPMA, requires free consent of the parties to the marriage. The Indian law presumes that, at the age of eighteen years, a person acquires the capacity to agree or disagree with an act by under-standing its nature and consequences.[65]

CMRA should have included the condition relating to free consent of the parties to a marriage when it raised the age of marriage for girls to eighteen years in 1978. The best practice would be to amend all the different marriage laws to include free consent of the parties as an essential prerequisite for a marriage to be valid. However, till such a change is brought about in all the personal laws, CMRA should be amended so as to make free consent of the parties an essential condition to a marriage with an overriding clause to nullify the contrary provisions of the existing personal laws. Any marriage without free consent of the parties should be declared null and void. Such an amendment to CMRA would also be in conformity with India's obligation under the Women's Convention.

As suggested above, instead of making piecemeal changes either in CMRA or in personal laws, the best solution would have been the enactment of a gender-just uniform civil code as provided in the Directive Principles of State Policy in the Constitution of India.[66] However, the issue of a uniform civil code is politicized to such an extent that at least in the near future there is no hope that any government would make efforts to enact it.[67] Therefore, in the present scenario, the most pragmatic approach would be to amend CMRA. This being a piece of secular and uniform legislation (at least in principle), objections to amend it would be the minimum.[68]

Registration of Marriage

At present, CMRA does not have a provision for registration of marriages. Under other personal laws there is such a provision. But non-registration does not affect the validity of the marriage. One of the best and most effective methods to control child marriages is to make the registration of marriage compulsory. It would assure the fulfilment of the condition as to the age as well as free consent of the parties to a marriage. Therefore, CMRA should be amended to include a provision regarding compulsory registration of marriages. In the absence of registration, the marriage should be declared as void and should not create any legal rights and obligations between the parties inter se.

Offences to be Cognizable

At present the offences under CMRA are cognizable only for the purpose of investigation. If offences would be declared as cognizable generally, the executive personnel would have the power to arrest, without a warrant of arrest from the court, persons who are organizing a child marriage. Such a measure in turn would help prevent the solemnization of child marriages. It would prove to be a major deterrent for prospective offenders. Therefore, the stipulation under CMRA that offences would be cognizable only for the purpose of investigation should be removed and all the offences should be declared cognizable at every stage.[69]

Ex-parte Injunction

CMRA at present does not make a provision for granting an ex-parte injunction for stopping a child marriage. The primary focus of the law should be more on preventing child marriages rather than punishing those who are involved in performing such marriages. Therefore, CMRA should make a clear provision for granting ex-parte injunction against solemnization of a child marriage.

Amendments in Rape Law

Contradictions in CMRA and the statutory rape law have already been discussed in detail.[70] A change in the legal value system on the age of marriage must also be reflected in the laws regulating rape and other sexual offences, which refer to the age of the victim for the expression of sexual consent. For preventing child marriages, it is necessary to punish a man for having sexual intercourse with a woman who is below the prescribed age for marriage. Therefore, the relevant section[71] of the Indian Penal Code should be amended so as to take away the unfettered right of a husband to have non-consensual sexual intercourse with his young wife.

Amendments in Guardianship Laws

The laws of guardianship of Hindus and Muslims and the one applicable to non-Hindus and non-Muslims, have a provision that the husband is the guardian of his minor wife. To have consistent legal policies under CMRA and guardianship laws, it is essential to amend this provision. Once the age of marriage for a girl is declared as eighteen years by CMRA, which is the age of majority under the Indian law,[72] there is no reason to provide for legal recognition of a minor wife. This provision should be deleted from HMGA, the Muslim personal law, and the Guardians and Wards Act.

Amendments in Other Laws

The problem of child marriage needs to be addressed comprehensively. A piecemeal approach by amending CMRA is not adequate. If the Indian government is seriously interested in eradicating the evil of child marriage, it must evaluate all laws that do not treat men and women equally. Unless women's human rights are recognized in all spheres to the fullest extent, the legal and social status of women will not improve. Therefore, all other laws that devalue women need to be amended. For example, laws relating to inheritance, divorce, guardianship and custody of children, equal payment in the organized and unorganized sectors, sexual harassment of women at work place, and equal opportunities for women in all spheres including political and economic spheres. Equally important is to legislate on those subjects which would accelerate empowerment of women, such as compulsory education.[73]

Legal Literacy

CMRA may not succeed in prohibiting child marriages even after rectifying the existing lacunae in it. The fundamental reason is that people who are expected to obey the law must be aware that such a law exists. In India, the extent of legal illiteracy is very high in those areas where child marriages are performed on a large scale. The National and Family Health Survey (NFHS) carried out in 1992–3 has pointed out that the legal minimum age for marriage is not widely known among women in India.[74] Overall, only one-third of the respondents could correctly identify the legal minimum age. According to NFHS, the provisions of CMRA are better known among urban and educated women.

People need to be informed about CMRA and its objects, and the ill effects of the practice of child marriage on young brides. Their consciousness needs to be raised. Thus the access to information is the first step in realizing the objects of the law. Unless they have knowledge of the provisions of the law, people cannot be expected to obey it.

Again, merely giving the information is not enough. A legal culture needs to be created. People need to be assured that laws are enacted for their benefit. Individuals, family members, and the community at large need to be mobilized to respect the law. Even the priests who perform the religious rituals in marriages should be made aware of their responsibilities towards society. This could be done in many ways. Television and radio can play a leading role and broadcast speeches of academics, doctors, health care providers, and popular leaders, discussions amongst people from all walks of life including students, experiences of victims, and success stories. The use of folk art can be another significant method to reach the rural masses. Even through creative art such as puppet shows and street plays it will be easy to spread the message about the correct age of marriage. Discussions can be initiated in women's clubs (*Mahila Mandals*) as well as in religious institutions.

Sensitizing the Judiciary

A sensitive judiciary could contribute toward realizing the goals of the law. It could take cognizance of social realities while interpreting the provisions of the law and could be more assertive while protecting and promoting the interests of the beneficiaries of the legislation. To sensitize the judiciary, judges need to be made conscious of their role. They have to be made gender sensitive and aware of social problems.

One of the important strategies that could be used for creating such consciousness among judges and lawyers would be to conduct training workshops for judicial personnel and lawyers. Educational institutions and voluntary organizations could contribute effectively by conducting such workshops. A gender-sensitized, human rights approach should be adopted in such workshops. Social scientists and legal personnel could be brought together in such a forum. Similar workshops could be arranged for legislators and executive personnel. Such an interdisciplinary approach would play an effective role in mobilizing them to interpret the law from women's point of view.

Brandeis Brief

Lawyers are an essential component of the judicial system. They need to assist the court to help it arrive at a conscious, reasoned decision. Particularly while handling any socio-legal issue, they need to argue a case in the broader context. The earlier discussion has pointed out that lawyers have not argued the issue of child marriage from the feminist perspective.[75] They have not relied on women's experience while arguing cases. They have not argued either from the perspective of violation of constitutional rights or of the human rights of adolescent girls. They have not brought to the notice of the courts the consequences of child marriage on the physical and psychological health of young girls or on their reproductive health, and their education and personal development. Nor have they argued how child marriage denies young girls an opportunity to choose their life partners.

It is the responsibility of lawyers to present a Brandeis Brief[76] before the courts by referring to all relevant extra-legal information on the issue of social and national importance. A Brandeis Brief makes use of social science and economic studies in addition to legal principles and case law. It is named after Louis D. Brandeis, a judge of the US Supreme Court, who as a lawyer persuaded the Court to uphold a statute stipulating a maximum ten-hour work day for women.[76a] Lawyers need to develop the methodology for using social science data to convince the court address the issue of child marriage more seriously by going beyond the technical interpretation of CMRA. The best strategy that lawyers could adopt to make the judiciary aware of the reality of adverse consequences of child marriages on young girls would be by initiating public interest litigation in the Supreme Court.

Initiating Public Interest Litigation

The Indian Supreme Court has developed a new jurisprudence of entertaining public interest litigation for perceiving violations of fundamental rights of vulnerable groups including those of children.[77] The Supreme Court has not only given a liberal interpretation to various fundamental rights mentioned in the Constitution, but has also revolutionized the processual jurisprudence so as to make the judicial process more easily accessible to all. It has liberalized the rules of locus standi, which stipulate that only persons having a direct interest in a matter may appear before the court in connection with it. Considering that a large number of people of India are poor and ignorant and lack the resources to invoke the judicial process for the enforcement of their fundamental rights, the Court has allowed social activists as well as social action groups to petition the court on their behalf. This is what has become known as public interest litigation.[78]

The Court has insisted that public officials must act in a manner consistent with the requirements of the Constitution, the directive principles of state policy, and the international treaties ratified by India.[79] The Supreme Court has shown its willingness to immerse itself in administrative detail in order to do justice to disadvantaged groups.[80] In the whole process the Court has given up its positivist approach and has departed from the adversarial procedure to become more proactive in protecting the fundamental rights of disadvantaged sections of the people.

The Supreme Court has made the maximum use of Article 21 for the realization of the human rights of many people. The Court has given liberal interpretation to its words. Article 21 states: 'No person shall be deprived of his life or personal liberty except according to procedure established by law.'[81] The Court has held that there were three types of rights contained in that article, namely (a) the right to life, (b) the right to personal liberty, and (c) the right not to be deprived of the rights mentioned in (a) and (b) except by procedure established by law.[82] The right to life included the right to live with dignity. From this emanated all the concomitant attributes of living with dignity such as the right to livelihood, the right to education, the right to health care, etc.

The liberal interpretation of Article 21 and the growth of public interest litigation changed the social profile of the Supreme Court from a body dealing with strictly legal issues to a body dealing with political, social, and economic issues. Based on this already established public interest litigation jurisprudence, a petition could be filed for the rights of protection of the young girls in the context of child marriage and its impact on their reproductive health and personality development.

In fact, a public interest petition was filed before the Rajasthan High Court[83] for issuance of directions to the State of Rajasthan to stop the menace of child marriage in an effective manner and to punish the officer responsible for not prohibiting child marriages. The government replied to the petition that it had taken 'all possible measures' to stop child marriages. A message from the chief minister of Rajasthan and the deputy inspector general of police was published in the newspapers appealing to the people not to marry off their girls below the age of eighteen years. The court was satisfied with the publication of the messages from the chief minister and the deputy inspector general of police. It opined that the executive personnel had fulfilled their duty by publishing the messages.

The court did mention in brief the evil effects of child marriage on education, development, and health of young brides in its judgment. The court suggested that the state government should consider the feasibility of appointing child marriage prevention officers[84] and the Central as well as the state government should consider the feasibility of making the provisions of the Act more stringent. But unfortunately, the court further commented:

> In my opinion, no amount of legislation can stop the solemnization of child marriages in contravention of the Act unless it is discarded by the society at large and this age-old custom is scrapped.[85]

The court was of the opinion that it was beyond the scope of the law to stop the evil of child marriages. It was satisfied just by the government publishing a message in the newspaper. It was too simplistic a solution to a deeply rooted social evil. Though limited, the law has a role to play. But it seems that the court was very pessimistic and undermined the role of the law as well as of the court by not issuing specific directions to the government making it answerable for the prevalent situation.

In fact, this would have been a good opportunity for the court to declare child marriage as violative of adolescent girls' human rights. The court could have held the government responsible for non-compliance with various international human right conventions. It could have asked the government to present a time-bound programme for preventing the age-old custom of child marriages. Unless the overlap between cultural norms and non-implementation of law is acknowledged by the court, the government can always make excuses and distance itself from the problem by placing the blame on recalcitrant cultural traditions that oppress women. The court should have understood the process of cultural legitimization and change, and assertion of family law within a political context. Instead, the judge commented that the petitioner had failed to make out any case against the state government.[86] To avoid such a comment from the court, the petitioner should have done proper homework by collecting enough social science data. She should have convinced the court to look at the problem from the feminist perspective and should have used constitutional and human rights arguments. She should have also referred to the most relevant international human rights instruments. But no such efforts were made. The High Court could also have taken the initiative to get proper information. But instead, the case was wound up almost summarily.

The next strategy could be to file a petition in the Supreme Court of India challenging the prevalence of child marriages.[87] With the help of the social science data on various aspects of child marriage including causes behind such practice and its impact on the reproductive health of adolescents as well as on their overall development, a strong case could be made before the Court. The following are the areas on which data with reference to adolescents—particularly married adolescents—could be presented before the courts:

— Incidence and prevalence of child marriage across the country,
— Scientific analysis of causes behind child marriages,
— Causes of unprotected and unwanted sexual relations,
— Unwanted pregnancies,
— Deaths during childbirth of adolescent girls,
— Miscarriages suffered by adolescent girls,
— Clandestine abortions,
— STDs including HIV/AIDS infection,
— Other maternal morbidities suffered by adolescents,
— Sexual violence and coercion faced by married adolescents,
— Availability of health services to adolescents particularly in the light of their special needs, and
— Availability of information on sex education to adolescents.

The epidemiological research findings on such issues are available to some extent in India.[88] Additionally, the experience of other countries on the issue of ill effects of child marriages could be brought to the notice of the court. The petition should also submit data on the positive impact of imparting information, education, and counselling on adolescents, and how it helps promote safe sex. A request could also be made in the petition for appointing independent persons as commissioners who could adopt an inquisitorial process that is more sensitive to the realities of sufferings of young girls, by which they could ascertain the validity of the claims made in the petition.[89]

Arguments could also be developed in the petition that state governments are responsible for providing alternatives to marriage for young girls. Such argument could be raised on the basis of data that would focus on the prevalent state of affairs of girls' education and opportunities available to them for career development, particularly for girls in rural areas. Scientific data on holistic personality development should also be included in such a petition. It should help suggest support mechanisms that need to be developed by the government for adolescent girls.

Apart from the use of such available data at the national and international level, other methodologies could also be adopted in such a petition. Expert opinions on various aspects of child marriages including its psychological impact could be brought before the court. Expert evidence on the social, economic, and other consequences of child marriages could also be recorded before the court. Expert medical opinion could be of great help to the court for understanding the true dimensions and gravity of the problem.

The petition should challenge the validity of child marriage under all the existing relevant Indian laws.[90] In addition to the argument that child marriage violates the fundamental and human rights of young girls, arguments could also be made by using the feminist methods, particularly, the feminist method of 'asking the woman question'. It could be argued that by not incorporating the women's experience the policy makers, law interpreters, and enforcers fail to grasp the gravity of the problem and hence fail to take a serious approach towards the issue of child marriages.

Through judicial activism, the Supreme Court of India has played the role of legitimizing and focussing attention on various social movements for social change and social justice.[91] If the national law and the Constitution are carefully studied along with the international human rights law, dynamically interpreted, and imaginatively applied to the existing realities there is hope that it would provide a basis for realization of the adolescent's human rights and in turn for the desired social change. A decision from the Supreme Court on such a public interest litigation might turn out to be a stepping stone in the process of realization of the adolescent's human rights.

The Supreme Court could ask the government to submit its plan of action for rectifying violation of human rights of girls. It could ask the government to make provisions in the budget for realizing the rights of adolescents. The government could be asked to submit a time-bound scheme for giving education and job skills to girls, providing user-friendly health care services as per the requirements of girls, enforcing the law, and creating awareness of the legal provisions.

The Role of Law

Law has been used to improve women's status in India right from the beginning of the nineteenth century. It started with the regulation passed for prohibiting sati by the British regime on the demand of social reformists in 1829.[92] It was then followed by the Widow Remarriage Act, 1856, by which Hindu widows were allowed to remarry. The issue of child marriage and the age of consent controversy took place in the latter half of the nineteenth century and the age of consent was raised in 1891. But it took a long time to enact the legislation on the prevention of child marriage. These laws were enacted in response to the demands of social reformers and were based on the idea that women needed *protection* from traditions and customs, which were harmful and unkind towards them.[93] It is interesting to note that though the social reformers demanded enactment of laws to eliminate social practices such as sati and child marriage, their focus was not exclusively on the legislative measures; they gave considerable importance to the education of women. Indeed, the power of law in the process of social reform was often cast within this broader context of education.[94]

In the beginning of the twentieth century when the national independence movement was taking shape, women's participation in the political process and women's suffrage were two important subjects. The social reform movement continued even during this period. The Child Marriage Restraint Act, 1929, the Hindu Women's Right to Property Act, 1937, the Dissolution of Muslim Women's Marriage Act, 1939, etc., were enacted before independence. However, the basis of these law reforms was the same as before—the protection of the women.

In post-independent India, law reforms took place on the principle of *equality* enshrined in the Constitution. Major changes were brought in the Hindu law of marriage, divorce, adoption, succession, and guardianship. Thereafter the major campaigns were launched in the late 1970s and 1980s to reform the personal laws, dowry law, rape law, and domestic violence law and to enact a uniform civil code, etc. In fact in the 1980–89 decade the maximum legislative activity to control violence against women took place.[95] Thus social reformers and women activists in India have used law again and again as an instrument of social reform.

But then a genuine question is how far have these laws succeeded in bringing real change in the lives of women? Are these laws based on women's experience? Are women being brought on an equal footing with men? Do these laws address inequalities based on gender, class, and caste? Do they address the structural inequalities? Do they alter the power relations or equations?

These and many more questions have been raised about the role of law in improving the status of women. Scholars of the sociology of law have studied the impact of law on society and have generally concluded that there are severe limitations on the role of law in bringing about change in any society.[96] Recently, efforts to theorize about the role of law from the feminist perspective have been made, and have given a new dimension to the subject.

An excellent review of various feminist approaches towards the role of law has been done by Ratna Kapur and Brenda Cossman.[97] They argue that there are three distinctive perspectives reflected in the literature on the subject: (1) Protectionism, (2) Equality, and (3) Patriarchy.[98] In protectionism the role of law is unproblematically asserted as protecting women. The assumption is that women are *naturally* weak, *naturally* different, and *naturally* in need of law's protection. In the second approach the relationship between law and women is seen as one of promoting equality.[99] And law is looked upon as an instrument of social engineering. In the third approach the role of law is analysed as an instrument of patriarchal oppression.[100] The focus of analysis is often on the legal regulation of sexuality and violence. However, these approaches according to the authors fail to capture the complex and contradictory nature of law.[101] On the one hand law does improve the status of women, and on the other, it has tremendous power to oppress them. It reinforces relations of subordination; at the same time it is an important source of resistance to oppression and change in women's status.

Keeping the complex role of law in mind let me ask a question: how successful has the law been in preventing child marriages by raising the age of marriage? Demographic information on the prevalence of child marriages in the last chapter has pointed out that the situation has not changed substantially. It is argued, particularly by social scientists, that whatever change has occurred since the enactment of the legislation is mainly due to modernization rather than due to law. They argue that law has failed to achieve its expected objective.[102]

While assessing the impact of CMRA, one must do so by critically analysing a number of factors. One, whether there are any lacunae left in the law. Two, whether other existing, relevant, and supportive laws have been amended to match the law in question. Three, to what extent people have knowledge of the new law. Four, whether the enforcment machinery is being made aware of the objects of the law and whether that machinery is working efficiently and responsibly. Five, whether the judiciary is sensitive enough to realize its role in the context of the purpose of the law. Six, to what extent economic and educative programmes support the law. Seven, whether the legislators are well informed about the broad objectives behind the need of curbing a particular mischief that is being addressed by them through the law. Ignorance or callousness on the part of legislators while laying down the policies and programmes supportive of law and the absence of a holistic approach to the issue affect substantially the success of any law. And lastly, whether Indian law complies with international obligations under the various conventions ratified by India.

Those who have argued that the law has failed to prevent child marriages probably do not evaluate it from these perspectives. The success of the law needs to be measured in the context of all these issues. Ultimately, one must keep in mind that the law is not *the* panacea for eliminating all social evils. It has certainly a positive, educative role, and many a times a symbolic role to play. It is equally true that unless legal rights are created, it is difficult to demand enforcement of those rights. But the law has its own limitations, particularly in the area of family relations and such issues where sentiments of people are involved. The law has limitations if it has to regulate deeply rooted beliefs, traditions, and customs.

I share the views expressed by Archana Parashar on the role of law in reforming society.[103] She defends strongly the continuing value of law for social reforms, although she does so from a perspective that recognizes the limitations of law. She argues that one must develop a more realistic appraisal of the limitations of the law. Much of the disillusionment with the ability of law to reform comes from 'inappropriate expectations' about its potential to bring about social change.[104] Legal rights operate within the complexities of the prevailing politico-economic system. Law reform may not remove the structural inequalities of the life systems, which make it difficult for individuals to realize their rights.[105] Parashar argues that instead of unrealistically expecting that the law can change the whole social system, it is more productive to realize that the law can induce or assist social change only to a certain extent.[106] Often social legislation is symbolic and may help create conditions which are conducive to such change.[107] Legislation sends a message that certain forms of behaviour are unacceptable. It gives language to the activists to negotiate with people, the government, and society at large.

Conclusions

The chapter has illustrated the half-hearted and piecemeal approach of the legislators in dealing with the practice of child marriage. They have not taken into account women's experiences and opinions. The patriarchal and discriminatory CMRA has not attempted to answer the woman question because such question has not been taken into consideration. By passing CMRA legislators have indicated their protective approach towards women. But they have failed miserably to translate even this approach into reality. In spite of the law being there in the statute book for more than seventy years, not much has changed in real life. No efforts have been made to synchronize the relevant provisions of all the laws dealing with the issue of age at marriage.

CMRA and other related laws need to be amended on the basis of the 'woman question'. The same age for both the parties, their free consent, compulsory registration of marriage, and marriage in contravention of any of these conditions to be void are the basic issues that must be addressed by CMRA and personal marriage laws.

Equally important is to keep in mind that merely enacting or reforming the law does not make people abide by it. Meaningful alternatives which are acceptable to people need to be provided. If a girl is not to be married off what is she to do? Young active adolescent girls' minds must be occupied in constructive work. The best alternative is to educate her properly to become a mainstream participant in building the nation. The government must create easy and compulsory access to education particularly in the rural areas. The parents and the community need to be convinced about the importance of education for girls. There has to be enough budgetary provision to implement these policies and law. In a democracy, it is the responsibility of civil society to make the government accountable for its duties. Until these goals are achieved, we all need to work relentlessly.

End Notes

[1] Article 44 of the Indian Constitution, see infra note 66.

[2] Section 2 of HMA defines the scope of the Act.

[3] Section 5 (iii) of HMA, as it was till 1978 amendment in CMRA. The ages fifteen years and eighteen years for girls and boys were in accordance with the provisions of CMRA before 1978.

[4] Section 6 of HMA provided a list of relations who could act as guardian for the purpose of marriage. This section was omitted in 1978. It became redundant. After 1978 a girl could marry only at the age of eighteen years, which is the age of majority. A girl can take the decision at this age on her own and is not required to obtain consent for the marriage.

[5] Section 18 (a) of HMA provides punishment to a groom as well as to the bride. It reads as follows: 'Every person who procures a marriage of himself or herself to be solemnized under this Act in contravention of the conditions specified in clauses (iii), (iv) and (v) of Section 5 shall be punishable—

(a) in the case of a contravention of the condition specified in clause (iii) of Section 5, with simple imprisonment which may extend to fifteen days, or with fine, which may extend to one thousand rupees or with both.'

Thus HMA punishes even the bride. CMRA does not punish the bride.

[6] Section 11: Void Marriages: Any marriage solemnized after the commencement of this Act shall be void and may, on a petition presented by either party thereto against the other party be so declared by a decree of nullity if it contravenes any one of the conditions specified in clauses (i), (iv) and (v) of Section 5. [5(i) lays down the condition of monogamy and 5(iv) and 5(v) cover the list of relations by blood and affinity amongst whom the marriage is prohibited.]

[7] Section 12: Voidable Marriages: (1) Any marriage solemnized, whether before or after the commencement of this Act, shall be voidable and may be annulled by a decree of nullity on any of the following grounds namely:

(a) ...

(b) that the marriage is in contravention of the condition specified in clause (ii) of Section 5; or

(c) ...

(d) ...

Thus it would be clear from reading Sections 11 and 12 that a child marriage is neither void nor voidable. So it is valid.

[8] AIR 1978 SC 1351; see also *V. Mallikarjunaiah* v. *H.C. Gouramma* AIR 1997 Kant. 77.

[9] Ibid. at 1358.

[10] 1980 Hindu Law Reporter (Punjab & Haryana) 157. The high courts of Himachal Pradesh, Orissa, Rajasthan, and Patna, also have taken the same position. See *Premi* v. *Daya Ram* AIR 1965 HP 15, *Durjyodhan* v. *Bengabati Devi* AIR 1977 Ori. 36, *Durga Bai* v. *Kedarmal* 1980 HLR (Raj.) 166, *Rabindra Prasad* v. *Sita Devi* AIR 1986 Pat. 128. The only exception is of the Andhra Pradesh High Court. In *Panchireddi* v. *Ganapatlu* AIR 1975 AP 193 the division bench of the AP High Court held that a child marriage was void. However, the full bench of the same high court in *Vankatarama* v. *State* AIR 1977 AP 43 overruled this decision. But it is interesting to note that again in *Katari Subba Rao* v. *Katari Seetha Mahalakshmi* AIR 1994 AP 364 the division bench of the same high court held that a child marriage was void. The court (p. 366) said, 'If there is a marriage of a girl who is below 12 years, it is a void marriage. It cannot be treated as a marriage at all.' It must be noted that this decision has come after the Supreme Court decision in *Lila* v. *Laxmi* in 1978 and constitutionally it will have no validity as per Article 141 of the Constitution. The decision of the SC is the law of the land and is binding on all the high courts.

[11] Ibid. at 160.

[12] Section 13 (2)(iv) of HMA.

[13] This was introduced in HMA in accordance with the recommendation of CSW.

[14] Section 2 (vii) of the Dissolution of Muslim Women's Marriages Act, 1939.

[15] AIR 1952 Madhya Bharat 30.

[16] Ibid. at 31.

[17] K.S.N. Murty, 'Marriage of Hindu Minors' (1969) *AIR Journal* 72 at 75.

[18] Section 18 (i) of HMA. Punishments for parents is laid down only in CMRA. As discussed earlier, CMRA does not punish the child bride but HMA does.

[19] The Supreme Court has declared it as valid in *Lila Gupta* v. *Laxmi Narain* AIR 1978 SC 1351 at pp. 1352, 1358; see also *Rabindra Prasad* v. *Sita Devi* AIR 1986 Patna 128 at p. 129: '... the marriage solemnized in violation of Sec. 5 (iii) remains unaffected. Neither the marriage is void nor voidable.'

[20] Section 5 of HMA: A marriage may be solemnized between any two Hindus, if the following conditions are fulfilled, namely:

(i) ...

(ii) at the time of the marriage, neither party—

(a) is incapable of giving a valid consent to it in consequence of unsoundness of mind; or

(b) though capable of giving a valid consent has been suffering from mental disorder of such a kind or to such an extent as to be unfit for marriage and the procreation of children; or

(c) has been subject to recurrent attacks of insanity.

(iii) ...

(iv) ...

(v) ...

[21] Paras Diwan, *Modern Hindu Law: Codified and Uncodified* (Allahabad: Allahabad Law Agency, 1993) at 191.

[22] Section 12 (1): Any marriage solemnized, whether before or after the commencement of this Act, shall be voidable and may be annulled by a decree of nullity on any of the following grounds, namely:

(a) ...

(b) ...

(c) that the consent of the petitioner ... was obtained by force or by fraud as to the nature of the ceremony or as to the material fact or circumstance concerning the respondent or

(d) ...

[23] Section 12 (2): Notwithstanding anything contained in sub-section (1), no petition for annulling a marriage—

(a) on the ground specified in clause (c) of sub-section (1) shall be entertained if—

(i) the petition is presented more than one year after the force has ceased to operate or, as the case may be, the fraud had been discovered; or

(ii) the petitioner has, with his or her full consent, lived with the other party to the marriage as husband or wife after the force has ceased to operate or, as the case may be, the fraud has been discovered;

[24] *Moore* v. *Valsa* 1 (1992) DMC 55.

[25] AIR 1964 Punj. 359.

[26] I (1992) DMC 96.

[27] Ibid.

[28] Meera Kosambi, 'Gender Reform and Competing State Controls over Women: The Rukhmabai Case, 1884–1888' 29 *Contributions to Indian Sociology* (1995).

[29] Article 328 of the Indian Constitution provides for adult suffrage and gives a person of eighteen years the right to vote. It reads: 'The election to the House of the People and to the Legislative Assembly of every State shall be on the basis of adult suffrage, i.e. to say, every person who is a citizen of India and who is not less than 18 years of age on such date... shall be entitled to be registered as a voter at any such election.'

According to Section 3 of the Indian Majority Act, 1875, the age of majority is eighteen years. However, Section 2 excludes application of this age in matters of marriage and divorce. It states: 'Nothing herein contained shall affect—

(a) the capacity of any person to act in the following matters (namely)— marriage, dower, divorce, and adoption; (b) ....'

According to Section 11 of the Indian Contract Act, 1872 'Every person is competent to contract who is of the age of majority according to the law to which he is subject and who is of sound mind ...'

The Hindu Minority and Guardianship Act states in Section 4(a): 'Minor means a person who has not attained the age of 18 years.'

[30] Section 6 of HMA gave a list of the persons entitled to give consent as guardians in marriage. And according to Section 5 (vi) as it stood before 1978, it was necessary that the guardian should give his consent to the marriage where the bride had not completed the age of eighteen years.

[31] Article 16(1): State Parties shall take all appropriate measures to eliminate discrimination against women in all matters relating to marriage and family relations and in particular shall ensure, on a basis of equality of men and women:

(a) the same right to enter into marriage;

(b) The same right freely to choose a spouse and to enter into marriage only with their free and full consent;

(c) ... (h) ....'

Article 1 of the Marriage Convention also explicitly provides for the consent of the parties to a marriage. It states: 'No marriage shall be legally entered into without the full and free consent of both parties, such consent to be expressed by them in person after due publicity and in the presence of the authority competent to solemnize the marriage and of witnesses, as prescribed by law.' But India has not signed it.

[32] Except the Dissolution of Muslim Women's Marriage Act, 1939.

[33] See Tahir Mahmood, *The Muslim Law of India* (New Delhi: Allahabad Agency, 1990) at 49; see also F.B. Tyabji, *Muslim Law*, 4th ed. (Bombay: N.M. Tripathi, 1968) at 52, where he mentions that the age of puberty for girls is nine years.

[34] See M. Hidaytullah (ed.), *Mulla Principles of Mahomedan Law*, 19th ed., (Bombay: N.M. Tripathi, 1990) at 233.

[35] Ibid. at 234–5. It is not available if a minor has been contracted in marriage by the father or father's father.

[36] Ibid.

[37] This is one of the grounds available to a wife for divorce under Section 2 (vii) of the Dissolution of Muslim Women's Marriages Act, 1939, and is interpreted strictly by the judiciary. A husband is not required to obtain similar confirmation from the court. See *Usman* v. *Budhu* AIR 1942 Sind 92, *Pirmohammad Kukaji* v. *The State of MP* AIR 1960 MP 24 *Sahib Ali Biswas* v. *Jinnatan Nahar* AIR 1960 Cal. 717, *Nizamuddin* v. *Huseni* AIR 1960 MP 212. See also Hidaytullah, note 160 supra at 235.

[38] A doubt could be raised as to whether the amended Act of 1978 is applicable to Muslims. The reason is that while amending the Act in 1978, it specifically mentioned that the provisions of the Act are to be read in HMA and ICMA. It did not mention so for Muslims.

[39] Tyabji, supra note 33 at 51–2.

[40] This age is different and is lower than the one required to enter into any civil contract under the Indian Contract Act.

[41] Section 60 of ICMA, 1872.

[42] See *Lakshmi Sanyal* v. *S.K. Dhar* AIR 1972 SC 2667. The Supreme Court held that Section 19 of the Indian Divorce Act, which provides grounds for declaring the marriage null and void, does not specify the age below the prescribed one, as a ground for nullity. However, the Supreme Court has not referred to Section 4 of ICMA, which mentions that marriage shall be void if the conditions prescribed are not complied with. Therefore, in spite of this provision the marriage below the prescribed age is not void but is valid according to the Supreme Court decision.

[43] Section 3 (1), emphasis added.

[44] Section (3) sub-section (2): Notwithstanding that a marriage is invalid under any of the provisions of sub-section (1), ...

[45] Section 18 states the grounds for nullity. It does not cover under-age marriage. There is no Supreme Court decision on this issue. Parsis in India generally marry at a late age. So the issue is more of academic interest.

[46] Section 4 (c) read with Section 24 of SPMA, 1954.

[47] Section 8: Registration of Hindu Marriages—

(1) For the purpose of facilitating the proof of Hindu marriages, the state governments may make rules providing that the parties to any such marriage

may have the particulars relating to their marriage entered in such manner and subject to such conditions as may be prescribed in a Hindu Marriage Register kept for the purpose.

[48] Section 8, sub-section (5): Notwithstanding anything contained in this section, the validity of any Hindu marriage shall in no way be affected by the omission to make the entry.

[49] Article 16: 1. State Parties shall take all appropriate measures to eliminate discrimination against women in all matters relating to marriage and family relations and in particular shall ensure, on a basis of equality of men and women:

(a) The same right to enter into marriage;

(b) The same right freely to choose a spouse and to enter into marriage only with their free and full consent;

(f) The same rights and responsibilities with regard to guardianship, wardship, trusteeship ... of children ...;

(h) The same rights for both spouses in respect of the ownership, acquisition, management ... enjoyment and disposition of property ...;

2. The betrothal and the marriage of a child shall have no legal effect, and all necessary action, including legislation, shall be taken to specify a minimum age for marriage and to make the registration of marriages in an official registry compulsory.

[50] Declaration, note 90 in Chapter Two and accompanying text.

[51] Section 4(a).

[52] Section 2: The provisions of this Act shall be in addition to and not, save as hereinafter expressly provided, in derogation of the Guardians and Wards Act, 1890.

[53] Section 17: (1) In appointing or declaring the guardian of a minor, the court shall, subject to the provisions of this section, be guided by what, consistently with the law to which the minor is subject, appears to be for the *welfare of the minor.*

[54] Section 21: A minor is incompetent to act as guardian of any minor except his own wife or child or ....

[55] Section 10.

[56] Emphasis added.

[57] The staff of the minister of law and justice, which prepares the draft and submits it to the Cabinet, has the primary responsibility of reviewing the existing laws before drafting any amendment. Then the responsibility is in the Cabinet ministers. Thirdly, it is on the parliamentarians of the ruling party and lastly, but not unimportantly, the responsibility falls on the opposition party members

of Parliament. They are all expected to do proper homework before attending the Parliament sessions. However, when such significant lapses occur on their part, it obviously reflects on their irresponsible attitude.

[58] Mahmood, supra note 33 at 51–2. See also Tyabji supra note 33 at 48.

[59] Ibid.

[60] The situation is the same in Pakistan and Bangladesh. However, experience from Sri Lanka is worth noticing as it is altogether different. There the law of guardianship has never been connected with child marriage. Laws and policies have undermined child marriage, though the statutory minimum age of marriage is as low as twelve years for girls. Sri Lanka's policies on providing accessible facilities for registration of marriage and free education from primary to university level has contributed to female literacy and has thus eliminated child marriage at least in non-Muslim communities. See Goonesekere, Chapter Two note 77.

[61] For detailed discussion see Chapter Two, note 63 and accompanying text.

[62] One can learn from the experiences of those countries, particularly from Asia, which have already declared child marriage void. For example, in Indonesia child marriage is void. It was done so in 1991. Similar is the situation in Sri Lanka. It is interesting to note that in both these countries the prescribed age of marriage for a girl is much lower than in the Indian law. But in reality percentage of girls marrying below eighteen years is much less than in India. See Goonesekere, Chapter Two, note 77.

[63] See Chapter Two, p. 54 et al.

[64] There are Acts, which have been drafted in this manner. For example, to nullify the effect of the decision of the Supreme Court in the *Shah Bano* case (*Mohd. Ahmed Khan* v. *Shah Bano Begum* AIR1985 SC 945), The Muslim Women (Protection of Rights on Divorce) Act was enacted in 1986. It took away the right of Muslim divorcees to claim maintenance from their ex-husbands under Section 125 of the Criminal Procedure Code. To oust the jurisdiction of Section 125 of the Criminal Procedure Code, the new Act used a non-obstante clause while defining its scope in Section 3. Section 3 begins with a non-obstante clause, 'Notwithstanding anything contained in any other law', which overrides the jurisdiction of other laws.

[65] See supra note 29.

[66] Article 44 of the Constitution of India states, 'The State shall endeavour to secure for the citizens a *uniform civil code* throughout the territory of India'. In India, except the matters relating to family law, viz., marriage, divorce, guardianship, inheritance, and adoption, there is already a uniform civil law. But only in family matters religion-based personal laws apply. Uniform civil code in Article 44, therefore, refers to uniform family law.

[67] See Jaya Sagade, 'Uniform Civil Code' (1991) 43 *Social Action* 501; Vasudha Dhagamwar, *Uniform Civil Code* (New Delhi: Indian Law Institute, 1990).

[68] One may argue that in a given set-up certain changes (e.g. a provision for free consent and compulsory registration of marriage) that I am suggesting to CMRA would be more appropriate in the marriage laws rather than in CMRA. But I am suggesting those changes in CMRA for many reasons. Firstly, the Marriage Convention covers the three issues, namely marriage age, free consent, and registration of marriage together and the Women's Convention also covers these aspects in one article, indicating that these three aspects are complementary to each other. Secondly, I am suggesting a change in the title of CMRA to widen its scope. Thirdly, in the Indian context, these changes are practically viable for political reasons.

[69] Under the Protection of Civil Rights Act if the police fail to take cognizance of an offence after a complaint is lodged, he himself is held guilty of committing the offence under the Act. On a similar ground amendment can be introduced in the Act. Similar is the provision under Section 498A of the Indian Penal Code, which defines cruelty to a married woman.

[70] See Chapter Two at p. 37 and 63.

[71] Section 375.

[72] Supra note 29.

[73] It is worth learning from the experience of other countries particularly from the South-Asian and Asian regions. Sri Lanka and Indonesia are the two countries where the high rate of literacy and attendance in schools due to compulsory education policy have contributed to a great extent in delaying marriages. See also UNDP Report on Human Development 2000.

[74] International Institute for Population Sciences (IIPS), *National Family Health Survey (NFHS) 1992–93 India* (Mumbai: IIPS, 1995) at 81–82.

[75] See Chapter Two at 60 et al.

[76] See Erikson Rosemary and Simpson Rites, *Use of Social Science Data in Supreme Court Decisions* (Chicago: University of Illinois, 1998) at 6.

[76a] *Muller* v. *Oregon*, 208 US 412, 28 s.ct. 324 (1908).

[77] *Sheela Barse* v. *Union of India* AIR 1986 SC 1773.

[78] Through public interest litigation, issues of human rights, governance, and environment are brought before the Court.

[79] *Sheela Barse* v. *Secretary, Children Aid Society* AIR 1987 SC 656.

[80] See G.L. Peiris, 'Public Interest Litigation in the Indian Subcontinent: Current Dimensions' (1991) 40 *International Comparative Law Quarterly* 66.

[81] Article 21 of the Indian Constitution.

[82] *Maneka Gandhi* v. *India* AIR 1978 SC 597.

[83] *Sushila Gothala* v. *State of Rajasthan* AIR 1995 Raj. 90.

[84] Government of Gujarat has added provision for Child Marriage Prevention Officers by adding Section 13 to CMRA in 1973.

[85] Supra note 83 at 91.

[86] Ibid. at 93. The day of *akha teej* (according to the Hindu calendar) is considered to be an auspicious day for performing child marriages in India. It was on 13 May in the year 1994. The petition came up for admission on 12 May 1994. So the judge commented that if the petitioner was really interested in seeking any direction from the court, she should have approached the court earlier.

[87] Particularly in states like Rajasthan where child marriages are performed on mass scale on *akha tij* (an auspicious day in the month of April/May) and the state fails to take action to prevent solemnization of such marriages.

[88] See Shireen Jejeebhoy, 'The Importance of Social Science Research in the Promotion of Sexual and Reproductive Choice of Adolescents' (1999) 18 *Medicine and Law* 255. And wherever data are not available, social scientists should generate data by carrying out research in relevant areas.

[89] The court could make such innovations by taking advantage of the words 'by appropriate proceedings' in Article 32.

[90] CMRA, HMA, PMDA, ICMA, Muslim personal law, and Jewish Law.

[91] See S.P. Sathe, *Judicial Activism in India* (New Delhi: Oxford University Press, 2002).

[92] See S.P. Sathe, *Towards Gender Justice* (Bombay: SNDT Women's University, 1993) at 2, 3.

[93] See Ratna Kapur and Brenda Cossman, *Subversive Sites: Feminist Engagements with Law in India* (New Delhi: Sage Publications, 1996) at 51.

[94] Ibid.

[95] Flavia Agnes, 'Protecting Women against Violence? Review of A Decade of Legislation, 1980–89' (1992) 27 *Economic and Political Weekly WS* 19.

[96] See J.N.D. Anderson (ed.), *Changing Law in Developing Countries* (London: George Allen and Unwin, 1963); Upendra Baxi, *Towards a Sociology of Indian Law* (New Delhi: Satvavahan Publication, 1986); M.D.A. Freeman, *The State, the Law and the Family* (London: Tavistock, 1984); C. Smart, *Feminism and the Power of Law* (London: Routledge, 1989).

[97] See supra note 93 at 21–43.

[98] Ibid. at 22.

[99] Ibid. at 24.

[100] Ibid. at 27.

[101] Ibid. at 30.

[102] See for instance Malini Karkal and Irudaya Rajan, 'Age at Marriage: How Much Change' (1989) 24 *Economic and Political Weekly* 505; Shireen Jejeebhoy, 'Adolescent Sexuality and Fertility' (1996) 447 *Seminar* 16 at 18.

[103] Archana Parashar, *Women and Family Law Reforms in India: Uniform Civil Code and Gender Equality* (New Delhi: Sage, 1992) at 30.

[104] Ibid. at 31.

[105] Ibid.

[106] Ibid.

[107] Ibid.

4

Child Marriage and
International Human Rights

Introduction

In this chapter, I explore how human rights established in international human rights treaties and the Constitution of India can be applied to prevent child marriages in India. The language and the concept of human rights have been developed through the struggle of individuals and groups. Many individuals find human rights empowering because they provide means by which individuals can legitimately assert their interests.[1] Human rights that are backed by the Indian Constitution have become the source of realization of the rights of the disadvantaged and have not merely remained aspirations. The present study analyses not only those human rights that are obviously violated by child marriage but covers more comprehensive wrongs involving a broad spectrum of human rights to address both causes and consequences of child marriages.

The challenge here is not only to identify those rights that might be infringed but also to suggest possible remedies. State parties to international conventions are under a legal obligation to ensure that domestic legislation conforms to international human rights. State parties are also obligated to investigate and remedy the conduct of individuals in violation of these human rights. My goal is to suggest ways by which the government might be held accountable for its failure to prevent child marriages and suggest strategies for remedying violation of human rights of those young girls.

A number of international human rights treaties that have addressed the issue of age at marriage are based on the Universal Declaration of Human Rights (UDHR) adopted in 1948. The primary international human rights conventions[2] concerning the young girls' human rights are the Convention

on the Elimination of All Forms of Discrimination against Women, 1979
(Women's Convention)[3] and the Convention on the Rights of the
Child, 1989 (Children's Convention).[4] These conventions manifest the
fundamentals of UDHR and reassert UDHR's two legally binding
covenants, the International Covenant on Civil and Political Rights, 1966
(ICCPR)[5] and the International Covenant on Economic, Social and Cultural
Rights, 1966 (ICESCR).[6] Besides, other international treaties that are
significant in the discussion are the Convention on Consent to Marriage,
Minimum Age for Marriage and Registration of Marriages, 1962 (Marriage
Convention)[7] and the Supplementary Convention on the Abolition of
Slavery, the Slave Trade, and Institutions and Practices Similar to Slavery,
1956 (Slavery Convention).[8]

The major international human rights conventions have established
committees to monitor the compliance of state parties with treaty obli-
gations. Under the Women's Convention, there is a Committee on the
Elimination of Discrimination against Women (CEDAW) and under the
Children's Convention, there is a Committee on the Rights of the Child
(CRC). Besides, there are the Human Rights Committee (HRC) under
ICCPR and the Committee on Economic, Social and Cultural Rights
(CESCR) under ICESCR. These committees receive periodic reports that
state parties are required to submit to show how they have responded through
their laws, policies, and practices to comply with the respective conventions.
To assist countries in their reporting obligations, CEDAW, HRC, and
CESCR have developed a series of General Recommendations/Comments.[9]
These recommendations/comments develop the standards of performance
applicable to measure the compliance with human rights norms.

Another important international mechanism that has evolved for raising
human rights grievances is a complaint procedure.[10] For instance, the
individual complaint procedure is established under the First Optional
Protocol to ICCPR. Recently, an Optional Protocol to the Women's
Convention has been adopted by the General Assembly.[11] A provision is
made for the receipt of individual complaints by the monitoring body
concerned. However, an individual cannot lodge such a complaint unless
she/he has exhausted domestic remedies. The views or recommendations of
the UN treaty bodies are not formally binding on the state parties as a
matter of international law.[12] India has so far not ratified any of the optional
protocols to the UN treaties.[13]

Apart from these mechanisms,[14] the UN has evolved another mechanism to arrive at a consensus for the advancement of human rights of individuals. It has sponsored a number of international conferences to address the issue of human rights. The World Conference on Human Rights held in Vienna (the Vienna Conference) in 1993 focussed on human rights of women among other matters. The International Conference on Population and Development (ICPD) held in Cairo in 1994 and the Fourth World Conference on Women (FWCW) held in Beijing in 1995, are the two major conferences, which focussed on women's right to sexual and reproductive health. These conferences specifically developed the standards for the promotion of the human rights of adolescent girls.

Nearly ten years have passed since the Cairo and Beijing conferences took place. International agencies have taken account of what has been achieved by these international conferences for realizing women's human rights. The United Nations General Assembly has passed resolutions regarding future actions that need to be undertaken by governments, voluntary organizations, civil society, and international agencies.

Obligations of the Government to Implement Human Rights

Individuals expect protection from the state. They count on the state for their safety and well-being.[15] Human rights violations by the state, therefore, add an element of insult and indignity to the sufferings of individuals. The primary object of international human rights law is not to punish states, but to see that states comply with their obligations, which they have accepted by ratifying the international human rights treaties, and thus prevent future violation of human rights. The compliance mechanisms for international human rights law respect the unique character of human rights treaties and ensure that the remedies afforded serve to deter future violations and uphold the legal order that the treaties create.

The international law of state responsibility for human rights violation has evolved significantly in recent times.[16] By ratifying or acceding to the international conventions, state parties accept the legal duty to abide by the conventions and thereby become obliged to take steps to protect the exercise and enjoyment of human rights, to investigate violations, and to provide effective remedies to victims. It is worth exploring which acts of violations of women's human rights are imputable to state parties.

For instance, child marriage performed by private individuals does not necessarily implicate the state. However, when the state tolerates or excuses child marriages by not prosecuting those who are responsible for contracting child marriages, the state bears the responsibility, as marriage is a state-sanctioned institution. The state is responsible not directly for contracting child marriages, but for its own lack of diligence in preventing through its executive, legislative, or judicial organs the private act of contracting child marriage. The state is also responsible because child marriage violates specific human rights that are binding on the state as a matter of international law. The responsibility of states is not only that they themselves should not violate human rights, but that they should meet international obligations to deter and condemn such violations perpetrated by private persons.[17]

All human rights impose three types or levels of obligations or duties on state parties—the obligation to respect, protect, and fulfil human rights:[18]

— Obligation to *respect* rights by which states are prohibited from interfering with the protection, promotion, and enjoyment of human rights. These are negative obligations.

— Obligation to *protect* rights by which states are required to prevent harm to individuals from all including private parties. These are positive obligations.

— Obligation to *fulfil* rights by which states are required to take affirmative measures for realization of human rights including appropriate legislative, administrative, budgetary, judicial, promotional, and other measures. These are again positive obligations.

Obligation to Respect Rights

A state violates its negative obligation when it passes any legislation which intrudes into the rights of individuals. The violation of the negative obligations could be evidenced even by a single incident. For example, if a law is passed by which access to information or service regarding family planning is denied to adolescents, or if mandatory requirement of the parental consent or notification for such information or services is required by the law, such law would violate a state's negative obligation towards the adolescents. The duty to respect young girls' rights obliges state parties not to take any action which would restrict their autonomy or intrude into their privacy.

Obligation to Protect Rights

The duty to protect rights requires state parties to take positive actions to prevent the violation of rights committed by all including private individuals.[19] For instance, the human rights of young girls are violated by the parents when they force them to enter into child marriages. State parties in such a situation are required to take positive actions on behalf of the young girls against those who violate their rights. State parties are legally responsible if they fail to exercise *due diligence* in controlling private actors.

Obligation to Fulfil Rights

There is a direct positive obligation on state parties to enact appropriate legislation and provide administrative, budgetary, and economic measures for the full realization of human rights. In the case of young girls, for example, state parties are required to protect their right to education, information, and development by taking necessary steps such as passing legislation to provide compulsory education.

India has ratified all the above-mentioned conventions[20] and is, therefore, under an obligation as a matter of international law to respect, protect, and fulfil human rights of the girls referred to in it. Such ratification puts an obligation on the Indian state to bring its legislation and policies in line with the standards of the treaty concerned. Moreover, effective implementation of these laws and policies is essential to ensure compliance with these treaties. The standards laid down in these conventions do not automatically become a part of Indian domestic law so as to create rights in favour of individual citizen. The Indian Parliament is required to enact legislation to give effect to the rights incorporated in these conventions. This is implicit from Article 51(c) and Article 253 of the Constitution. Article 51(c) reads: 'The State shall endeavour to foster respect for international law and treaty obligations in the dealings of organised peoples with one another.' Article 253 of the Constitution gives 'power to Parliament to make any law for implementing any treaty, agreement or convention with any other country or countries or any decision made at any international conference, association or other body'. By referring to these provisions, it would be worth analysing India's efforts to comply with international treaties.

The judicial colloquia on the subject of the domestic application of international human rights norms have evolved a number of principles concerning the role of the judiciary in advancing international human rights.

These principles are known as the 'Bangalore Principles'[21] which have inspired the Indian Supreme Court to develop a jurisprudence for advancing human rights. The Supreme Court of India has stated: 'Any international convention not inconsistent with the fundamental rights and in harmony with its spirit is to be read into these provisions to enlarge the meaning and content thereof, to promote the object of constitutional guarantee.'[22] Within the international human rights paradigm, recently, the Supreme Court has explored how sexual harrasment of women at the workplace amounts to violation of their human rights. It has quoted Articles 11 and 24 of the Women's Convention and has adopted General Recommendation 19 on 'Violence against Women' of CEDAW, to set guidelines and requirements for processing sexual harrasment complaints, that are meant to fill a gap in the law.[23] These guidelines are applicable to both private and public employers until the Indian Parliament passes suitable legislation on the subject. Through this decision, the Supreme Court has paved the way for the domestic application of women's international human rights law. Moreover, the Indian Parliament has enacted the Protection of Human Rights Act in 1993 for better implementation of human rights and has established the National Human Rights Commission. It is worth understanding what efforts the Commission has made for preventing child marriages.

Methodology

In the following pages, I discuss the various human rights of young girls as defined in international human rights conventions that are violated as a result of child marriages. Such analysis is done by adopting various steps. I have clustered these human rights around the harm that results from the existence of the practice of child marriage as well as around the various kinds of harm suffered by individuals as a consequence of child marriages. In the process I identify and analyse the relevant articles of UDHR, ICCPR, ICESCR, the Women's Convention, Children's Convention, Marriage Convention, and Slavery Convention. I also refer to the general recommen-dations/comments adopted by the treaty-monitoring bodies and their concluding observations on the country reports. I also mention the relevant parts of the Cairo Programme of Action (POA) and the Beijing Platform of Action (PLA) that were evolved at the international conferences.

I then analyse the extent to which the Indian state has complied with its obligation under the treaties that it has ratified for promoting the human rights of young girls, particularly in the context of child marriage. I try particularly to analyse it on the basis of the feminist method 'asking the woman question'. At the end of the discussion on each right, in case of any deficiencies, the measures that need to be adopted in future by the Indian government are suggested. I also suggest on what counts the treaty-monitoring committees should demand more information from the Indian government so as to improve India's performance and thereby ensure realization of human rights of young girls. The discussion bears in mind and refers to the provisions of the Indian Constitution and decisions of the Supreme Court.

Before going into the specifics of the young girls' human rights in the context of child marriage as addressed by the international human rights conventions, I review very briefly the historical evolution of international human rights instruments including women's and children's human rights conventions. I also examine the two other equally important conventions, the Slavery Convention and the Marriage Convention that were adopted by the General Assembly, in 1956 and 1962 respectively, even prior to the adoption of two major international human rights instruments, namely, the International Covenant on Civil and Political Rights and the International Covenant on Economic, Social and Cultural Rights.

Evolution of International Human Rights

The constitutional document of the United Nations (UN), the Charter of the United Nations, came into force in 1945. It does not include a bill of rights but contains as one of the goals of the United Nations Organization the promotion of human rights and fundamental freedoms for all, without discrimination as to race, sex, language, or religion.[24] The commitment of the United Nations to human rights was first reflected in the Universal Declaration of Human Rights (UDHR), which was adopted by the General Assembly in 1948.[25] The foundation of UDHR was to reaffirm faith in fundamental human rights and in the dignity and worth of the human being. UDHR itself is not a legally enforceable instrument but legal recognition is given to it through a number of international treaties.[26] With UDHR, the individual person became the subject of international law.

The primary relevance of the Universal Declaration to the discussion in this chapter is its emphasis on the right to equal protection. Article 2 of UDHR reads: 'Everyone is entitled to all the rights and freedoms set forth in this Declaration, without distinction of any kind, such as race, colour, sex, language, religion, political or other opinion, national or social origin, property, birth or other status.' Another most relevant article of UDHR is Article 16 (1) which reads: 'Men and women of full age, without any limitation due to race, nationality or religion, have the right to marry and found a family. They are entitled to equal rights as to marriage, during marriage and its dissolution.' Article 16(2) states: 'Marriage shall be entered into only with the free and full consent of the intending spouses.' The Commission on Human Rights—a body established under the authority of the United Nations Charter, set the goal of drafting the International Bill of Human Rights to create specific human rights standards in response to the general principles enshrined in UDHR. Initially, the idea was to draft one single convention on human rights. But eventually two separate instruments were developed: the International Covenant on Civil and Political Rights (ICCPR) and the International Covenant on Economic, Social and Cultural Rights (ICESCR).[27] Both these conventions were adopted by the General Assembly in 1966 and entered into force in 1976.

All these human rights documents vest rights in every individual human being on the basis of her/his being *human*. Article 1 of UDHR states: 'All human beings are born free and equal in dignity and rights. They are endowed with reason and conscience and should act towards one another in a spirit of brotherhood.'[28] The application of human rights is universal and is evident in the title of UDHR and in the statement of its preamble that 'rights and freedoms are a common standard of achievement for all peoples and all nations'.[29] The preamble of ICCPR and ICESCR reiterates that 'these rights derive from the inherent dignity of the human person and they are universal as they belong to all humans'.[30]

Evolution of the Women's Convention

In the evolution of human rights law, the formal notion of equality between men and women was central to human rights since 1945 when the Charter of the United Nations[31] was formulated. It was reaffirmed in 1948 by UDHR,[32] followed by ICCPR[33] and ICESCR[34] in 1966. ICCPR mentions that equality before the law and the principle of non-discrimination are enforceable rights. It states:

> All persons are equal before the law and are entitled without any discrimination to the equal protection of the law. In this respect the law shall prohibit any discrimination and guarantee to all persons equal and

effective protection against discrimination on any ground such as race, sex, language, religion, political or other opinion, national or social origin, property, birth or other status.[35]

However, though these provisions referred to women's rights and other provisions appeared to be *gender-neutral*, they did not in fact protect and benefit women as they did men. By and large civil and political rights—the so-called first generation rights—held a privileged position in the human rights law and practice, despite formal recognition by the international community of the interdependence of these first generation rights and the second-generation rights, namely the economic, social, and cultural rights.

Abuse suffered by individuals at the hands of the state was the overwhelming concern for the UN during its first two decades. As men were active in the public sphere, to which women had no access, the first-generation rights were not actually applied to women's human rights. Women's impaired access to political institutions almost kept them out of the human right discourse in the initial phase of the development of human rights jurisprudence. In fact, prioritization of civil and political rights resulted in neglect of gender-specific abuses in private life, and it marginalized women's rights.[36] Their experiences and perspectives were largely, though not entirely, absent from the international human rights discourse.

In this context, it is important to consider two aspects of the public/ private distinction. There is a clear dichotomy between the public/private human rights discourse, which is one of the principal theoretical barriers in realizing women's human rights.[37] One aspect of the dichotomy is the political, legal, and social process, which constructs the public and private domains. The public sphere of law, economics, politics, intellectual, and cultural life is regarded as the province of men and the private sphere of home, family, and health is relegated to women. This assignment entrenches women's inequality in relation to men. Moreover, the privacy of domestic life makes women's concern invisible and ensures preservation of the status quo. The second aspect is the theoretical distinction in international law between conduct that is attributed to the state and for which the state is held liable by the international community, and the conduct of private persons that does not directly implicate the international obligations of the state. The demarcation of public and private life within society is an inherent political process that both reflects and reinforces power relations, especially the power relations of gender, race, and class.[38]

Until the Women's Convention was adopted by the UN General Assembly, women's experiences and perspectives were largely, but not entirely, absent from the international human rights discourse. The international community and the traditional human rights lawyers did not take the structural causes and systemic nature of women's subordination and oppression into account. Women's experiences and their sufferings and disadvantages were neglected mainly because the private sphere of familial relationship was considered to be out of the purview of the human rights debate. Consequently, women's problems and concerns were not central to the rights framework. The invisibility of women led to the feminist struggle for women's human rights. It was not until the late 1960s and 1970s that progress was made in international fora towards the meaningful articulation of women's human rights.[39]

In 1967, the international community addressed the issue of the subordination of women in the Declaration on the Elimination of Discrimination against Women which was adopted unanimously by the UN General Assembly. It highlighted the then existing legal, institutional and social methods that violated women's rights and emphasized the need to protect those rights. Women's distinct roles and their special needs were focussed on in this Declaration.[40] The Declaration advanced the setting of standards for women's rights significantly. It also served as a basis for creating a legally binding convention for women's human rights.

Right from 1967 onwards, the process of adopting a convention on the rights of women gained momentum. As a first step, the UN General Assembly declared the year 1975 as International Women's Year. The UN Commission on the Status of Women (CSW), a Charter-based body, took an initiative in 1974 for drafting the convention. Finally, the Convention on the Elimination of All Forms of Discrimination against Women (Women's Convention) was adopted by the General Assembly in 1979 and it came into force in 1981. The Convention established an international bill of rights for women, and state parties agreed as a matter of international law to guarantee the enjoyment of those rights. The Optional Protocol to the Women's Convention was opened for signature on 10 December 1999, Human Rights Day and came into force on 22 December 2000.[41]

The Women's Convention defines discrimination against women as

> any distinction, exclusion or restriction made on the basis of sex which
> has the effect or purpose of impairing or nullifying the recognition,

enjoyment or exercise by women, irrespective of their marital status, on a basis of equality of men and women, of human rights and fundamental freedoms in the political, economic, social, cultural, civil or any other field.[42]

It lays down obligations upon state parties to eliminate discrimination in national constitutions or other legislation, to take steps to ensure the practical realization of this principle,[43] and most importantly to modify or abolish customs and practices that discriminate against women.[44] By reading Articles 2(f) and 5 together, state parties agree to reform personal laws. These articles strongly reinforce the commitment to eliminate all forms of discrimination, since many pervasive forms of discrimination against women rest not on law as such but on legally tolerated customs and practices. For instance, in India the customary practice of child marriage of girls is prevented through legal measures, but is not declared illegal and invalid. As a ratifying state party, India is under an obligation to reform the law regarding age of marriage.

The standard of treatment of women required by the Convention is that of equality,[45] but is not limited to formal equality.[46] It endorses substantive equality that accounts for social, economic, and educational inequalities and seeks to eliminate such inequalities through positive measures. For instance, to ensure women's effective right to work, state parties are required to take appropriate measures.[47] The Convention provides specific guarantees of women's equality in identified areas where gender-based discrimination has been especially detrimental such as political life,[48] education,[49] health services,[50] and the family.[51] The monitoring power under the Convention is given to the Committee on the Elimination of Discrimination Against Women (CEDAW).[52] Recently the Optional Protocol to the Women's Convention has also come into force by which CEDAW will be able to address individual complaints too.[53]

Evolution of the Children's Convention

The Preamble of the Charter of the United Nations gave special emphasis to the future by proclaiming: 'We the peoples of the United Nations determined to save succeeding generations from the scourge of war ... have decided to combine our efforts to accomplish these aims ...' The Charter names as one of its purposes 'Observance of human rights and fundamental freedoms *for all* without discrimination as to race, sex, language, or religion'.[54]

Three years later, in 1948, UDHR enunciated the entitlement of 'all members of the human family'[55] to enjoy human rights and fundamental freedoms. UDHR also referred specifically to children's rights. It stated that children are entitled to special care and assistance.[56] The initial concern for children's rights was linked with women's rights.[57] These provisions of the Charter and of UDHR were developed in the following years to reflect more specifically the rights of the child. Education was envisaged by UDHR as the tool for the full development of the human personality.[58]

In 1959, the UN adopted a specific declaration of the Rights of the Child and focussed on children as persons entitled to rights in their own capacity. However, being merely in the form of a declaration of policy, it had no binding force.[59] The declaration emerged as political rhetoric in the absence of focus on how to realize those rights. Later human rights instruments, namely ICCPR (1966)[60] and ICESCR (1966), did articulate the rights to cover children[61] and were binding on the states that ratified these instruments. However, the issue of protecting children's rights in international law was not raised until 1979.

In 1979, the Women's Convention was adopted by the UN General Assembly. It addressed the issue of gender discrimination against women throughout their lifespans thereby recognizing that women included girls and adolescents.[62] It addressed the issue of discrimination against women and girls in the family.[63] It included a conceptual framework on the family and parental responsibilities for children, which provided a space for focussing on the interests and the rights of the girl child.[64] The Women's Convention was followed by a declaration that 1979 was to be designated as the International Year of the Child. Ten years later, in 1989, the UN General Assembly adopted the Convention on the Rights of the Child (Children's Convention). The Children's Convention had the largest number of signatories on the day it was opened for signature.[65] It is the most comprehensive treaty and protects the entire range of human rights: civil, political, economic, social, cultural, and humanitarian. The monitoring power under the Convention is given to the Committee on the Rights of the Child.

Article 1 of the Children's Convention states that 'a child means every human being below the age of eighteen unless, under the law applicable to the child, majority is attained earlier'. The Children's Convention recognizes that children are entitled to human rights in their own right. It endorses the two basic principles, namely the 'best interests of the child' and the 'evolving capacities' of the adolescent. Article 3(1) of the Convention states: 'In all actions concerning children, whether undertaken by the public or private social welfare institutions, courts of law, administrative authorities or legislative bodies, the best interests of the child shall be a primary consideration.' Article 5 of the Convention also requires that

> States Parties shall respect the responsibilities, rights and duties of parents or where applicable, the members of the extended family... or other persons legally responsible for the child, to provide, *in a manner consistent with the evolving capacities of the child, appropriate direction and guidance* in the exercise by the child of the rights recognised in the present Convention.[66]

Reading of these two articles indicates that children incapable of judgment are entitled to appropriate direction and guidance from parents or guardians. Legitimate parentalism may be exercised over children who need protection against their liability to make decisions that would injure them or harm their important interests, because their own inexperienced judgment lacks adequate insight or foresight.[67] However, state parties are required to respect the rights of parents when they guide their children appropriately. If parents do not act in the best interests of their children, state parties have an obligation to intervene in the best interests of the children. For instance, when young girls are given in marriage by their parents, they are neither acting in the best interests nor are they respecting their wishes to decide not to marry at young age.

Evolution of the Slavery and Marriage Convention

The origin of the Marriage Convention requiring state parties to prescribe the minimum age of marriage, consent of the intended spouses, and the registration of the marriage could be traced back to the Supplementary Convention on the Abolition of Slavery, the Slave Trade, and Institutions and Practices Similar to Slavery, 1956. The international community laboured to eliminate slavery through the creation of numerous treaties, conventions, and protocols.[68] An ad hoc committee based on the Charter of the Economic and Social Council (ECOSOC) was appointed in July 1949 to survey the field of slavery and other institutions and customs resembling slavery that were restrictive of the liberty of a person and that tended to subject that person to a state of servitude.[69] Amongst other things, it identified the purchase of wives, involving involuntary subjection of a woman to a man not of her choice as one of such practices. The ad hoc committee submitted its report in 1951 to ECOSOC and recommended the preparation of a new supplementary convention on slavery and other forms of servitude. The report was discussed by ECOSOC[70] and a drafting committee was appointed to prepare a draft of such a convention.

ECOSOC thereafter convened a conference of plenipotentiaries in 1956 to complete the draft on slavery and similar practices.[71] The conference discussed amongst other issues, the issue of the servile form of marriages involving the sale of brides and equated it with practices similar to slavery.[72] Eventually the Supplementary Convention on the Abolition of Slavery, the Slave Trade, and Institutions and Practices Similar to Slavery (Slavery Convention), was adopted in 1956 and it came into force in 1957. The Convention took cognizance of the practice of servile forms of marriage along with other practices and mentioned that all measures should be taken for its abolition.

Considering the importance of the issue of marriage law that affects women more severely than men, ECOSOC thereafter referred the issue of servile marriages to CSW for further action. CSW prepared a draft of the Convention on the Consent to Marriage, Minimum Age for Marriage and Registration of Marriages for consideration of ECOSOC and presentation to the UN General Assembly. The UN General Assembly adopted the Marriage Convention in 1962 and it entered into force in 1964.

The Marriage Convention promotes marriage as a consensual institution and requires the establishment of a minimum legal age for marriage and official recording of marriages. It outlaws child marriages and betrothal before puberty. But it does not specify the minimum age for marriage.[73] However, the UN General Assembly passed a resolution titled 'Recommendation on Consent to Marriage, Minimum Age for Marriage and Registration of Marriages' in 1965. It recommended that states should take legislative action to specify a minimum age for marriage, which in any case shall not be less than fifteen years of age.[74] The provision as to marriageable age and full and free consent was also incorporated in Article 23 of ICCPR and Article 16 of the Women's Convention.[75]

However, neither of these conventions recommended a minimum age for marriage. There is no provision to establish a monitoring body under the Slavery and Marriage Conventions. Therefore, the actual practice of application of the Slavery and Marriage Conventions to child marriage has not developed.[76]

International Human Rights and Child Marriage[77]

Human rights are the rights of individuals in society. To call them *human* implies that all human beings have them, equally and in equal measure, by virtue of their inherent human dignity, regardless of sex, race, age, social class, economic position, religion, culture, or other parameters. Implied in one's human dignity, human rights are inalienable and imprescriptible. Human rights are rights, not just aspirations, and are not dependent on privilege. As *rights*, they imply that they are claims *as of right* and *entitlements*.[78] Thus they are the instruments through which particularly powerless individuals and groups can claim human dignity.

Marriage is a state-sanctioned institution. Therefore, failure on the part of a state to address the prevention of child marriages of young girls is an indication of social injustice. It is a result of exclusion of injustices that women experience. In the subsequent chapters, I try to establish that with the human rights approach such injustice could be remedied. My argument is that human rights are denied to young girls when they are given in marriage by their parents for social, cultural, religious, and economic reasons as child marriage causes multiple harm to these girls. Child marriage

— takes away their autonomy in respect of the choice of a life partner and the right to decide the timing of the marriage;

— may expose them to violence and abuse which may result in emotional and psychological problems and sometimes even in desertion and divorce;

— creates problems for their reproductive health in terms of maternal mortality and morbidity;

— does not give them the opportunity to decide freely and responsibly the number and spacing of their children;

— reaffirms stereotypes of women in child-bearing roles;

— takes away their right to education which in turn:

- denies them the opportunity to become economically independent,
- undermines their self-confidence,
- hampers their decision-making power,
- affects their overall well being, and

> – hinders their ability to participate to the fullest extent in the of life activities,

and thereby violates human rights of young girls.

The harm resulting from child marriage can be classified into two broad categories:

— Harm caused by the existence of the institution of child marriage itself and

— Harm resulting to individuals as a consequence of actual child marriages.

Consequences of child marriage could be further classified into:

— Consequences on health particularly reproductive health and

— Consequences on the overall development of young girls.

Each kind of harm takes away one or the other human right of young girls. These human rights can be analysed in a variety of ways. Human rights originating in the various international human rights instruments including women's and children's conventions are clustered around these categories of harm.

The purpose of clustering human rights around these various kinds of harm is to develop arguments against the traditional practice of child marriage. Such arguments would establish how child marriage violates the human rights of young girls and would help in turn advance their human rights. Hereinafter, I intend to explore the application of these international human rights through the discrete and legally distinguishable categories of rights, at the same time emphasizing the interdependence of these rights. As the effects are vast in each of the two broad categories mentioned above, these are discussed in detail in two separate chapters.

End Notes

[1] Rebecca Cook et al., *Advancing Safe Motherhood Through Human Rights* (Geneva: World Health Organization, 2001) at 4.

[2] Treaties, conventions, covenants are the different terms which are used interchangeably.

[3] Convention on the Elimination of All Forms of Discrimination against Women, G.A. Res. 34/180, UN GAOR, 34th Session, No. 46 at 193, UN Doc.A/ 39/45 (1979) (entered into force, 3 September 1981) entered into force for India on 8 August 1993.

[4] Convention on the Rights of the Child, G.A. Res. 44/25 (XLIV), UN GAOR, 44th Session, Supp. No. 49 at 167, UN Doc. A/44/49 (1989) (entered into force, September 1990) entered into force for India on 11 January 1993.

[5] International Covenant on Civil and Political Rights, G.A. Res. 2200A (XXI), UN Doc.A/6316 (1966) (entered into force, 23 March 1976) entered into force for India on 10 July 1979.

[6] International Covenant on Economic, Social and Cultural Rights, G.A. Res. 2200A (XXI), (entered into force, 23 March 1976) entered into force for India on 10 July 1979. There are also other regional Conventions, viz., The European Convention on Human Rights, The American Convention on Human Rights, and The African Charter on Human and Peoples' Rights. These are not discussed here as the focus of the book is on India.

[7] Convention on Consent to Marriage, Minimum Age for Marriage and Registration of Marriages, G.A. Res. 1763 A (XVII) (1956) (entered into force, 9 December 1964). India has not ratified it.

[8] Supplementary Convention on the Abolition of Slavery, the Slave Trade, and Institutions and Practices Similar to Slavery, G.A. Res. 608 (XXI) (1956) (entered into force 30 April 1957). India ratified it on 23 June 1960.

[9] United Nations, International Human Rights Instruments, Compilation of General Comments and General Recommendations Adopted by Human Rights Treaty Bodies, HRI/Gen/1/Rev.2, 29 March 1996.

[10] Andrew Byrnes, 'Enforcement Through International Law and Procedure', in Rebecca Cook (ed.), *Human Rights of Women* (Philadelphia: University of Pennsylvania, 1994) at 195.

[11] The UN General Assembly Resolution A/54/4 on 6 Oct 1999 has entered into force on 22 December 2000.

[12] For instance, under Article 8 of the Optional Protocol to the Women's Convention, state parties are required to submit their observations to CEDAW. However, normally it is expected that state parties will be inclined to follow the recommendations and comments of the Committee. See Torkel Opsahl, 'The Human Rights Committee' in Philip Alston (ed.), *The United Nations and Human Rights: A Critical Appraisal* (Oxford: Clarendon Press, 1992) 431.

[13] This aspect is not discussed in detail in the following pages.

[14] There are other mechanisms such as the Communication Procedure of the Commission on the Status of Women and ECOSOC Resolution 1503

intended to receive information on the human rights situation in individual countries. However, both are little known and therefore little used. See Byrnes, supra note 10 at 205. The third important mechanism adopted is of the thematic special rapporteur who is appointed by the Commission on Human Rights. See Chapter Five, note 121 and accompanying text.

[15] R. Pound, *Social Control Through Law* (London: Oxford University Press, 1942) at 25.

[16] Kamminga, *Inter-State Accountability for Violations of Human Rights* (Philadelphia: University of Pennsylvania Press, 1992) at 486.

[17] Rebecca Cook, 'State Accountability under the Convention on the Elimination of Discrimination against Women' in Cook (ed.), supra note 10 at 228 (238).

[18] Maastricht Guidelines on violation of economic, social, and cultural rights. See also Rebecca Cook and M.F. Fathalla, 'Duties to Implement Reproductive Rights' (1998) 67 *Nordic Journal of International Law* 1.

[19] See *X. and Y. v. The Netherlands,* 1985 European Court of Human Rights Series A, Vol. 91.

[20] Except the Marriage Convention. See supra notes 3–8.

[21] For the text, see Commonwealth Secretariat and Interights, *Developing Human Rights Jurisprudence: Conclusions of Judicial Colloquia on the Domestic Application of International Human Rights Norms* (London: Commonwealth Secretariat, 1992).

[22] *Vishaka* v. *State of Rajasthan* AIR 1997 SC 3011 at 3014. It is interesting to note that this case was filed by a group established by a voluntary organization named Vishaka. Vishaka filed this case after an incident of rape of a social worker that took place in Rajasthan. Bhavari Devi was working as a *sathin* (social worker) in the social welfare department of the government of Rajasthan. Her job was to create awareness about CMRA and to prevent child marriages. She was taught a lesson for this work. She was gang-raped by the so-called high-caste people who did not like her intervention in their personal matters. There is no direct reference to the reasons for the gang-rape case in the judgment. But the court mentioned in the beginning (at 3012) that the immediate cause for the filing of the writ petition was an incident of alleged brutal gang-rape of a social worker in a village of Rajasthan.

[23] Ibid. at 3014, 3015.

[24] See in particular the Preamble and Articles 1, 13, and 55 of the UN Charter, 1945. The concern with human rights including women's rights is reinforced by references in the Charter to work that the organization is empowered to undertake. See Article 56 which mentions that states pledge

themselves to take action for the achievement of human rights and other social development goals. Article 68 indicates establishment of commissions in the economic and social fields and for the promotion of human rights.

[25] Universal Declaration of Human Rights, G. A. Res. 217A (III), UN Doc.A/810 (1948).

[26] It is now viewed as a normative instrument reflecting customary international law that imposes legal obligations on all states. See John Murphy, 'Introduction to Universal Declaration of Human Rights' in Carol E. Lockwood, et al. (eds), *The International Human Rights of Women* (New York: American Bar Association, 1998) at 138.

[27] The separation into two documents occurred due to the ideological differences in the attitudes of the states towards the importance of protecting political and economic rights. See Lynn P. Freedman, 'Human Rights and Women's Health', in M. Goldman and M. Hatch (eds), *Women and Health* (New York: Academic Press, 1999) 428 at 431. In order to overcome the disagreement between Eastern and Western bloc nations over the value of socio-economic rights, two separate instruments were created. See Barbara Stark, 'Introduction to International Covenant on Economic, Social and Cultural Rights', in Lockwood, supra note 26 at 215.

[28] Article 1.

[29] Preamble.

[30] Preamble.

[31] Article 2.

[32] Article 2.

[33] Article 2, 3.

[34] Article 2, 3.

[35] Article 26.

[36] Charlotte Bunch, 'Women's Rights as Human Rights: Toward a Re-Vision of Human Rights' (1990) 12 *Human Rights Quarterly* 486.

[37] See Donna Sullivan, 'The Public/Private Distinction in International Human Rights Law', in Julie Peters and Andrea Wolper (ed.), *Women's Rights Human Rights*, (New York: Routledge, 1995) 126.

[38] Ibid. at 127–8.

[39] Though there were a number of other international treaties that came into force on specific aspects of women's lives. These include, The Discrimination (Employment and Occupation) Convention, 1958; The Convention against Discrimination in Education, 1960; the Equal Remuneration Convention, 1951; the Supplementary Convention on Slavery, 1956; the Convention for the

Suppression of the Traffic in Persons and of the Exploitation of the Prostitution of Others, 1949; the Convention on the Nationality of Married Women, 1957; the Convention on the Political Rights of Women, 1954; etc.

[40] See Lockwood, supra note 26 at 245–50.

[41] United Nations, *Optional Protocol to the Convention on the Elimination of All Forms of Discrimination against Women*, UN Doc. A/Res/54/4.

[42] Article 1 of the Women's Convention.

[43] Ibid. Article 2 (a).

[44] Ibid. Articles 2 (f) and 5.

[45] Ibid. Article 3.

[46] Ibid. Article 4.

[47] Ibid. Article 11.

[48] Ibid. Article 7.

[49] Ibid. Article 10.

[50] Ibid. Article 12.

[51] Ibid. Article 16.

[52] Ibid. Article 17.

[53] See supra note 11.

[54] Article 55(c) of the UN Charter.

[55] Preamble of the UN Charter.

[56] Article 25 (2) of the UDHR: Motherhood and childhood are entitled to special care and assistance.

[57] Ibid.

[58] Article 26 (1): Everyone has the right to education .... (3) Parents have a prior right to choose the kind of education that shall be given to their children.

[59] Though it is argued that it has become part of customary international law. See Sohn, 'The New International Law: Protection of Rights of Individuals Rather than States' (1982) 32 *American University Law Review* 1 at 17.

[60] See for example, Article 14 of ICCPR that provides safeguards concerning the administration of justice.

[61] See for example, Article 10 of ICESCR that speaks of special protection to children. Article 12 is concerned with the highest attainable standard of physical and mental health and specially mentions that the states are obliged to take steps for reduction of the still-birth rate and of infant mortality and for the healthy development of the child.

[62] See The Committee on the Elimination of Discrimination Against Women (CEDAW), General Recommendation 24, UN GAOR, 1999, Doc. No. A/54/38/Rev.1, Para 8.

[63] Article 16 of the Women's Convention.

[64] Article 16(1)(d) of the Women's Convention.

[65] See Cynthia Cohen and Per Miljeteig Olssen, 'Status Report: United Nations Convention on the Rights of the Child' (1991) 8 *New York Law School Journal of Human Rights* 367.

[66] Emphasis added.

[67] Rebecca Cook and Bernard Dickens, 'Recognising Adolescents' 'evolving capacities' to exercise choice in reproductive healthcare' (2000) 70 *International Journal of Gynaecology and Obstetrics* 13 at 15.

[68] For example, the 1890 General Act for the Repression of the African Slave Trade, the 1919 Treaty of Saint-German-en-Laye, the Slavery Convention, 1926, the Forced Labour Convention, 1930.

[69] (E/-1617).

[70] UN Yearbook 1951 at 504.

[71] UN Yearbook 1956 at 228–9.

[72] Nina Lassen, 'Slavery and Slavery-Like Practices: United Nations Standards and Implementation' (1988) 57 *Nordic Journal of International Law* 197 at 201.

[73] See at 151.

[74] General Assembly Resolution 2018 (XX) of 1 November 1965.

[75] For detail discussion, see at 151 et al.

[76] HRC has taken up the issue of child marriage with India but has not yet questioned it as a form of slavery.

[77] See generally, International Planned Parenthood Federation, *Charter on Sexual and Reproductive Rights* (1995).

[78] Louis Henkin, 'Where are we going from here?' in Martin (ed.), *International Human Rights Law and Practice: Cases, Treaties and Materials*, 21–3 (Cambridge: Kluwer Law International, 1997).

5

Human Rights Violated by the Custom of Child Marriage

Introduction

Child marriage violates a number of human rights of young girls that can be separately identified in various human rights conventions. These rights include the right to equality, right to marry and found a family, right to liberty and security, and right to be free from slavery. Right to equality can be discussed under the sub-headings: right to sexual and gender non-discrimination and right to non-discrimination on the ground of age. And finally I intend to discuss how the intersectionality of sex, gender, and age are compounded by cultural and traditional customs and what the country is obliged to do in order to ensure that Indian children are not denied their human rights.

Right to Equality

The prohibition of discrimination is among the most fundamental principles of international human rights law. As stated in the UN Charter, one of the four overarching purposes of the UN is 'to achieve international co-operation in promoting and encouraging respect for human rights and for fundamental freedoms for all without distinction as to sex, race, language, or religion'.[1]

The Universal Declaration and the two UN Human Rights Covenants, ICCPR and ICESCR, require governments to prohibit discrimination of any kind in the exercise of protected rights, such as on grounds of sex, race, colour, language, religion, political or other opinion, national or social origin, property, birth, or other status.[2]

The right of women to equality with men (as distinct from the right to non-discrimination) has received attention since the advent of the United

Nations. In its first preambular paragraph, the UN Charter 'reaffirms faith' in a number of fundamental principles, including the 'equal rights of men and women'.[3] Article 3 of both ICCPR and ICESCR obliges state parties 'to undertake to ensure the equal rights of men and women to the enjoyment' of all the rights set forth in each covenant. The Women's Convention in its title itself focuses on the elimination of *all forms* of discrimination against women. It recognizes the right to protection against discrimination on the ground of sex and gender.[4] The Children's Convention endorses the right to non-discrimination on the ground of sex[5] as well as on the ground of age.[6]

Right to Non-discrimination on Grounds of Sex and Gender

Discrimination on the ground of sex is prohibited under all the international human rights conventions.[7] In fact, it has been argued that the prohibition of sexual discrimination is now part of customary international law which binds all the states even without their express ratification of a treaty.[8] The main treaty stating various rights included within the overarching right of women to the enjoyment of human rights on the basis of equality with men is the Women's Convention. It obliges state parties 'to pursue by all appropriate means and without delay a policy of eliminating discrimination against women' and to 'take in all fields ... all appropriate measures ... to ensure the full development and advancement of women, for the purpose of guaranteeing them the exercise of the enjoyment of human rights and fundamental freedoms on a basis of equality with the men'.[9] Discrimination against women is defined in Article 1 as:

> [A]ny distinction, exclusion or restriction made on the basis of sex which has the effect or purpose of impairing or nullifying the recognition, enjoyment or exercise by women, irrespective of their marital status, on a basis of equality of men and women, of human rights and fundamental freedoms in the political, economic, social, cultural, civil or any other field.

The definition has several distinctive features. First, it states that women are entitled to enjoy human rights on the basis of equality with men, and not merely freedom from discrimination on the ground of sex.[10] Second, the right to equal enjoyment extends to rights in any field including economic and social.[11] Third, it extends to the protection of measures that have the effect of improving women's equal enjoyment of rights.[12]

Thus the Women's Convention addresses discrimination on the grounds of biological as well as political, social, economic, and cultural constructs, which account for the disadvantage that women suffer. Article 3 of the Women's Convention reads:

> States Parties shall take in all fields, in particular in the political, social, economic and cultural fields, all appropriate measures, including legislation to ensure the full development of and advancement of women ...

It characterizes women's inferior status and oppression not just as a problem of inequality between men and women but rather as a function of sex and gender discrimination against women.[13] It moves from a sex-neutral norm to the recognition of the fact that the law must respond to the special needs of women by understanding the pervasive and systemic nature of discrimination against them. Article 5 of the Women's Convention states:

> States Parties shall take all appropriate measures:
>
> (a) to modify social and cultural patterns of conduct of men and women with a view to achieving the elimination of prejudices and customary and all other practices, which are based on the idea of inferiority or the superiority of either of the sexes or on stereotyped roles for men and women.

Thus, it goes beyond the UN Charter, UDHR, ICCPR, and ICESCR to address the disadvantaged position of women in all areas of their lives. The Women's Convention identifies the need to confront the social causes of women's inequality by addressing 'all forms' of discrimination that women suffer.[14] It thereby accounts for women's life experiences. It requires 'States Parties to eliminate even the private discrimination against women by any person'.[15]

The practice of child marriage of girls violates the right to equality on the ground of sex as well as gender. It violates the right in both forms of equality—formal as well substantive equality. The prohibition against sex discrimination has largely been interpreted to require that likes be treated alike or those similarly situated are to be treated equally.[16] Within this prevailing conception, equality is equated with sameness. When the two are same, they are to be treated equally. Any difference in treatment to individuals or groups constitutes discrimination. This is a formal equality. The practice of child marriages of girls when looked at from this narrow perspective of formal equality treats them differently from boys of their age and thus discriminates against them on the ground of sex and violates their right to formal equality. Even the laws of many countries[17] that prescribe a lower age of marriage for girls than boys discriminate on the ground of sex and thereby violate the right to non-discrimination on the ground of sex provided in ICCPR and ICESCR, the Women's Convention, and the Children's Convention.

It is not only on the basis of formal equality that the practice of child marriage of girls could be challenged. It violates substantive equality too. The focus of substantive equality is not simply on equal treatment but rather on the actual impact of the practice on individuals or groups. The focus is not on sexual discrimination but on gender discrimination. The focus is not on the sameness or difference, but rather on disadvantage. The central inquiry of substantive equality approach is whether the practice in question contributes to the disadvantage. Accordingly, discrimination consists of treatment that further disadvantages a group that has historically and socially experienced systemic oppression.[18] The object of the substantive equality approach is to eliminate the existing inequality in day-to-day life suffered by the disadvantaged and seeks to eliminate it by positive measures. The Women's Convention as pointed out earlier addresses the formal as well as substantive equality and discrimination based on sex and gender.

The concept of gender is constructed by social, economic, and cultural considerations. The girl child is discriminated against from the earliest stage of life through her childhood and into adulthood.[19] The first lesson that a female child is made to learn is that the differential treatment between her and her brothers is a fact of life.[20] The practice of preference for a male child is a deeper form of discrimination perpetrated against the girl child. Lineage continuity and succession to property are some of the considerations underlying the desire to have sons. Another reason for the girls child's inferior status in her family is that since by custom a daughter, on her marriage, is expected to leave the parents' home to join her husband's home, parents depend on their sons for material support during their old age.

The practice of child marriage usually victimizes girl children. Girls are perceived as burdens by their parents. Child marriage of their daughters relieves them of the responsibilities attached to raising a girl. At the same time, as the girl's parents are relieved of their burden, the groom's parents also benefit because they gain an unpaid slave and often a dowry.

As discussed earlier,[21] the purpose of the marriage is transference of father's dominion over a woman in favour of her husband. This transfer is then expected to take place at an early age so as to allow her to adapt to her socially determined position.[22] Another reason for child marriage of girls is to control her sexuality[23] and reproduction, which is at the heart of unequal gender relationships. Through culturally embedded concepts of virginity and chastity, women's sexuality is not only controlled by men but is often a symbol of the honour and status of a family.[24] The society has undue concern about female virginity, and awareness of its absence severely hampers the marriage prospects of girls. The practice of child marriage reduces the possibility of any suspicion regarding the virginity of a young girl. Marriages are arranged, therefore, either immediately after or sometimes even before she attains puberty.

These social, economic, and cultural justifications for child marriage adversely affect the girl children's health, education, and development as pointed out in earlier chapters. It contributes to their already low position in the family and society, subordinates them further, and thereby results in the denial of substantive equality to them, discriminates against them, and aggravates their systemic oppression.

Article 2(f) of the Women's Convention calls upon state parties to '[T]ake all appropriate measures, including legislation, to modify or abolish existing laws, regulations, customs and practices which constitute discrimination against women'.[25] The Women's Convention further calls upon, through Article 5, the elimination of all cultural practices, which are based on the idea of the inferiority of women or stereotyped roles of men and women. It calls upon state parties to take all appropriate measures:

> (a) To modify the social and cultural patterns of conduct of men and women, with a view to achieving the elimination of prejudices and customary and all other practices, which are based on the idea of the *inferiority or the superiority* of either of the sexes or on *stereotyped roles* for men and women ....[26]

Articles 2(f) and 5(a) of the Women's Convention when read together put an obligation on state parties to take appropriate measures to modify cultural practices, such as child marriage, by passing or reforming legislation, taking steps for effective enforcement of such legislation, and making efforts to change the attitudes of people to those cultural practices. These provisions of the Women's Convention, therefore, reiterate a feminist viewpoint and require state parties to take appropriate measures to remedy a situation where women's experiences have so far been excluded.

Apart from this, young girls are denied the same degree of choice as men in countries where marriages are arranged by parents. They have little say in deciding the timing of their marriage or selecting their spouse. Their minds are conditioned and a psychological framework is built up in such a way that they feel duty-bound to respect the decision of their parents. In case of arranged marriages of young girls the question of their choice, therefore, becomes irrelevant. When parents find a groom for their young daughter, they do not ask for her consent. Even if they ask, it does not mean much in reality, as culturally daughters are groomed to believe that parents always act in their *best interest*.

At the same time, it is equally true that selection of a groom largely depends upon the class and caste to which the parents belong. Economic, social, and educational positions are inevitable factors that restrict the choice by the parents of a groom for their daughter. Woman's lack of independent status by any of these considerations further reduces her chance of having any say in the matter of her marriage. As a consequence, when a child marriage takes place, the right to choose the husband is denied to a girl and thereby her autonomy is not respected. As a result, she is discriminated against on the grounds of sex at the point of entering into marriage. It violates her right to equality at the point of entering into marriage as stipulated in Article 16(1) of the Women's Convention. Article 16(1) calls upon state parties

> [T]o take all appropriate measures to eliminate discrimination against women in all matters relating to marriage and family relations and in particular to ensure, on a basis of equality of men and women:
>
> (a) The same right to enter into marriage
>
> (b) The same right to freely choose a spouse and to enter into marriage only with their free and full consent.

In this connection, CEDAW's General Recommendation 21 on 'Equality in Marriage and Family Relations' on Article 16(1)(a) and (b) of the Women's Convention is very significant. It observes:

> A woman's right to choose a spouse and enter freely into marriage is central to life and to her dignity and equality as a human being. An examination of States Parties' reports discloses that there are countries, which on the basis of custom, religious beliefs or the ethnic origins of

particular groups of people, permit forced marriages or remarriages .....
Subject to reasonable restrictions based for example on a woman's youth
or consanguinity with her partner, a woman's right to choose when, if,
and whom she will marry must be protected and enforced at law.[27]

Even before the Women's Convention, ICCPR and ICESCR emphasized
free consent of the parties to a marriage. Article 23 of ICCPR states:

> (3) No marriage shall be entered without the free and full consent of
> the intending spouses.
>
> (4) States Parties to the present Covenant shall take appropriate steps
> to ensure equality of rights and responsibilities of spouses as to
> marriage, during marriage.

Article 10(1) of ICESCR also reiterates: 'Marriage must be entered into
with free consent of the intending spouses.'

Thus all three conventions specifically guarantee to men and women
the equal right to enter into marriage with free and full consent. Child
marriage violates this right. Free consent is not only the one that is without
force or coercion. But it has a positive element in it. It has to be an informed
consent exercised on the basis of free will.[28] To exercise free, full, and informed
consent for entering into a marriage, a person needs to have the physical
and mental capability to understand the meaning and responsibility of
marriage. A person has to have proper information about the other spouse,
the pros and cons of the proposed marriage and its repercussions on future
life. A person needs to be in an open environment with proper opportunity
to express her will. Obviously, as a *child*, she lacks such understanding due
to her underdeveloped physical and mental capacity. And even if she has
such understanding, the parents do not assign importance to it and ignore
her evolving capacities.[29]

HRC in its General Comment 28 on the Equality of Rights between
Men and Women mentioned that:

> States are required to treat men and women equally in regard to marriage
> in accordance with Article 23 .... Men and women have the right to
> enter into marriage only with their free and full consent, and States
> have an obligation to protect the enjoyment of this right on equal basis.
> *Many factors may prevent women from being able to take the decision to
> marry freely.* One factor relates to the minimum age for marriage. That
> age should be set by the State on the basis of equal criteria for men and
> women. These criteria should ensure women's capacity to make an

informed and uncoerced decision. A second factor in some States may be that either by statutory or customary law a guardian, who is generally male, consents to the marriage instead of the woman herself, thereby preventing women from exercising a free choice.[30]

HRC through this comment has responded to the realities of life that prevent women from freely taking decisions about their marriages. There are many factors that restrict them, such as young age, economic dependence, and powerlessness. Older men in the family many a times take the decision about their marriages on their behalf. Marriage being a state-sanctioned institution, there is an obligation on state parties to ensure that men and women are treated equally in regard to marriage and to take appropriate measures. HRC has reiterated this obligation of state parties by taking cognizance of women's experiences.

One of the legal ways to assure a bride's free and full consent to the marriage is to make the registration of marriage compulsory. Registration of marriage is certainly a critical issue because it offers a point at which states can be involved in preventing discrimination in marriage against women. States can pass a law by which a marriage could be allowed to be registered only when the conditions regarding age and consent of the parties are fulfilled. Otherwise, such a marriage should have no legal effect.

Right to Non-discrimination on the Ground of Age

Various adverse consequences of child marriage on girls have been discussed in detail in earlier chapters. Girls are far more likely than boys to be married early and to much older men. Culturally, it is expected that a man should be older than his wife, and in many countries this practice is supported by law.[31] Not only are young girls affected disproportionately, but the practice of child marriage also has consequences for them that it does not have for boys when they are married at a much younger age than boys. In Chapter One I have discussed in length the adverse consequences on the health, education, development, and status of young girls because of child marriage.[32]

There is no provision in CRC which specifically bans the practice of child marriage. However, Article 2.2 of the Children's Convention places a duty upon state parties

[T]o take all appropriate measures to ensure that the child is protected against *all forms of discrimination* or punishment on the basis of the status, activities, expressed opinions, or beliefs of the child's parents against, legal guardians or family members.[33]

All forms of discrimination would mean discrimination on the basis of age also. When young girls are given in marriage, they are discriminated against on the basis of age as compared to older boys in which case the discrimination is compounded by sex. State parties are required to take legal as well as extra-legal steps to protect young girls from such discrimination.

Intersectionality of Sex, Age, and Gender Discrimination

The above discussion shows that young girls are discriminated against on the basis of age and sex, as well as gender. Women are discriminated against on the basis of sex and gender in marital relations, but the young girls are further discriminated against on the basis of their age. The Intersectionality of these three grounds results in discrimination against girl children qualitatively as well as quantitatively.[34] Such discrimination is additionally compounded by cultural and traditional justifications and is supported by the patriarchal social system.[35] That is the reason behind its securing legitimacy and continuation in spite of international efforts to denounce it. As emphasized by Crenshaw, there is a need to demarginalize the intersection of age, sex, and gender that will help preclude child marriage of girls.[36]

No social group has suffered greater violation of its human rights in the name of culture than women. A cultural explanation of the gendered social practice of child marriage has to be challenged by asking 'the woman question'. Only when women are kept at the centre of the discussion can the gender complexity of the cultural argument be exposed.[37] Articles 2(f) and 5(a) of the Women's Convention are premised on the notion that where cultural constructs of gender are an obstacle to the achievement of woman's equality, it is the cultural practice that has to give way. Woman's rights are not to be sacrificed in situations where their realization requires modifying social and cultural patterns of behaviour.[38] Women's experiences in fact need to be reflected while defining the cultural norms.

In 1993, the Vienna Conference declared that human rights of women should form an integral part of the United Nations human rights activities.[39] In 1995, the Fourth World Conference on Women succeeded in bringing about a new international commitment to the goals of equality and development for all women everywhere, and moved the global agenda for the advancement of women into the twenty-first century. The Beijing Declaration and the Platform for Action adopted unanimously by representatives from 189 states, is a powerful agenda for women's empowerment and gender equality. It spelt out twelve critical areas of concern.[40] The Beijing Platform for Action defined a set of strategic objectives and spelled out actions to be taken by governments, the international community, non-governmental organizations, and the private sector for the removal of the existing obstacles to women's advancement. The girl child was one of the special categories to which the Beijing Platform for Action paid attention. Governments, through their commitments, recognized at Beijing that human rights of the girl child are an inalienable, integral, and indivisible part of universal human rights, and must be promoted, protected, and recognized at all stages of the life cycle.

The need to eliminate all forms of sex and gender discrimination against women was an integrative and universal theme in POA[41] and PLA[42]. Both the documents urged the states 'to eliminate all forms of discrimination against the girl child and the root causes of son preference, which result in harmful and unethical practices'. Countries which have endorsed POA and PLA and the state parties that have ratified the Women's and Children's Convention are thus duty-bound to address these issues for the protection of young girls' rights. Governments committed themselves to take effective steps for mainstreaming of gender which called for the re-examination of society in its entirety and its basic structure of inequality. The focus was, therefore, no longer limited to women and their status in society but was committed to restructuring institutions and political and economic decision making in society as a whole.

As a follow-up to the Beijing Conference, ECOSOC[43] and the General Assembly[44] requested the Commission on the Status of Women to identify emerging issues, trends, and new approaches to issues affecting the situation of women or the equality between women and men that required urgent consideration. The UN General Assembly then called for a special session to review the progress made in the five years since the Beijing Platform of Action was adopted. The special session, which became popularly known as 'Beijing +5', was convened under the theme 'Women 2000: Gender Equality, Development and Peace for the Twenty-first Century'.[45] It provided the opportunity for governments and civil society to share good practices and to examine current challenges and obstacles encountered in the implementation of the Beijing Platform for Action.

Governments and the international community once again reaffirmed their commitment to the Platform for Action and a common development agenda with gender equality as an underlying principle. They recognized that efforts towards ensuring women's advancement needed to combine a focus on women's conditions and basic needs with a holistic approach based on equal rights and partnership, along with the promotion and protection of all human rights and fundamental freedoms. There is a clear endorsement of women's experience. Certain areas such as education, social services and health, including sexual and reproductive health, and violence against women and girls were identified as requiring focussed attention. Thus in pursuance of the Beijing +5, a binding commitment has been made by the countries. Considering the major focus areas that were identified by Beijing +5, one can see that child marriage is certainly a priority issue. It remains to be seen how governments are going to respond in practice.

Therefore, at the cost of repetition, it is necessary to mention that compulsory registration of marriage is the best solution to reduce the severity of intersectionality of various grounds of discrimination against the girl child that is caused due to child marriage. Countries which have ratified the above-mentioned international human rights conventions, particularly the Women's Convention, are duty-bound to enact legislation that stipulates the minimum age of marriage, free consent of girls, and compulsory registration of marriage. Such legislation has to declare that non-compliance with any one of the three conditions would make the marriage void.

Right to Equality: India's Obligation

The Indian Constitution makes the right to equality a fundamental right for all citizens. Article 14 of the Constitution states: 'The State shall not deny to any person equality before law or the equal protection of the laws within the territory of India.' Article 15 speaks about prohibition of discrimination. It reads:

(1) The State shall not discriminate against any citizen on grounds only of religion, race, caste, sex, place of birth, or any of them.

(2) ...

(3) Nothing in this article shall prevent the State from making any special provision for women and children.

However, it is one thing to guarantee equality in the Constitution and another thing to make it a social reality. Indian tradition and culture are so male-dominated that even after more than fifty years of the Constitution, women generally experience inequality throughout their lives. Child marriage is one such example where girl children face discrimination through legislation as well as cultural and traditional practices. Once the girl is given in child marriage, she is denied equal opportunity, unlike her counterpart, to education and further development. Additionally, she is likely to face problems regarding her mental and physical well-being, including her reproductive health. Thus her marriage at a young age discriminates against her in all possible ways and takes away her right to equality. Legitimacy to the practice of child marriage is a clear indication of denial of recognition of her experience. Therefore, the cultural explanation of gendered social practice of child marriage has to be challenged by applying the woman question. Only when women are kept at the centre of the discussion that the gender complexity of the cultural argument can be exposed.

India has legislation—the Child Marriage Restraint Act (CMRA)—that specifies different minimum age for marriage—eighteen years for a girl and twenty-one years for a boy—which in itself is discriminatory on the basis of sex.[46] Thereby it violates young girls' right to formal equality assured by Article 14 of the Indian Constitution and discriminates on the ground of sex. CMRA does not provide for the registration of marriages, nor does it require the free consent of the parties to a marriage. In the absence of such provisions it is difficult to ascertain whether the girls are able to take freely the decision for their marriage. Apart from CMRA, the other existing marriage laws, based on religion do not mention the consent of the parties to a marriage and do not provide for the compulsory registration of marriages.[47] In the absence of such provisions in CMRA or in personal laws, it is difficult to ascertain the exact percentage of child marriages and more difficult to control such marriages.

Apart from the constitutional provisions and domestic legislation on the minimum age of marriage, India has ratified ICCPR and ICESCR and particularly the Women's Convention and Children's Convention and is, therefore, duty-bound to protect the rights of girl children to non-discrimination on the grounds of sex, gender, and age. Marriage is a matter that falls within the purview of religion-based personal laws in India and as discussed earlier in detail, all these personal laws discriminate against women on the basis of sex as well as religion.[48] India has filed a declaration to Article 16 of the Women's Convention.[49] The declaration reads:

> (i) With regard to Articles 5 (a) and 16 (1) of the Convention on the Elimination of All Forms of Discrimination against Women, the Government of the Republic of India declares that it shall abide by and ensure these provisions in conformity with its policy of non-interference in the personal affairs of any community without its initiative and consent.[50]

India has thereby excused herself from not eliminating the discrimination based on sex, gender, and religion in the field of personal laws.

Analysis from the feminist perspective of CMRA, personal laws of marriage, and the Indian government's position vis-a-vis the international human rights instruments substantiates an argument that the government is not prepared to review its laws and the practices that are derogatory to women in the name of culture and religion. The practice of son preference, differential treatment between a girl and her brother, neglect of her health and education, overall inferior status in the family, and undue concern about her sexuality are some of the important reasons for child marriage. The state has not valued these experiences of women and hence has not initiated effective measures, including legal, to change the attitude of people, though child marriages of girls are taking place on a large scale and are adversely affecting their future lives.

India filed an initial report before CEDAW,[51] which was considered in January 2000.[52] The Government of India did not make any direct reference in its report to the issue of child marriage. CEDAW also did not raise the issue of child marriage directly. However, it commented in its concluding observations on the religion-based personal laws and sexual discrimination. However, CEDAW raised a question in this context and enquired about the steps taken by the Indian government to adopt a gender-just uniform civil code.[53] The reply given by the government was that the policy of the government was of non-interference in the matters of personal laws and would continue to be the same, unless the initiative for changes in the laws came from the respective communities themselves.[54] CEDAW commented:

> The Committee notes that steps have not been taken to reform the personal laws of different religious and ethnic groups in consultation with them so as to conform with the Convention. The Committee is

concerned that the Government's policy of non-intervention perpetuates sexual stereotypes, son preferences and discrimination against women.[55]

CEDAW also expressed its concern about the declaration made by India on Article 16 (1) of the Women's Convention. CEDAW commented:

> The Committee urges the Government to withdraw its declaration to Article 16(1) of the Convention and to work with and support of women's groups as members of the community in reviewing and reforming these personal laws. The committee also calls upon the government to follow the directive principles in the Constitution and Supreme Court decisions and enact a uniform civil code.[56]

India has also filed a declaration regarding registration of marriage provided in Article 16(2) on compulsory registration of marriages.[57] The declaration states:

> With regard to Article 16 (2) of the Convention on the Elimination of All Forms of Discrimination against Women, the Government of the Republic of India declares that though in principle it fully supports the principle of compulsory registration of marriages, it is not practical in a vast country like India with its variety of customs, religions and level of literacy.[58]

The declaration is worded in such a way that there is no commitment to change the situation in future.

Arguments have been made in Chapter Three in support of compulsory registration of marriages.[59] Even the National Commission for Women in its Marriage Bill, 1994 recommended to the government that registration of marriages should be made compulsory to prevent child marriages. CEDAW expressed its concern about the registration of marriages in the following words:

> India has not yet established a comprehensive and compulsory system of registration of births and marriages. The Committee notes the inability to prove those important events by documentation on trafficking, child labour and *forced or early marriage*.[60] The Committee calls upon the Government to provide adequate resources and establish a system of compulsory registration of births and monitor implementation in co-operation with women's groups and local bodies. It urges the Government to withdraw the reservation to Article 16(2) of the Convention.[61]

CEDAW also referred to the Marriage Bill drafted by the National Commission for Women in 1994 and called upon the Government on India to strengthen law enforcement and introduce reforms proposed by the National Commission for Women.[62] The Marriage Bill has declared child marriage void. In the light of these comments, India is obligated to make the registration of marriages compulsory. Reservations or declarations to any of the international treaties are not supposed to be incompatible with the object and purpose of the Conventions.[63] The declaration filed by India to Article 16(1) is the best illustration of such incompatibility. HRC in its General Comment 24 on issues relating to reservations or declarations made upon ratification has mentioned in clear terms that

> The Covenant consists not just of the specified rights, but of important supportive guarantees. These guarantees provide the necessary framework for securing the rights in the Covenant and are thus essential to its object and purpose. Reservations designed to remove these guarantees are thus *not acceptable*.[64]

It further stated that

> Domestic laws may need to be altered properly to reflect the requirements of the Covenant; and mechanisms at the domestic level will be needed to allow the Covenant rights to be enforceable at the local level.[65]

Regarding the effect of unacceptability of the reservation, it mentioned that the reservation would generally be severable, in the sense that the Covenant would be operative for the reserving party without the benefit of the reservation.[66] At the end HRC mentioned that states should also ensure that the necessity of maintaining reservations be periodically reviewed and that they be withdrawn at the earliest possible moment.[67]

By implication CEDAW should also judge the incompatibility of any of the reservations or declarations filed by India. India's declaration is incompatible with the object of Article 16 of the Convention as the religion-based personal laws in India do discriminate against women. Further, not declaring child marriage void by not amending the existing laws is against Article 16(2) of the Women's Convention. And by not providing for the compulsory registration of marriages and excusing itself from making it so in future by filing the declaration in respect of Article 16, India is defeating the object of this article. Even the language of the declaration is such that there is no possibility of changing the situation in future. India's declaration on Article 16, therefore, should be treated as not acceptable by CEDAW.

As mentioned by HRC, the result is that India would not be able to claim any benefit under the declaration and would be responsible to answer to CEDAW.

Therefore though, CEDAW, has touched upon the issue of child marriages in India in an indirect manner, in future it should address the issue more directly. It should declare child marriage a discriminatory and harmful cultural practice, should recommend the necessary changes in the existing laws, and ask more forcefully for the withdrawal of the reservations by communicating that these are incompatible with the Convention, and hence unacceptable.

In its concluding observations on India's report, CRC noted the persistence of discriminatory social attitudes and harmful traditional practices towards girls, including female infanticide, selective abortions, low school enrolment and high dropout rates, and *early and forced marriages.*[68] It expressed concern about the religion-based personal laws, which perpetuate gender inequality in areas such as marriage, divorce, custody and guardianship of infants, and inheritance, prevalent in India.[69] CRC recommended:

> In accordance with Article 2 of the Convention, the Committee encourages the State party to ensure the enforcement of protective laws. The Committee encourages the State party to continue its efforts to carry out comprehensive public education campaigns to prevent and combat gender discrimination, particularly within the family. To assist in these efforts, political, religious and community leaders should be mobilized to support efforts to eradicate traditional practices and attitudes, which discriminate against girls.[70]

CRC, while expressing its concern about the health of adolescents commented:

> The Committee is concerned that the health of adolescents, particularly girls, is neglected, given, for instance, a very high percentage of early marriages, which can have a negative impact on their health. Adolescent suicides, especially among girls ... are serious concerns for the Committee.[71]

It recommended

> [T]he State party strengthens the existing National Reproductive and Child Health Programme, targeting the most vulnerable groups of the

population .... The Committee recommends continued allocation of resources to the poorest sections of society and continued co-operation with and technical assistance from, *inter alia*, WHO, UNICEF, UNAIDS and civil society.[72]

CRC recommended that India should continue its efforts to carry out extensive campaigns to combat harmful traditional practices, such as *child marriages*, and to inform, sensitize, and mobilize general public opinion on the child's right to physical and mental integrity, and safety from sexual exploitation.[73]

CRC, in its concluding observations, has expressed its serious concern regarding the high percentage of child marriage of girls prevalent in the country. CRC has clearly mentioned that the practice of child marriage is discriminatory and violates human rights of girl children guaranteed under the Children's Convention. Its recommendations need to be pursued by voluntary organizations and civil society.

India also participated in the Fourth World Conference on Women at Beijing in 1995 and its follow-up done in the year 2000 through the preparatory committee and special session, popularly referred to as Beijing +5. As mentioned before, the protection of the human rights of girls was approved as one of the twelve critical areas by Beijing and Beijing +5 to be focussed on during the next five years. Eradication of child marriage in India, therefore, certainly needs the attention of the government.

International treaty-monitoring bodies—particularly CEDAW, CRC, and HRC—have taken cognizance of the gendered conditions that facilitate or permit child marriage through their concluding observations and General Recommendations/Comments. India is under obligation to respond to these recommendations. The state needs to prevent child marriages by making all efforts including legislative changes. It needs to bring in more flexibility in its policies so as to adopt the feminist thoughts that demand space for women's considerations—their interests, experiences, and values. Only if such an attitude is adopted by the state, there is a possibility of fulfilment of human rights of young girls.

Right to Marry and Found a Family

Article 16.1 of UDHR states: '[M]en and women of *full age* have the right to marry and found a family.'[74] Article 23.2 of ICCPR states: '[T]he right of men and women of *marriageable age* to marry and found a family shall be recognized.'[75] Article 16(2) of the Women's Convention states: '[T]he marriage of a *child* shall have no legal effect.'[76]

The terms *full age*, *marriageable age*, and *child* are neither defined nor explained by the respective international instruments. The Children's Convention defines 'child' as '... every human being below the age of 18 years ....'[77] By referring to this definition the minimum marriageable age could be interpreted as eighteen years. Therefore, the right of young girls to marry at a 'marriageable age', 'full age', or when they become adult is violated when they are married off before they attain the age of eighteen years.

These conventions recognize the right to marry but with a restriction on the age of parties. Rebecca Cook has rightly pointed out that laws requiring a minimum age for marriage are not inconsistent with the right to marry and found a family. The right to marry and to become parents is a right of adults rather than of children or adolescents.[78] An act of founding a family is not merely a biological function. It is much more than that. It involves planning, timing, and spacing for the good of the whole family. The right to found a family incorporates the right to augment the survival prospects of the conceived child.

However, as discussed previously, marriage at an early age denies all such opportunities to young girls.[79] They are forced to enter into motherhood and family responsibility as soon as possible after the marriage for which they are unprepared. Being inexperienced, they are unable to work for the betterment of the family. They neither have the capacity to negotiate with their spouse nor do they have sufficient information and means to delay the birth of their first child. Thereby, they are denied the right to decide freely and responsibly on the number and spacing of their children recognized under Article 16(1)(e) of the Women's Convention[80], as well as the right to found a family.

The right to marry includes the right not to marry. Young girls have the right not to be married off. CEDAW, in its concluding observations on the report of Ethiopia expressed 'great concern' about the prevalent practice of child marriage and suggested that the age of marriage be the same for boys and girls.[81] It identified deep-rooted customs, traditions, and illiteracy as major obstacles in the implementation of the Convention.[82]

While commenting on the report of Indonesia, CEDAW expressed its concern over the discrimination in the laws regarding age of marriage and health, including the requirement of the husband's consent for sterilization or abortion.[83] Similar was the comment on the report of the Republic of Korea.[84]

Though CEDAW's concern regarding the practice of child marriages is expressed in the concluding observations, there is further scope to develop these concluding observations more systematically. There are countries where the problem of child marriage is in existence on a large scale. But CEDAW does not refer to the problem of child marriage while adopting concluding observations on the report of those countries where child marriage exists.[85] CEDAW could ask for more data from the reporting countries relating to child marriage, such as legal provisions regarding the age at marriage, free and informed consent of the parties to the marriage, and registration of marriage. It could also confirm the factual situation by referring to the demographic data on age at marriage, awareness about the law, and special efforts, if any, made for improving conditions that compel child marriages.[86]

The general recommendations of CEDAW on violence, health, marriage, and family relations have contributed to assessing which human rights mentioned in the Convention are violated. In its General Recommendation 19 on 'Violence against Women,'[87] CEDAW commented that gender-based violence is a form of discrimination within the meaning of Article 1 that identifies eight rights and freedoms.[88] CEDAW emphasized that discrimination is not restricted to action by government but also by 'any person'. The state should be held responsible for private acts if it fails to act with due diligence to prevent the violation of the rights or to investigate and punish the acts of violence.

CEDAW has not directly referred to the practice of child marriage as a form of family violence. However, while commenting on Articles 2(f), 5, and 10(c) it referred to the traditional attitudes by which women are regarded as subordinate to men or as having stereotyped roles perpetuating widespread practices involving violence, such as family violence and abuse, and forced marriage. It noted that the effect of such violence is to deprive women of equal enjoyment of human rights and to help retain them in subordinate roles and such violence contributes to their lower level of education, skills, and work opportunities.[89]

CEDAW has referred to forced marriage.[90] Force is implicit in child marriage as young girls are pressurized to get married either by not being asked for their consent or by ignoring their wishes. CEDAW has recommended that state parties should take effective legal measures to protect women from violence in the family[91] as well as preventive measures to change the attitudes concerning roles and status of men and women.[92] Through these observations CEDAW has focussed on gendered conditions that facilitate or enable forced marriages. This is exactly what the woman question does. However, in future, CEDAW in its general recommendation, instead of referring only to forced marriages, should also refer specifically to child marriage as a form of domestic violence.

The Vienna Conference also stressed the importance of working towards the elimination of violence against women in public and private life. It urged state parties to eradicate any conflicts between the rights of women and the harmful effects of certain traditional or customary practices, cultural prejudices, and religious extremism.[93]

As already mentioned, though the Women's Convention declares that 'the marriage of a child shall have no legal effect', it does not define 'child' and thereby does not stipulate a minimum age of marriage. CEDAW commented on Article 16(2) while giving its General Recommendation 21 on 'Equality in Marriage and Family Relations':

> Article 16(2) and the provisions of the Convention on the Rights of the Child preclude States Parties from permitting or giving validity to a marriage between persons who have not attained their majority. In the context of the Convention on the Rights of the Child, "a child means every human being below the age of 18 years, unless, under the law applicable to the child, majority is attained earlier". Notwithstanding this definition and bearing in mind the provisions of the Vienna Declaration, the Committee considers that the minimum age of marriage should be 18 years for both man and woman. When men and women marry, they assume important responsibilities. Consequently, marriages should not be permitted before they attained full maturity and capacity to act. According to the World Health Organization, when minors, particularly girls, marry and have children, their economic autonomy is restricted.[94]

It further commented:

> Some countries provide for different ages for marriage for men and women. As such provisions assume incorrectly that women have a different rate of intellectual development from men, or that their stage of physical and intellectual development at marriage is immaterial, these provisions should be abolished.[95]

CEDAW also recommended that state parties should require compulsory registration of all marriages.[96] In order for state parties to comply with the Women's Convention they have to pass legislation declaring: (a) eighteen to be the age of marriage for women and men, (b) registration of marriage to be compulsory, and (c) marriage to be void in case of non-compliance with either of these conditions. This would help in the fulfilment of women's right to marry and found a family.

CEDAW further noted with alarm the number of reservations to the whole or part of Article 16 that state parties have entered. It especially referred to reservations entered to Article 2, claiming that the compliance might conflict with a commonly held vision of the family-based, inter alia cultural and religious belief or the country's economic or political status.[97] CEDAW recommended to state parties to gradually withdraw their reservations.[98]

These various general recommendations when read together do indicate CEDAW's concern about the issue of child marriage. However, considering the magnitude and serious repercussions of child marriage, it would be in the interest of girl children all over the world that CEDAW should adopt a General Recommendation on child marriage. It could be worded on similar lines to CEDAW's General Recommendation on Female Circumcision. The reason is that female circumcision is also a similar traditional practice performed on young girls without their consent and justified on the basis of culture. It is harmful to their health and has serious social repercussions on their life.[99] CEDAW's General Recommendation 19 on Violence against Women could also be relevant as a guideline for drafting such recommendation on child marriage. Violence against women violates a variety of human rights covered by the Women's Convention and so does child marriage. The recommendation could be divided into three parts: Introduction; Comments on specific articles of the Women's Convention that are relevant to child marriage, e.g. Articles 2, 3, 5, 10, 12, 14, and 16; and lastly, specific recommendations. Such specific recommendations could be worded as follows:

    (a) That state parties take appropriate legal measures with a view to eradicating the practice of child marriage. Such measures could include:

        (i) Passing of legislation or amendment of existing legislation on marriage providing for the minimum age of eighteen years for both the parties, for free and informed consent of the parties, for compulsory registration of marriage, and declaring a marriage void in the absence of compliance with such provisions;

(ii) Introduction of a provision that would give a woman the right to maintenance to be claimed from the man to whom she was married and/or his parents;

(iii) Introduction of a provision for implementation of these measures through training of the judiciary and administrative personnel.

(b) That state parties take appropriate and effective measures with a view to creating awareness about the harmful practice of child marriage. Such measures could include:

(i) Collection and dissemination of basic data about child marriages;

(ii) Support of women's organizations for the elimination of child marriages;

(iii) Encouragement of politicians, officials responsible for implementation of laws, professionals, and religious and community leaders at all levels including the media to co-operate in influencing attitudes towards eradication of child marriage, the encouragement of religious leaders being for the positive interpretation of religious texts;

(iv) Introduction of appropriate educational and training programmes and seminars based on research findings about the problems arising from child marriage.

(c) That state parties take appropriate measures for creating enabling conditions to prevent child marriages.

(d) That state parties include in their national health policies appropriate strategies aimed at eradicating child marriage. For implementation of such strategy, special training about harmful effects of child marriage could be given to health personnel.

(e) That state parties invite assistance, information, and advice from appropriate organizations of the United Nations system to support and assist efforts to eliminate child marriages including providing alternatives for girls.

(f) That state parties include in their reports to the Committee under Articles 16 of the Women's Convention information about measures taken to eliminate child marriage.

Apart from CEDAW, other treaty bodies have also commented on the age of the parties to a marriage. HRC, in General Comment 19, mentioned that the age of marriage should be such as to enable each spouse to give his or her free and full personal consent in a form and under conditions prescribed by law.[100] HRC also mentioned that the right to equality in the family and in marriage includes the right to found a family that implies freedom from compulsory and child marriage, and to access information and education about health and reproduction.[101] It also said that the protection of children under Article 24 could extend to consideration of prevention of early pregnancy and child marriage, by raising the age of marriage for girls.[102] The above comments of CEDAW and HRC indicate that these committees have analysed the situations leading to child marriage not merely from the point of view of avoiding discrimination on the ground of sex but also by taking into consideration what women are forced to face in real life.

The Children's Convention, drafted as a gender-neutral convention, has not directly addressed the issue of child marriage. It does not specifically require state parties to prohibit child marriage. However, it could be argued that the Children's Convention does not recognize any right of parents to marry off their daughter as a child. It does respect their rights and duties to make provision for their children, and considering children's evolving capacities[103] to give appropriate directions and guidance to them in the exercise of their rights.[104] Parent's legal power to discharge their duties in the *best interest* of children is underscored by the Convention. Article 18.1 reads:

> States Parties shall use their best efforts to ensure recognition of the principle that both parents have common responsibilities for the upbringing and development of the child. Parents ... have the primary responsibility for the upbringing and development of the child. The *best interests* of the child shall be their basic concern.[105]

To pursue the best interests of children, parents have to take care of their children's health, education, development, and their overall well-being to the best of their capacities. They have to groom their children in such a way that they become responsible adults in future. The parents, therefore, according to the 'best interests' principle are under a legal obligation not to marry off their children below the age of eighteen years.

The Children's Convention also puts an obligation on all state agencies to take all appropriate measures to protect the child from all forms of abuse, neglect, or maltreatment while in the care of parents. Article 19.1 reads:

> States Parties shall take all appropriate legislative, administrative, social and educational measures to protect the child from all forms of physical or mental violence, injury or abuse, neglect or negligent treatment, or maltreatment or exploitation, including sexual abuse, while in the care of parents ....

Article 3.1 of the Children's Convention requires state parties to act in the 'best interests' of the child. It states:

> In all actions concerning children, whether undertaken by public or private social welfare institutions, courts of law, administrative authorities or legislative bodies, the best interest of the child shall be a primary consideration.

When parents give their girl child in marriage, it cannot be accepted that they act in the 'best interest' of their daughter. In fact, child marriage is a form of physical as well as mental violence against a girl child committed at the domestic level by her own parents. State parties are responsible in such a situation to take proper measures against the parents to protect the best interest of the girl child.

Article 24.3 of the Children's Convention requires state parties 'To take all effective and appropriate measures with a view to abolishing *traditional practices* prejudicial to the health of children.'[106] It is mentioned time and again that the practice of child marriage is justified on the basis of culture and traditions. Thus, in pursuance of Article 24.3, it is an obligation of state parties to abolish the practice of child marriage in the best interest of children.

In addition, Article 12 of the Children's Convention requires state parties 'To assure to the child who is capable of forming his or her own views the right to express those views freely in all matters affecting the child ....' The customary practice of child marriage, prevalent in the absence of law or in the absence of effective enforcement of law, violates the right mentioned in Article 12. When girls are compelled to enter into marriage against their will or before they are capable of consenting to marriage, their right to expression is violated.

Though the Children's Convention has not dealt explicitly with child marriages, challenges to the practice of child marriage could be read in many of its provisions by interpreting it according to its object and purpose of protecting the child. In pursuance to these various articles, CRC has given increasing attention to raising and enforcing the legal age at marriage in the concluding observations on the reports of the state parties.[107] It has drawn attention to the discrepancies in the domestic laws detrimental to young girls. CRC has also addressed on a number of occasions the conflict between parental rights of authority and children's best interest.[108]

CRC has expressed its anxiety on a number of occasions about the justification of the practice of child marriage in the name of culture and traditions prevalent in various countries. For example, while commenting on the report of Nepal, CRC noted that there were 'Persistent discriminatory attitudes towards girls, as reflected in the son preference, the persistence of child marriages, the notably lower school attendance of girls and their higher dropout rate.'[109] CRC also noted the discrepancy in the minimum age of marriage for girls and boys in Nepal.[110] It expressed its concern on the report of Lebanon in the following words: 'The Committee is worried by the widespread practice of child marriage and the related consequences of high child mortality rates and the negative impact on the health of young girls bearing children at young age.'[111] On the report of Indonesia, CRC expressed concern over the national legislation providing for a discriminatory age of marriage for women and men, in violation of Article 2 of the Children's Convention.[112]

On the Nigerian report CRC expressed its concern regarding the practice of child marriage and recommended a review of the compatibility of customary, regional, and local laws with the Children's Convention and to engage with the eradication of violation of the rights of children.[113]

Similarly, while commenting on the report of Guatemala, CRC observed: 'The low age of marriage for girls, which is different than boys, is, in the Committee's view, incompatible with the principles and provisions of the Convention.'[114] CRC was also concerned with the situation prevalent in Zimbabwe. It highlighted the situation of female victim of practices such as *ngozi* (girl child pledging), *lobola* (bride price), and child marriage.[115]

While commenting on the practice of child marriage in Kuwait, CRC recommended that the state party should undertake all appropriate measures, including legal measures, to prevent and combat this traditional practice that is harmful to the health and well-being of girls and development of the family.[116] It urged the Government to undertake awareness-raising campaigns with a view to changing attitudes. CRC has contributed significantly by recognizing child marriage as a 'harmful traditional practice'. Such comment was made while delivering the concluding observations on the reports of Ghana[117] and Ethiopia.[118]

CRC has instituted a practice in its Fall Session of holding a General Discussion Day on a topic of interest to state parties.[119] It has often discussed the need to raise and enforce the legal age at marriage in such general discussions. Reports of these general discussions mention the issue of child marriage and pregnancy, forced marriage, sexual abuse, female genital mutilation (FGM), etc.[120] These reports also mention a variety of steps that should be taken by state parties for rectifying these situations.

Another international mechanism through which concern has been expressed on the issue of child marriage is the reports of the special rapporteur appointed on 'Violence against Women, its Causes and Consequences'.[121] In her report, she has focussed on the traditional practices through which women are subjected to violence.[122] Among such practices mentioned by her are childhood marriage, son preference, and FGM. She has argued in her recent report that these practices should be construed as a definite form of violence against women and should not be justified on grounds of tradition, culture, or social conformity.[123]

Another Special Rapporteur on 'Traditional Practices Affecting the Health of Women and Children'[124] has focussed on traditional practices, such as child marriage and FGM, which are harmful to health and argued for their eradication as they constitute a definite form of violation of human rights.[125] Referring to these reports the UN has repeatedly called for the complete eradication of such customs.

Right to Marry: India's Obligation

The Indian law on the age of marriage complies partly with Article 16 (2) of the Women's Convention by laying down the minimum age for marriage. Article 16(2) mentions:

> The betrothal and the marriage of a child shall have no legal effect, and all necessary action, including legislation, shall be taken to specify a minimum age for marriage and to make the registration of marriages in an official registry compulsory.

India contravenes thus the provisions of the Women's Convention in three respects. One, by not prescribing the same age for both a girl and a boy; two, by not declaring child marriages to be void and having no legal effect; and three, by not making registration of marriages compulsory. India thereby has failed in substance to comply with her obligations under Article 16 (2) of the Women's Convention.

As already mentioned in the previous discussion, the Indian government submitted its report to CEDAW and had a hearing in January 2000. CEDAW recommended through its concluding observations that the proposals of the National Commission for Women on law reform be used in preparing new legislation in critical areas, within a timeframe.[126] The National Commission for Women has recently prepared a draft on uniform marriage laws in which child marriage is declared void and of no legal effect.[127]

As mentioned earlier, CEDAW expressed its concern about the non-existence of a comprehensive and compulsory system of registration of births and marriage, which in turn could prevent effective implementation of laws that protect girls from child marriage. CEDAW urged the government to withdraw its declaration to Article 16(2).[128] In the light of these comments it is now the responsibility of civil society and women's organizations to encourage the government to respond to these comments. Voluntary organizations working for the promotion of the rights of girl children need to take the responsibility for implementation of the recommendation regarding registration.

Even HRC explained in its concluding observations on the report submitted by India:

> While acknowledging measures undertaken to outlaw child marriages ... the Committee remains gravely concerned that legislative efforts are not sufficient and that measures designed to change the attitudes which allow such practices should be taken. The Committee therefore recommends that the Government take further measures to overcome these problems ...[129]

India submitted her initial report to CRC in 1999.[130] CRC gave its concluding observations on 28 January 2000.[131] CRC in its concluding observations noted the persistence of discriminatory social attitudes and harmful traditional practices in respect of girls, including female infanticide, selective abortions, low school enrolment and high dropout rates, early and forced marriages, and religion-based personal laws which perpetuate gender inequality in areas such as marriage, divorce, custody and guardianship of infants, and inheritance.[132] It encouraged state parties to continue their efforts to carry out comprehensive public education campaigns to prevent and combat gender discrimination, particularly within the family. To assist in these efforts, it requested state parties to mobilize political, religious, and community leaders, so that they could support efforts towards eradicating traditional practices and attitudes, which discriminate against girls.[133]

In the light of Article 12 of the Children's Convention, CRC noted that the views of the child are accorded insufficient importance, especially within the family.[134] It encouraged the state to promote and facilitate within the family respect for the views of children and their participation in all matters affecting them, in accordance with Article 12 of the Convention. In this regard, CRC recommended that through training programmes in community settings, the state should develop skills for teachers, social workers, and local officials in assisting children to make and express their informed decisions and to have their views taken into consideration.[135] These observations and recommendations are quite significant in the light of promoting the rights of young girls to express their decisions about their future. If implemented as suggested by CRC, these recommendations would help prevent child marriages of young girls.

In the light of Article 1, CRC expressed its concern about the various age limits set by law that are not in accordance with the general principles and other provisions of the Convention. Of particular concern to CRC was the poorly enforced minimum-age standard with reference to CMRA. It recommended that India should make greater efforts to enforce the minimum-age requirements.[136] Thus, CRC has explained what is required on the part of the Indian government to comply with the Children's Convention in the area of child marriage. Similar to CEDAW and HRC, CRC has also adopted a feminist perspective and a pragmatic approach to assimilate women's interests in its concluding observations. Efforts are needed now on the part of the government to respond to it.

Right to Liberty and Security

The right to liberty and security is provided to everyone in Article 3 of UDHR. It states, 'Everyone has right to life, liberty and security of person.' The right to liberty is one of the strongest defences of individual integrity.

Child marriage encroaches on the right to liberty of a child bride, as she has no freedom to say 'no' to her marriage that is arranged by her parents. She has no freedom to choose her life partner. In addition, on marriage, she loses control on her future life too. Thus, child marriage is restrictive of the liberty of the girl child subjecting her to a state of servitude and, therefore, is very significant in the context of the lives of young girls. Her freedom regarding whom to marry and when to marry is taken away by her parents when the decision is taken for her by them.

All the major human rights conventions provide for the right to liberty. For instance, Article 9.1 of ICCPR states, 'Everyone has the right to liberty and security of person ... No one shall be deprived of his liberty except on such grounds and in accordance with such procedure as are established by law.' Articles 37 (b) and (c) of the Children's Convention also provide for the right to liberty. It states:

(a) ...
(b) No child shall be deprived of his liberty unlawfully or arbitrarily ...
(c) Every child ... shall be treated with humanity and respect for the inherent dignity of the human person and in a manner, which takes into account the needs of persons of his or her age.

However, an individual's right to liberty so far has been interpreted only in the context of misuse of the power by the state. Even HRC in its General Comment 8 has observed: 'Article 9, which deals with the right to liberty and security, has often been somewhat narrowly understood in reports by States Parties and they have given therefore the incomplete information.'[137] The right is extremely relevant in the context of child marriages, as within the private sphere of the family, the right to liberty and freedom of the young girl is not respected by her parents. Marriage being a state-sanctioned institution, there is a responsibility on the state to prevent violation of such rights. Article 1 of the Women's Convention that defines discrimination against women is worth taking note of here. It includes any restriction on fundamental freedoms of women in any field on the basis of sex:

For the Purpose of the present Convention, the term "discrimination against women" shall mean any distinction, exclusion or restriction made on the basis of sex which has the effect or purpose of impairing or nullifying the recognition, enjoyment or exercise by women, irrespective of their marital status, on a basis of equality of men and women, *of human rights and fundamental freedoms in the political, economic, social, cultural, civil or any other field.*[138]

And Article 3 requires:

> States Parties shall take in all fields, in particular in the political, social, economic and cultural fields, all appropriate measures, including legislation to ensure the *full development* of and advancement of women, for the purpose of guaranteeing them the exercise and enjoyment of human rights and *fundamental freedoms on a basis of equality with men.*[139]

These two articles read together make it clear that women are entitled to enjoy fundamental freedoms equally with men in all fields, which means that it would cover the freedom to choose whom to marry and when. Child marriage of girls discriminates against them by not giving the same freedom as that enjoyed by boys. State parties, by tolerating the practice of child marriage, violate their obligation to guarantee fundamental freedoms as required by Article 3 of the Women's Convention. Even those state parties that enact law prohibiting child marriage as required by Article 3, but do not enforce it effectively violate their obligation. In order to comply with Article 3, state parties have to take steps for effective enforcement of such a law.

When young girls participate in the marriage ceremonies, they comply with what is proposed by their parents. One may argue that such participation amounts to the *consent* of a girl to the marriage. However, any consent presupposes capacity to understand not only the act itself, but as importantly the consequences of such an act, particularly so when it has consequences on physical conditions and opportunities that last a lifetime. Attainment of such capacity is doubtful in the case of young girls. Besides, such consent could be meaningful only, if it is free and informed. Obviously, both these elements are lacking when parents take the decisions on behalf of their daughters. Parents behave contrary to their responsibility when they themselves arrange the marriage of their young daughters. They certainly do not act in the *best interests* of their young daughters. By giving young girls in marriage, parents take away their liberty[140] and jeopardize their security.

On the other hand, there is a positive obligation on state parties to take appropriate measures for the advancement and development of women in all fields of life. Child marriage curtails opportunities for such development. Therefore, state parties commit a breach of their duty at two levels. At one level they fail when they do not stop child marriage of girls. They fail at the second level by not providing opportunities for development of women. Such an analysis of the right to liberty can emerge only when the feminist method—asking the woman question—is adopted. The woman question alone can challenge the traditional conception that the right to liberty relates only to the misuse of the state power. It can demand that the right to liberty needs to be interpreted in such a way as to extend it even to those situations where the right is encroached within the family and by the members of the family. Child marriages occur as a result of such encroachment on the right of young girls at the hands of the parents within the family. The state party, by tolerating the practice of child marriage, allows the parents to violate the right to liberty and freedom and thereby fails in its obligation to guarantee fundamental freedoms as required by Article 3 of the Women's Convention.

Such an interpretation has not been done so far by any of the monitoring committees in the context of child marriages. However, in future these committees need to adopt such a feminist analysis of the right to liberty of young girls that would require the state parties to take action for the prevention of child marriages.

Right to Liberty: India's Obligation

Article 21 of the Indian Constitution covers the right to liberty along with the right to life.[141] However, the Indian state has yet to analyse adequately the practice of child marriage as a violation of young girls' right to liberty and security. There are a number of reasons for this situation. The practice of child marriage has been followed for centuries and is presumed to be an integral part of the culture. The government might not be politically interested in disturbing a practice which is so deeply rooted in society. Additionally, a group against whom the practice is performed is vulnerable, not vocal, and is politically dormant. As a result, the state has not shown enough commitment to protect the rights of adolescents. This fact is well reflected in the available demographic data that indicate the prevalence of the practice of child marriage on a large scale in India.[142] It exhibits negligence of the Indian state in the effective enforcement of CMRA and thereby the denial of the right to liberty and security to young girls.

The Indian judiciary also has not played an effective role in holding the state responsible and accountable for its neglect. Neither have the academicians nor lawyers argued before the court that child marriage is violative of the child bride's right to liberty and security. The international treaty monitoring bodies such as CEDAW or CRC or HRC have not addressed in their concluding observations on the report of India how child marriages violate the right to liberty and security. These committees need to develop such arguments in future. The Indian judiciary needs to participate more actively in denouncing the practice of child marriage by referring to the international conventions as well as the Constitution of India.[143]

Right to be Free from Slavery

Child marriage not only encroaches on the liberty and security of individual girls but also drives them to the state of servitude.[144] It usually forecloses opportunities for education and income generation, thus fostering a state of dependence of the girl child on her husband for her livelihood. In exchange, she is put into a de facto state of servitude to keep his house, make food for him, and bear and rear his children.

The Slavery Convention considers the servile form of marriage as a practice similar to slavery and mentions that all measures shall be taken for its abolition. Article 1 of the Slavery Convention reads:

> Each of the States Parties shall take all practicable and necessary legislative and other measures to bring about the abolition or abandonment of the following institutions and practices, where they still exist and whether or not they are covered by the definition of slavery convention signed at Geneva on 25 September 1926:
>
> (a) ...
>
> (b) ...
>
> (c) Any institution or practice whereby:
>
> (i) *A woman without a right to refuse*,[145] is promised or given in marriage on payment of a consideration in money or in kind to her parents, guardian, family or any other person or group; or
>
> (ii) ...
>
> (iii) ...
>
> (d) Any institution or practice whereby a child or young person under the age of 18 years, is delivered by either or both of his natural parents or by his guardian to another person, whether for reward or not, with a view to the exploitation of the child or young person or of his labour.

Encroachment on liberty and servitude being the basic ingredients of slavery, child marriage results in violation of the right to be free from slavery. To control such derogatory practices, Article 2 of the Convention declares:

> With a view to bringing to an end the institutions and practices mentioned in Article 1(c) States Parties undertake to prescribe, where appropriate, a suitable minimum age of marriage, to encourage the use of facilities whereby consent of both the parties to a marriage may be freely expressed in the presence of a competent civil or religious authority, and to encourage the registration of marriages.

Thus right back in 1956, the international community equated servile forms of marriages with a practice that is similar to slavery. The Slavery Convention defines slavery and a person of servile status as:

> (a) "Slavery" means, as defined in the Slavery Convention of 1926, the status or condition of a person over whom any or all of the powers attaching to the right of ownership are exercised, and "slave" means a person in such condition or status.
>
> (b) "A person of servile status" means a person in the condition or status resulting from any of the institutions or practices mentioned in Article 1 of this Convention.[146]

Notably, state parties are not permitted to make reservations to the Slavery Convention.[147] Thus, no country may legally permit slavery or slavery-like practices within its borders.[148]

Child marriage is a form of enslavement. Being under the control of the parents the girl child is denied the right to refuse such marriage. Parents or guardians transfer their ownership over their daughter to the husband. On marriage, she loses her freedom and independence for the rest of her life, a vital ingredient of slavery. She is viewed as property of her husband and is owned by him.[149] He has total control over her life. She becomes a victim of his domination. A child bride could also be viewed as a source of unpaid and free labour. She is required to prove her worth through work, which often results in exploitation of her labour. She becomes a forced labourer—another form of slavery—as a result of child marriage.[150] This not being enough, she also has to submit to intercourse upon demand, and must endure the risks of repeated pregnancies and childbirth. In the whole process, obviously, she has no say, no right to refuse, as her wishes are not valued and her evolving capacity is ignored. As a result, she remains throughout her life in the state of servitude resulting in violation of her right to be free from servitude that is mentioned in Article 8 of ICCPR.[151] Article 8 of ICCPR states:

1. No one shall be held in slavery; slavery and slave trade in all their forms shall be prohibited.
2. No one shall be held in servitude.

However, HRC has not expanded so far the term 'servitude' in the context of child marriage. It could do so in future while adopting its General Comment on Liberty as well as while formulating their concluding observations.

The practice of child marriage itself can be termed as a form of cultural and social slavery—slavery that is conditioned by social norms and custom, the roots of which are embodied in the patriarchal social set-up, the reason being that social and cultural norms are defined by men. Women are denied any role while defining these norms. The patriarchal social structure is set to work in a manner where women's experiences and their opinions are not counted, and in fact, are deliberately left out. To change the form of this cultural slavery, in addition to the passing of the law prohibiting child marriages, civil society has to work for creating a gender-just society.[152]

Right to be Free from Slavery: India's Obligation

India has ratified the Slavery Convention. Therefore, it is bound to take all measures to abolish slavery in any form. However, child marriage has not been thought as a practice similar to slavery either by the legislators or by the judiciary. In fact it has not been looked upon as a serious crime against the human dignity of young girls. The practice of child marriage brings the young brides to the state of servitude and enslaves them for the rest of their lives. These realities could be understood only when perceived from the perspective of the young brides. The policy makers, judicial personnel, and executives, therefore, need to step into the shoes of the married young girls, to understand the miserable lives that they endure. Looking at the practice of child marriage through the feminist lens alone would make them realize that the practice of child marriage is similar to slavery.

There is no provision appointing any monitoring body that would look into the actual practice of application of the Slavery Convention. The monitoring function is left to state parties to negotiate improved compliance on a bilateral basis. Any other state party to the Convention could raise the issue with India and negotiate to stop this servile form of marriage. And in case of failure on the part of the Indian government, it could refer the matter to the International Court of Justice.[153] Another international body that could challenge the practice of child marriages as a form of servile marriage in India is HRC. HRC did express its concern about child marriages in its Concluding Observations on the Report of India.[154] However, it did not refer to the practice of child marriage as a form of servile marriage nor as slavery under Article 8 of ICCPR. In future, HRC could recommend to the Government of India that the practice of child marriage being a practice similar to slavery, more serious steps be taken to prevent it in the country. Besides, it could be argued in a case before national fora like the Supreme Court and the National Human Rights Commission that child marriage is a form of slavery and therefore needs to be abolished.

End Notes

[1] UN Charter, Article 1; see also Article 55(c).

[2] Article 2 of the Universal Declaration, Article 2.2 of ICESCR, Article 2.1 of ICCPR.

[3] We the peoples of the United Nations determined to save succeeding generations from the scourge of war ..., and to reaffirm faith in the fundamental human rights, in the dignity and worth of the human person, in the equal rights of men and women and of nations of large and small ... have resolved to combine our efforts to accomplish these aims ....

[4] Articles 1 to 5 of the Women's Convention.

[5] Article 2.1.

[6] Article 2.2: right to non-discrimination on the ground of other status such as age.

[7] See generally, Anne Bayefsky, 'The Principle of Equality or Non-discrimination in International Law' (1990) 11 *Human Rights Law Journal* 1.

[8] See Ian Brownlie, *System of Nations: State Responsi lity* (Oxford: Clarendon Press, 1983) at 81.

[9] Articles 2 and 3 of the Women's Convention.

[10] Rebecca Cook, 'International Protection of Women's Reproductive Rights' (1992) 24 *New York University Journal of International Law and Politics* 645 at 678–9.

[11] Ibid.

[12] Ibid. Also, The Human Rights Committee has explained the prohibition of discrimination in ICCPR to have essentially the same meaning. Human Rights

Committee, General Comment 28 Para 2, 5, 7-HRC, General Comment 28, UN GAOR 2000, UN Doc. A/55/40, Annex VI at 133.

[13] T.K. Sundari Ravindran, 'Engendering Health' (2000) 489 *Seminar* 34.

[14] See Rebecca Cook, *Women's Health and Human Rights*, (Geneva: WHO, 1994) at 19–20.

[15] Article 2(e).

[16] See Kathleen Mahony, 'Canadian Approaches to Equality Rights and Gender Equality in the Courts' in Cook, Chapter Four, note 10 at 437 (442).

[17] See Introduction at xxv–xxvi.

[18] Ratna Kapur and Brenda Cossman, 'Women, Familial Ideology and the Constitution' in Ratna Kapur (ed.), *Feminist Terrains in Legal Domains* (New Delhi: Kali for Women, 1996) 61at 64.

[19] Beijing Platform for Action, Report of the Fourth World Conference on Women, Beijing, September 1995, UN Doc A/CONF.177/20 (1995) at 112, Para 259; M. Mukhopadhyay and Sliver Shackles, *Women and Development In India* (Oxford: Oxfam, 1984) at 11.

[20] Ibid. Mukhopadhyay at 11–12.

[21] See Chapter One at 8.

[22] Malini Karkal and Irudaya Rajan, 'Age at Marriage: How Much Change' (1989) 24 *Economic and Political Weekly* 505.

[23] Michael Koeing, 'Patriarchy, Women's Status and Reproductive Behaviour in Rural North India' (1992) 24 *Demography India* 145. See Report of the Special Rapporteur on Violence against Women submitted in January 2002, E/CN.4/ 2002/83 Para 103.

[24] See Purnima Mane, 'Socialisation of Indian Women in their Childhood: An Analysis of Literature' (1991) 52 *Indian Journal of Social Work* 81.

[25] Article 2(f).

[26] Article 5(a), (emphasis added).

[27] CEDAW, *General Recommendation* 21, UN GAOR, 1994, Doc. No. A/ 47/38 Para 16.

[28] Free will and determinism had philosophical connotations that are not discussed here.

[29] See Article 5 of the Children's Convention.

[30] HRC, General Comment 28, UN GAOR 2000, UN Doc.A/55/40, Annex VI, 133, Para 23, (emphasis added).

[31] See Appendix to Introduction at xlii.

[32] See Chapter One at 14 et al.

[33] Emphasis added.

[34] See Kimberlé Crenshaw, 'Demarginalizing the Intersection of Race and Sex: A Black Feminist Critique of Antidiscrimination Doctrine, Feminist Theory and Antiracist Politics' (1989) *University of Chicago Legal Forum* 139 and *also* Kimberlé Crenshaw, 'Mapping the Margins: Intersectionality, Identity Politics and Violence against Women of Colour' (1991) 43 *Stanford Law Review* 1241; Colleen Sheppard, 'Grounds of Discrimination: Towards an Inclusive and Contextual Approach' (2001) 80 *The Canadian Bar* 893.

[35] M. Eaton, 'Patently Confused: Complex Inequality and *Canada* v. *A. G. Canada*' (1994) 1 *Rev. of Constitutional Studies* 203 at 231.

[36] Crenshaw, supra note 34 at 151.

[37] Arati Rao, 'Politics of Gender and Culture in International Human Rights', in Julia Peters and Andrew Wolper (ed.), *Women's Rights, Human Rights* (New York: Routledge, 1995) 169.

[38] Ann Elizabeth Mayer, 'Cultural Particularism as a bar to Women's Rights: Reflections on the Middle Eastern Experience' in Peters, note 37, 176 at 179.

[39] GENERAL A/CONF.157/23 at I-1.

[40] Some of the most relevant areas were: education; social services and health, including sexual and reproductive health; the HIV/AIDS pandemic; violence against women and girls; the persistent and increasing burden of poverty on women; vulnerability of migrant women including exploitation and trafficking; the development of strong, effective, and accessible national machinery for the advancement of women; and the formulation of strategies to enable women and men to reconcile and share work and family responsibilities equally.

[41] Para 4.16, 4.25.

[42] Para 97, 277.

[43] E/1996/6.

[44] A/Res/52/231.

[45] A/55/341. It was held in New York, 5–9 June 2000.

[46] See Chapter Three at 76 et al. and 89.

[47] Except the Muslim personal law. See the discussion in Chapter Three at 77 et al.

[48] See Chapter Three at 74 et al.

[49] *UN Treaty Collection: Treaty Reference Guide.* It gives Definitions of Terms used in the UN Treaty Collection (www.untreaty.un.org/English/guide.asp). The term 'declaration' is used for various international instruments. However, declarations are not always legally binding. The term is often deliberately chosen

to indicate that the parties do not intend to create binding obligations but merely want to declare certain aspirations.

[50] Declaration of India to the Women's Convention.

[51] CEDAW/C/IND/1.

[52] CEDAW/C/SR/452, 453, and 462.

[53] CEDAW, 22nd Session, Jan 2000, *Response to Questions on India's First Report on CEDAW*, (Permanent Mission of India to the UN, New York, 2000) (hereinafter Response GOI) Question no. 68, at 34.

[54] Ibid. at 36.

[55] CEDAW/C/2000/1/CRP.3/Add.4/Rev.1, 1 Feb 2000, Para 31.

[56] Ibid. Para 32.

[57] It is interesting to note that at the drafting stage on the Women's Convention, India supported the principle of the registration of marriages. Lars Adam Rehof, *Guide to the Travaux PréParatoires of the United Nations Convention on the Elimination of All Forms of Discrimination against Women* (The Netherlands: Martinis Nijhoff Publisher, 1993) at 184.

[58] Declaration of India to Article 16.

[59] See Chapter Three at 89.

[60] CEDAW/C/2000/1/CRP.3/Add.4/Rev.1, 1 Feb 2000, Para 33; emphasis added.

[61] Ibid. Para 34.

[62] CEDAW/C/2000/1/CRP.3/Add.4/Rev.1, 1 Feb 2000, Para 30.

[63] Article 19(3) of the Vienna Convention on the Law of Treaties. It stipulates that where a reservation is not prohibited by the treaty or falls within the specified permitted categories, a state may make a reservation provided it is not incompatible with the object and purpose of the treaty.

[64] HRC/GEN/1/Rev.2, 4 November 1994, Para 11, emphasis added.

[65] Ibid. page 45, Para 12.

[66] Ibid. page 47, Para 18.

[67] Ibid. page 48, Para 20.

[68] Concluding Observations of the Committee on the Rights of the Child: India, 23/02/2000, CRC/C/15/Add.115 Para 32. Emphasis added.

[69] Ibid.

[70] Ibid. Para 33.

[71] Ibid. Para 50.

[72] Ibid. Para 51.

73 Ibid. Para 77.

74 Emphasis added.

75 Emphasis added.

76 Emphasis added.

77 Article 1 of the Children's Convention. According to WHO, a child is a person who is below eighteen years of age.

78 Cook, supra note 14 at 32.

79 See Chapter One at 21 et al.

80 Article 16(1)(e): States Parties shall ensure that women enjoy equal rights to decide freely and responsibly on the number and spacing of their children and to have access to the information, education and means to enable them to exercise these rights.

81 CEDAW, A/51/38 Para. 149 and 159.

82 CEDAW, A/51/38 Para. 134–63, 9 May 1996 (15th Session), Concluding Observations on the combined initial, second, and third periodic reports of Ethiopia CEDAW/C/ETH/1–3 and Add.1.

83 CEDAW, A/53/38 Para. 284, 14 May 1998 (19th Session), Concluding Observations on the report of Indonesia.

84 CEDAW, C/1998/II/L.1/Add.8 Para. 36, 8 July 1998 (19th Session), Concluding Observations on the report of the Republic of Korea.

85 For example, in Nigeria more than 50 per cent of girls are married before eighteen years of age. But there is no reference to it in the concluding observations on the report of Nigeria. See CEDAW/C/1998/II/L.1/Add.6 Nigeria, 7 July 1998.

86 CEDAW needs to refer to its standard format for giving concluding observation on a country report. Reference to such a format for concluding observations would help to prevent any relevant issue from being lost sight of, as has happened in the case of child marriages.

87 CEDAW, *General Recommendation 19*, Violence against Women, UN GAOR, 1992, Doc. No. A/47/38.

88 See Article 1.

89 *General Recommendation 19*, supra note 87, Para 11.

90 Ibid.

91 Ibid. Para 24 (r).

92 Ibid. Para 24 (t) (ii).

93 GENERAL A/CONF.157/23 at II-38.

94 *General Recommendation 21*, supra note 27, Para 36.

[95] Ibid. Para 38.

[96] Ibid. Para 39.

[97] Ibid. Para 41.

[98] Ibid. Para 43.

[99] *General Recommendation* 14 on Female Circumcision, UN GAOR 1990 DOC No A/45/38.

[100] ICCPR General Comment 19, Protection of the family, the right to marriage and equality of the spouses (Article 23): 27/07/90.

[101] These are the observations made by HRC in the *Round Table of Human Rights Treaty Bodies on Human Rights Approaches to Women's Health, with a Focus on Sexual and Reproductive Health and Rights*, (UNDAW/UNFPA/UNHCHR) New York, 1996. See Summary of Proceedings and Recommendations, at 23.

[102] Ibid.

[103] Article 5 of the Children's Convention.

[104] Article14.2 of the Children's Convention. See also Corinne A.A. Packer, 'Preventing Adolescent Pregnancy: The Protection offered by International Human Rights Law' (1997) 5 *International Journal of Children's Rights* 46.

[105] Emphasis added.

[106] Emphasis added.

[107] Cynthia Price Cohen, 'The United Nations Convention on the Rights of the Child: A Feminist Landmark' (1997)29 *William and Mary Journal of Women and the Law* 29 at 55.

[108] See Concluding Observations of CRC: October 30, 1996, 13th Session—(a) Morocco, CRC/C/15/Add.60 Para 13, 25; (b) Slovenia, CRC/C/15/Add.65 Para 10; (c) Nigeria, CRC/C/15/Add.61 Para 13; and (d) Mauritius CRC/C/15.Add.64 Para 13.

[109] Concluding Observations of CRC: Nepal, 12th session, Para. 12, CRC/C/15/Add.57 Para 17, 7 June 1996.

[110] Ibid.

[111] Concluding Observations of CRC: Lebanon, Committee on the Rights of the Child, 12th session, Para 16, CRC/C/Add.54, 7 June 1996.

[112] Concluding Observations of CRC: Indonesia, CRC/C/15 Add.7 Para 9, 11,18; 18 October 1993.

[113] Concluding Observations of CRC: Nigeria, CRC/C/Add.54 Para. 26, 1995.

[114] Concluding Observations of CRC: Guatemala, 12th session, CRC/C/Add.58 Para. 15; 7 June 1996.

[115] Ibid.

[116] Concluding Observations of CRC: Kuwait, 19th session, CRC/C/15/Add.96 Para. 28; 26 October 1998.

[117] Concluding Observations of CRC: Ghana, 19th session, U.N. Doc. CRC/C/15/Add.73 Para. 21, 42; 18 June 1997.

[118] Concluding Observations of CRC: Ethiopia, 14th session, U.N. Doc. CRC/C/15/Add.67 Para. 14, 24 January 1997.

[119] The purpose is to bring together experts on particular topics that can augment the knowledge of committee members.

[120] Cohen, supra note 107.

[121] The UN Commission on Human Rights, a Charter-based body, established by the Economic and Social Council (ECOSOC) (one of the principal organs of the United Nations created under the Charter of the United Nations) has innovated extra-conventional procedures for better realization of human rights. By one of such procedures a special rapporteur could be appointed either for a country or for a theme by the UN commission. Such a rapporteur has been appointed on violence against women. The rapporteur receives communications about alleged incidences of gender-specific violence against women that have not been effectively addressed through national legal systems. She then uses this information to have an open dialogue with governments for finding solutions. She is required to submit an annual report to the Commission on Human Rights. In turn these reports are submitted to the General Assembly through the ECOSOC which urges member states to look into violation of women's human rights and to take all possible measures for the enforcement of these rights.

[122] E/CN.4/1996/53,Para 54. She has again argued for eradication of sexual violence against the girl child in her report of the year 1997–E//CN.4/1997/47, Introduction and Para 8 and 9.

[123] E/CN.4/2002/83. Report of the Special Rapporteur on Violence against Women, 'Cultural practices in the family that are violent towards women', submitted in January 2002, Para 55–7, 111.

[124] The Sub-commission on the Prevention of Discrimination and Protection of Minorities, another Charter-based body, established by the Commission on Human Rights under the authority of the Economic, Social and Cultural Council in 1946 has also appointed a special rapporteur who has submitted his report on 16 February 1998.

[125] E/CN.4/Sub.2/1998/11, Para 7; see also E/CN.4/Sub.2/1997/10.

[126] CEDAW/C/2000/1/CRP.3/Add.4/Rev.1, 1 February 2000, Para 30; see Chapter Two at 56–7.

[127] National Commission for Women, Section 3 and 8 of the Draft on Marriage Bill, 1994.

[128] CEDAW/C/2000/1/CRP.3/Add.4/Rev.1, 1 February 2000, Para 32.

[129] Concluding Observations of HRC on India: CCPR/C/79/Add.81 at Para 16; 4 August 1997.

[130] CRC/C/28/Add.10, 7 July 1997. There is hardly any commitment for effective enforcement of the Act or to improve upon reproductive health services or status of young girls.

[131] Concluding Observations of CRC on India: CRC/C/15/Add.115, 23 February 2000.

[132] Ibid. Para 32.

[133] Ibid. Para 33.

[134] Ibid. Para 34.

[135] Ibid. Para 35.

[136] Ibid. Para 26.

[137] General Comment 8 on 'Right to Liberty and Security of Persons', HRC/Gen. I/Rev.2, 29 March 1996.

[138] Emphasis added.

[139] Emphasis added.

[140] Cook, supra note 14 at 29.

[141] See at 178 et al.

[142] See Chapter One at 4 et al.

[143] In the following pages there is a detailed comment on the role of the Indian judiciary. See later at 212 et al.

[144] See Debbie Taylor, *Servile Marriages: Institutional Slavery*, Anti-Slavery Report, 1994.

[145] Emphasis added.

[146] Article 7 of the Slavery Convention.

[147] Article 9 of the Slavery Convention.

[148] Article 10: Any disputes arising between States Parties that are not settled through negotiation 'shall be referred to the International Court of Justice at the request of any one of the States parties to the dispute.' However, this has not occurred, and historically, states parties have been reluctant to intervene. See Roger J.R. Levesque, 'Sexual Use, Abuse and Exploitation of Children: Challenges in Implementing Children's Human Rights' (1994) 60 *Brook. L. Rev.* 959 at 998; *also* Amy Small Bilyeu, 'Trokosi—the Practice of Sexual Slavery in

Ghana: Religious and Cultural Freedom vs. Human Rights' (1999) 9 *Indiana International and Comparative Law Review* 457 at 483.

[149] See Section 497 of the Indian Penal Code that defines the offence of adultery. It says that a man commits adultery if he has sexual intercourse with a *married* woman. It is not so if he does so with unmarried or divorced or widowed woman. One man commits this offence against another man with whose wife he had intercourse. The proprietary aspect of marital relations is quite evident in this. For comments see S.P. Sathe, *Towards Gender Justice*, (Bombay: SNDT University, 1993) at 13–14, 40–1. See Ladan Askari, 'The Convention on the Rights of the Child: The Necessity of Adding a Provision to Ban Child Marriage', (1998) 5 *Journal of International and Comparative Law* 123 at 126–7; Malini Karkal, 'Invisibility of the Girl Child in India' (1991) 52 *Journal of Social Work* 5; and Debbie Taylor, *Servile Marriages: Institutional Slavery*, Anti-Slavery Report, 1994.

[150] Article 2 of the Forced Labour Convention defines forced labour as, 'For the purposes of this Convention the term "forced or compulsory labour" shall mean all work or service which is exacted from any person under the menace of any penalty and for which the said person has not offered himself voluntarily', Convention (No. 29), adopted on 28 June 1930 by the General Conference of the International Labour Organization (ILO) at its fourteenth session. Entered into force 1 May 1932.

[151] Kirsten Backstrom, 'The International Human Rights of the Child: Do They Protect the Female Child?' (1996–97) 30 *George Washington Journal of International Law and Economics* 541 at 549–50; see also Bart Rwezaura, 'Protecting the Rights of the Girl-child in Commonwealth Jurisdictions' in Andrew Byrnes (ed.), *Advancing the Human Rights of Women: Using International Human Rights Standards in Domestic Litigation* (London: The Commonwealth Secretariat, 1997) at 114.

[152] Berta Esperanza HernAndez-Truyol, 'Women's Rights as Human Rights—Rules, Realities and the Role of Culture: A Formula for Reform' (1996) 21 *Brooklyn Journal International Law* 605 at 663–6. See also Special Rapporteur on Violence against Women, supra note 122, Para 123–30.

[153] Article 10 of the Slavery Convention. However, historically, state parties have been reluctant to intervene in the internal and private matters of another state party.

[154] Concluding Observations of HRC on India, supra note 129.

6

The Girl Child's Right to Development: Adverse Consequences of Child Marriage

Introduction

When girl children are married off at an early age they are denied their human rights, their right to be children. Apart from the human rights injustices such as discrimination and loss of freedom, young brides face serious health hazards, sometimes even to the extent of losing their lives as a consequence of pregnancies that come too early in their lives because of child marriage. Hereinafter, I shall examine violation of those human rights that result as a consequence of child marriage. I have classified these as

— consequences of child marriage on reproductive health and

— consequences of child marriage on the development of young girls.

I have analysed different rights under various international conventions that are violated as consequences of child marriage. As regards reproductive health, the rights that are violated are the right to life and survival, the right to the highest attainable standard of health, and the right to information. As regards the development of young girls, the most relevant right is the right to education.

Rights Affecting Reproductive Health

Right to Life

Adolescent pregnancy is identified as one of the root causes of high maternal mortality in developing countries.[1] Almost 99 per cent of maternal deaths occur in developing countries.[2] The most obvious human right violated by preventable death is young girls' right to life, also explicated as the right to survival. Therefore, avoidance of child marriage would help promote the right to life of young girls.

The right to life and survival is the foundation of all other human rights. Article 3 of UDHR states: 'Everyone has the right to life, liberty and security of person.' Article 6(1) of ICCPR recognizes right to life in the following words: 'Every human being has the inherent right to life. This shall be protected by law. No one shall be arbitrarily deprived of his life.' And Article 6 of the Children's Convention states:

> 1. States Parties shall recognise that every child has the inherent right to life.
> 2. States Parties shall ensure to the maximum extent possible the survival and development of the child.

The wording of ICCPR is different from that of the Children's Convention. It protects an individual from violation of the right to life at the hands of the state and is confined to the due process of law before submission to capital punishment.[3] This consideration of the right to life is essentially philosophized by men. Feminist scholars have argued that such interpretation ignores the historical reality of women that persists in the developing regions of the world where almost 580,000 women are estimated to die each year from pregnancy-related causes.[4]

The Human Rights Committee has noted:

> The right to life has been too often narrowly interpreted. The expression 'inherent right to life' cannot be properly understood in a restrictive manner, and the protection of this right requires that states adopt positive measures.[5]

The right to life does not, therefore, mean to prevent intentional killing only but it encompasses measures that are needed to protect life against unintentional losses. It is very significant to note the way the Children's Convention has articulated the right to life in two clauses. It says that every child has the inherent right to life. The term 'inherent' indicates that it is a natural fundamental right. If any action is taken against the children, in private or public, the state is duty-bound to protect children from inhuman treatment or abuse. Considering the potential danger to the life of young girls resulting from child marriage, the state is under obligation to protect their right to life by preventing parents from arranging the marriage of their underage daughters. Additionally, the second part of Article 6 puts an obligation on state parties to ensure to the maximum extent possible the survival and development of the child. Thereby the state parties are not only to prevent child marriages but there is a positive obligation to fulfil the right to development of the girl children.

The Human Rights Committee also expressed its view that it was desirable to take 'all possible measures' to reduce infant mortality and increase life expectancy.[6] For the same reasons, state parties are also obliged to take 'all possible measures' to reduce maternal mortality, including measures to prevent child marriages.

The right to life is denied to those adolescent girls who die each year because of pregnancy-related causes that are preventable by delaying the first birth. All pregnancies carry some health risks, but these are higher in case of young girls because in the majority of such cases the pregnancy is ill-timed and is unwanted. Their bodies are not mature enough to face the burden of pregnancies. It is shown worldwide that adolescents who give birth are three times as likely to die in childbirth, as are women aged 20–29 under similar circumstances.[7]

A young girl's right to life entitles her not to be married off at an early age. After the marriage, the sexual relationship between the young wife and her husband is inevitable. As a consequence, she becomes pregnant and due to her underdeveloped pelvic structure, she suffers from many complications during and after pregnancy, sometimes to the extent of losing her life during childbirth. This results in violation of her fundamental right to life. Therefore, as a consequence of child marriage, the right to survival is denied to the young girl.

It must also be noted that the anaemic condition of women is another important cause of maternal death. The discrimination against girl children in terms of unequal allocation of family and community resources between them and boys leads to malnutrition and anaemia. Equitable distribution of available resources between girls and boys in a family would help mitigate their anaemic condition which in turn would help reduce maternal deaths. Truly speaking, much could be accomplished by changing the customary practices and social attitudes towards women. Young women could survive the pregnancies if they were not forced into child marriages.

The Cairo Programme of Action, POA, has also reaffirmed that 'Everyone has the right to life'.[8] The governments, particularly those of the developing countries, who have endorsed POA and the Beijing Platform of Action, PLA, are therefore duty-bound to reduce maternal mortality. The countries, where child marriage is a social norm, need to take serious efforts to prevent child marriages. Such efforts would result in a substantial reduction in maternal deaths and would ensure the right to life of young girls.

Right to Life: India's Obligation

Article 21 of the Indian Constitution guarantees to all the right to life. It states: 'Protection of life and liberty: No person shall be deprived of his life or personal liberty except according to the procedure established by law.' The Supreme Court of India has interpreted this right very liberally, particularly in the course of public interest litigation, and widened its scope to remedy violations of human rights of those who have been the victims of political oppression, social tyranny, and economic exploitation.[9] Through public interest litigation, the court's intervention was sought successfully against inhuman working conditions in stone quarries in *Bandhua Mukti Morcha* v. *Union of India*.[10] In *Consumer Education and Research Centre* v. *Union of India* the Supreme Court intervened for controlling occupational hazards and diseases affecting workers in the asbestos industry.[11] It got the CBI to inquire into the alleged police atrocities.[12] The court expanded the right to life to encompass the right to live with dignity in *All India Imam Organisation* v. *Union of India and Others*.[13] Pavement dwellers' right to livelihood was recognized by the Supreme Court in the *Olga Tellis* case.[14] The Court also expanded the right to life in Article 21 to include the right to health[15] and right to education.[16]

The Supreme Court declared in *Parmananda Katara* v. *Union of India*[17] that it is an obligation of those who are in charge of the health of the community to preserve life. So when an accident occurs, doctors, whether government or private, are duty-bound to provide essential services. The right to life is not restricted only to prevent intentional killing, but also to protect life against unintentional loss and preventable deaths. However, it has still not included preventable maternal deaths in the right to life. The reason probably is that no such legal claim has so far made its way to the Supreme Court. If such a case is brought before the Supreme Court, by applying the reasoning in the *Parmananda Katara* case, it would be logical to claim the right to emergency obstetric care on behalf of those needy women against the Indian state as well as private doctors. They could be made liable to provide emergency services in future.

In India, most adolescent pregnancies occur within marriage.[18] Thus, married young girls' right to life is violated when they succumb to complications arising out of pregnancies.[19] Parents, who marry off their young daughters before they attain the legal age of marriage, indirectly compel them to have sexual relationship with their husbands. As a result, they become pregnant and face the risk of death during pregnancy and childbirth. Failure on the part of the government to enforce CMRA against parents makes young girls victims of avoidable death due to the cultural practice of child marriage, as a consequence of which they are denied the right to life. The Indian state so far has not looked at the issue of child marriage from such a perspective. It would be worth trying to approach the Supreme Court for holding the government liable for its inaction for not enforcing CMRA.

Young girls who are married off at a young age also suffer from a number of maternal morbidities.[20] Besides, they lose the opportunity of education and economic independence. This ultimately results in the denial of their right to live with dignity. Thus, the jurisprudence evolved around Article 21 of the Indian Constitution could very well be applied to prove how child marriages deny the right to life and right to live with dignity to young girls. However, to prove such a claim in the court, it would be essential to do proper homework. Enough empirical data to support such arguments is not available today. If data could be collected through proper social science methods, it would help substantiate the claim more meaningfully.

Data could be collected for a certain period, regarding the profile of brides who were below the age of eighteen years at the time of marriage. It should cover:

— Education,
— Food intake,
— Quality of food,
— General health,
— Reproductive health,
— Major illnesses,
— Major issues relating to maternal morbidity,
— Reproductive health,
— Social and economic background of their families including how many women in the family got married below the legal minimum age, and

— Status of women in those families.

Additional information on the following would be helpful:

— Incidence and prevalence of child marriage across the country,
— Causes behind child marriages,
— Causes of unprotected and unwanted sexual relations,
— Unwanted pregnancies,
— Young girls' deaths during childbirth,
— Causes of death of girls in the age group of 13–20 years,
— Miscarriage suffered by the young girls,
— STDs including HIV/AIDS infection prevalent among them,
— Other maternal morbidities suffered by adolescents,
— Sexual violence and coercion among married adolescents,
— Availability of health services to them particularly in the light of their special needs,
— Availability of information on reproductive system to adolescents,
— Type of sex education available to girls in school and out of school, and
— Avenues open for career development and awareness.

Data from a control group would also be essential for comparative analysis.

A careful selection of the sample from different states of India would be a significant factor. Along with the percentage of child marriage, the law and order situation prevalent in these states, social and economic development index, and literacy level would be some of the other factors that would be required for scientific analysis. In addition, a few case studies from the field also would be of significance. On the basis of such data, a petition could be filed before the Supreme Court challenging the practice of child marriage. The foundation of such a petition could be a claim that child marriage violates various human rights and, therefore, needs to be stopped. The government could be asked to submit a time-bound action plan covering legal and extra-legal measures to control child marriages. Considering the previous response of the Supreme Court to public interest litigation, there is a great possibility of the Court issuing such directions to the government. However, care will have to be taken by voluntary organizations to pursue such directions until they are enforced effectively.

Besides, the decision in such public interest litigation would have tremendous potential for creating public awareness about the issue of child marriage. The public at large could be made aware of the adverse consequences of child marriage on young girls. Thereby it would help generate public opinion against the practice of child marriage.

The Right to the Highest Attainable Standard of Health

In Chapter One, I have discussed in detail the serious physical harm that young brides face as a result of sexual relations with their husbands. The impact of child marriage is much more severe on the reproductive health of girl children than of men due to biological differences. As pointed out earlier, early marriage and early childbirth are linked to high rates of pregnancy-related complications including risk to life, miscarriage, anaemia, obstructed labour, vesico- or recto-vaginal fistulas, incontinence, stillbirth, or risk to the life of the newborn.[21] Failure on the part of the state to prohibit child marriage, therefore, exposes the child brides to these health risks, and thereby results in a violation of their right to sexual and reproductive health. The right to reproductive health is an essential element of a woman's general right to health. Child marriage not only violates right to health but it seriously hampers the right to mental health too.

The right to the highest attainable standards of health is recognized by major international human rights instruments. Article 25 (1) of UDHR declares: 'Everyone has the right to a standard of living adequate for the health and well-being of himself and of his family ....' By Article 12 (1) of ICESCR, 'States Parties recognise the right of everyone to the enjoyment of the highest attainable standard of physical and mental health.'

Article 12 (2) of ICESCR urges state parties to take steps to achieve the full realization of this right and it includes, by way of illustration, what steps the state parties should take in certain areas. For instance, Article 12 (2)(a) requires state parties to make the provision for the reduction of the rate of stillbirth and of infant mortality and for the healthy development of the child.

Article 24 of the Children's Convention contributes in a very significant way to the children's right to health. Article 24 (1) of the Children's Convention reads:

> States Parties recognise the right of the child to the enjoyment of the highest attainable standard of health and to facilities for the treatment

of illness and rehabilitation of health. States Parties shall strive to ensure that no child is deprived of his or her right to access to such health care services.

Article 12 (1) of the Women's Convention prohibits all forms of discrimination against women in the delivery of health care. It provides:

> States Parties shall take all appropriate measures to eliminate discrimination against women in the field of health care in order to ensure, on a basis of equality of men and women, access to health care services, including those related to family planning.

All these articles focus on the right of access to health care services and require state parties to make available sufficiently good-quality health care services to all without any discrimination. CESCR's General Comment 14 on Health has significantly developed the understanding of what is required to implement the right. It has focussed on physical and economic access to information on health care, ethical and cultural acceptability, and good quality health services to all.[22] CEDAW's General Recommendation on Women and Health as well as the POA of Cairo and PLA of Beijing have also evolved standards of health that are to be complied with by state parties. CEDAW has mentioned:

> States parties should implement a comprehensive national strategy to promote *women's health throughout their life span* (emphasis added). This will include interventions aimed at both the prevention and treatment of the diseases and conditions affecting women, as well as responding to violence against women, and will ensure universal access for all women to a full range of high-quality and affordable health care, including sexual and reproductive health services.[23]
>
> States Parties should allocate adequate budgetary, human and administrative resources to ensure that women's health receives a share of the overall health budget comparable with that for men's health, taking into account their different health needs.[24]

CEDAW has further recommended to state parties that they should, in particular:

> (a) place a gender perspective at the center of all policies and programmes affecting women's health ...;
>
> (b) ensure the removal of all barriers to women's access to health services, education and information, including in the area of sexual and

reproductive health, and, in particular allocate resources for programmes directed at the adolescents for the prevention of and treatment of sexually transmitted diseases, including HIV/AIDS;

(c) prioritize the prevention of unwanted pregnancy through family planning and sex education and reduce maternal mortality rates through safe motherhood services and prenatal assistance;

(d) monitor the provision of health services to women by public, non-governmental and private authorisation, to ensure equal access and quality of care;

(e) require all health services to be consistent with the human rights of women, including right to autonomy, privacy, confidentiality, informed consent and choice;

(f) ensure that the training curricula of health workers include comprehensive, mandatory, gender-sensitive courses on women's health and human rights.[25]

These provisions take care of the right to health service of all and, therefore, include young girls also. However, how their right to health is affected by their marriage at a young age needs to be explored. The relationship between child marriage and the right to health services is a complex one. At one level, sufferings of young brides, particularly in developing countries, arising out of pregnancy-related complications such as miscarriage, anaemia, obstructed labour, vesico- or recto-vaginal fistulas indicate denial of such services to them.[26] It is an indication of the failure on the part of state parties to comply with their treaty obligations and of their failure to prevent violation of the right to health of young brides. The best option to comply with the right to health of young brides is to create such conditions that would not force her to face these health problems. It means that state parties should take all possible measures to prevent child marriages. However, until such efforts are made, state parties are under obligation to provide health care services to these young brides so as to minimize their sufferings.

At another level, it is also significant to note that there are a number of barriers that a young bride faces in her attempt to access health care services. For instance, she is likely to be unaware of the health complications that might arise out of pregnancy. And even if she is aware, she has no freedom to decide about her sexuality or childbearing as the decision to access the health care services is taken by others, such as her in-laws, on her behalf. The resultant effect is that when she is married off as a child her right to health is violated, first because of non-availability of services and next, because of restrictions put on her freedom by others. The best way to avoid such a situation, therefore, is to prevent her marriage when she is a child.

It is worth referring in this context to Article 24(3) of the Children's Convention. It reads: 'States Parties shall take all effective and appropriate measures with a view to abolishing traditional practices prejudicial to the health of children.' The traditional practice of child marriage being prejudicial to the right to the health of the young girl so given in marriage, state parties are duty-bound to take all appropriate measures to abolish the practice of child marriage. In the absence of such efforts on the part of the state parties, probably even effective health interventions may not be able to protect these young girls fully.

At this juncture it is important to realize that the right to health should be understood in the broader context as explained by the World Health Organization. The Constitution of the World Health Organization defines health as 'A state of complete physical, mental and social well-being and not merely the absence of disease or infirmity.'[27] The legal implication of this broad concept of health goes beyond the provision of medical and related health care services and focuses on the full range of human rights. Such an approach means that state parties are duty-bound to promote health-related services, and to prevent or remove barriers to realization of women's physical, mental, and social well-being. Removal of these barriers implicates a range of civil, political, economic, social, and cultural rights. The right to health is, therefore, closely related to and dependant upon the realization of other human rights such as the right to marry and found a family, and the right to life, dignity, equality, liberty, freedom, access to information, and education. Such a close connection developed between the right to health and other human rights indicates that the international community wants state parties to implement the right to health by keeping in mind the vulnerable position of women in a patriarchal society. This is further supported by CESCR through its General Comment 14 on Health. It has interpreted the right to health as:

> ... an inclusive right extending not only to timely and appropriate health care but also to the underlying determinants of health, such as access to adequate supply of food, nutrition, and access to health-related education and information, including on sexual and reproductive health. A further important aspect is the participation of the population in all health-related decision-making at the community, national and international levels.[28]

According to the CESCR,

> The right to health embraces a wide range of socio-economic factors and contains both freedoms and entitlements. The freedoms include the right to control one's health and body, including sexual and reproductive freedom, and the right to be free from interference. The entitlements include the right to a system of health protection, which provides equality of opportunity for people to enjoy the highest attainable level of health.[29]

CESCR has specifically mentioned that to fulfil the right to health there is a need to adopt effective and appropriate measures to abolish harmful traditional practices affecting the health of children, particularly girls, including child marriage, female genital mutilation, and preferential feeding and care of male children.[30] To pursue this goal, it recommended that state parties should provide a safe and supportive environment for adolescents that ensures the opportunity to participate in decisions affecting their health, to build life skills, to acquire appropriate information, to receive counselling, and to negotiate the health-behaviour choices they make. The committee further recommended that state parties should integrate a gender perspective in their health-related policies, planning, programmes, and research in order to promote better health for both women and men. According to the committee, a gender-based approach recognizes that biological and socio-cultural factors play a significant role in influencing the health of men and women.[31]

On the basis of these comments, it can very well be argued that a young girl's right to health is violated as a consequence of child marriage. She has no control over her body after the marriage and, thereby, she loses her sexual and reproductive freedom. As rightly pointed out by CESCR, child marriage interferes in her life, as there are long-lasting effects on her health.

Child marriage has a connection with the complex web of social, cultural, political, and economic factors. It is linked to deep and pervasive inequality based on gender. Inequality makes the control of women's reproduction by others possible. At the same time, such control reinforces inequality. This cycle of inequality and control works through multiple mechanisms. It is perpetuated most directly through patriarchal family systems, characterized by gender inequality that value women primarily for their services as wives and mothers. Such control is typically justified and maintained by cultural and religious systems that view patriarchal order as natural.[32] State parties, therefore, while promoting the right to health, are required to take measures to eradicate the practice of child marriage.

At this point, it is also significant to note that the right to health includes right to reproductive health. The term 'reproductive health' is explained by Dr M.F. Fathalla as follows:

> Reproductive health implies that people have the ability to produce, to regulate their fertility and to practice and enjoy sexual relationships. It further implies that reproduction is carried to a successful outcome through infant and child survival, growth and development. It finally implies that women can go safely through pregnancy and childbirth, that fertility regulation can be achieved without health hazards and that people are safe in having sex.[33]

POA adopted by ICPD in 1994 also reiterated:

> The reproductive health is a state of complete physical, mental and social well being and not merely the absence of disease or infirmity, in all matters relating to the reproductive system and its functions and processes. Reproductive health therefore implies that people are able to have satisfying and safe sex life and that they have the capability to reproduce and freedom to decide if, when and how often to do so. Implicit in this last condition are the rights of men and women to be informed and to have access to safe, effective, affordable and acceptable methods of their choice ... and the right of access to the appropriate health care services that will enable women to go safely through pregnancy and childbirth.[34]

Thus the right to reproductive health encompasses two key categories: the right to reproductive choice and the right to quality reproductive health care.[35] The right to reproductive choice involves the right to reproductive decision making, i.e. to control one's body and make decisions about childbearing, sexuality, and well-being. The right to reproductive health care entails a right to access to health services, including family planning and quality of care, which can be exercised on the basis of informed consent, free of discrimination, coercion, and violence.

However, in countries where child marriages are performed regularly on a large scale, neither the reproductive choice nor the right to reproductive health services can be availed of by a child bride because of lack of freedom to do so. Therefore, the best practice to protect her from violation of her right to reproductive health would be to prevent her marriage when she is a child. Even CEDAW, through its General Recommendation 24 on Women and Health has urged state parties to recognize interconnection between the right to health and child marriage as child marriage leads to physical and emotional harm arising from early childbirth.[36]

Emotional harm does not only result from childbirth at a young age but the fact of child marriage itself has a negative impact on the mental health of girls. The fact of child marriage along with the low levels of or no education, economic dependence, denial of decision-making power, inequality in the home, and sexual exploitation that takes place also seriously affects mental health.[37] The relationship between gender inequality and negative mental health consequences—particularly depression and anxiety— has been documented by health research.[38]

Recent WHO statistics show that mental health problems account for 11.5 per cent of disability-adjusted life years[39] lost compared to 10.7 per cent for infectious and non-infectious respiratory diseases, 10.3 per cent for cardiovascular diseases, 8.1 per cent for maternal and perinatal conditions, 6.1 per cent for STDs/HIV, and 5.8 per cent for cancer.[40] Depression, in particular, ranks as the fourth most serious disease worldwide.[41] In India, child marriage, and cultural constraints on female roles have been associated with depression.[42] In Pakistan young age at marriage, illiteracy, low income, and severity of physical abuse have been found to be significant predictors of anxiety and depression in women.[43] Based on these findings, state parties are duty-bound to take concrete measures for prevention of child marriages, which in turn would take care of mental health problems arising from such marriages.

In addition to the general recommendations/comments, the treaty-monitoring bodies, have taken serious cognizance of the young girls' right to reproductive health. For instance, while commenting on the report of Kuwait, CRC has recommended that the state should undertake all appropriate measures including legal measures, to prevent and combat the traditional practice of child marriage that is harmful to the health and well-being of girls and development of the family.[44] It urged the government to undertake awareness-raising campaigns with a view to changing attitudes. CRC made such comments earlier also while delivering the concluding observations on the reports of Ghana[45] and Ethiopia.[46]

Right to Health: India's Obligation

In Chapter One it has been pointed out with the help of demographic and epidemiological data and hospital-based studies in India that adolescent pregnancy that primarily occurs within marriage has seriously affected the health, particularly the reproductive health, of young brides. It has resulted in high rates of maternal mortality as well as morbidities. The Indian state is responsible for this situation because it has not successfully enforced CMRA, which in turn has forced young brides to suffer from maternal morbidities, sometimes even leading to death. At the same time, the state is also responsible, as it has failed to provide health care services to these girls.

In India, there is no comprehensive public health legislation that gives the right to health care to people though there is a National Health Policy declared in 1983.[47] The Constitution of India, under the directive principles of state policy, defines health in general as well as in specific terms. Article 47 of the Constitution states:

> Duty of the State to raise the level of nutrition and the standard of living to improve public health: The State shall regard the raising of the level of nutrition and standard of living of its people and the improvements of public health as among its primary duties ...

The directive principles, though not justiciable in the court, are fundamental in the governance of the country. There is a clear reflection of these principles in various policies mentioned above. Apart from Article 47, there are references to health-related matters in the Seventh Schedule of the Constitution, which includes the three lists—Union, State, and Concurrent. These lists provide the subject matters on which legislation can be framed by the union or the states exclusively and those matters over which the union and states have concurrent authority to legislate. The Constitution deals with the legislative relations between the Parliament and the states. Article 245 recognizes the power of the Parliament and of a legislature of a state to make laws for the whole or a part of India, or the state respectively. Article 246 states that the Parliament has exclusive power to make laws with respect to any matters in List I (Union List) of the Seventh Schedule. The legislature of any state has exclusive power to make laws with respect to any matters in List II (State List) of the Seventh Schedule. And both have the power to make laws with respect to any of the matters enumerated in List III (Concurrent List) of the Seventh Schedule.

The Concurrent List contains the following health-related matters[48]: population control and family planning, drugs and poisons, legal, medical, and other professions. Matters related to health care in the State List are[49]: public health, sanitation, hospitals, and dispensaries. The Union List does not contain any matter related to health care. A plain reading of Articles 245 and 246 with the Seventh Schedule would show that public health care does not fall within the purview of the Parliament. And ideally, it would be the responsibility of the state legislature to pass laws on health care.

However, there are various ways in which Parliament could take the initiative to introduce legislative reforms in the health care system within the existing constitutional framework. If the provision of universal health care is considered as an issue of economic planning, there is scope for the Parliament to legislate on health care within the constitutional boundaries because economic planning appears in the Concurrent List.[50] Additionally, social security and social insurance, and price control are other items included in the Concurrent List.[51] Under these headings, Parliament can certainly enact health legislation giving people a statutory right to health care.

In brief, the provision in the directive principles and the legislative items in the Concurrent List do give full scope to Parliament to pass a comprehensive legislation giving people the right to health care. However, the government has not made any efforts to enact such a legislation. In fact, if there is a will it would not be difficult for the Parliament to declare the right to health as a fundamental right. However, in the absence of a statutory and constitutional right to health, it would be important to analyse how the Supreme Court of India has evolved the right to health care.

The Supreme Court of India has been adopting an innovative and progressive attitude towards social injustice caused or condoned by the state since the late 1970s.[52] During this period it has departed from the traditional rule of *locus standi* and has allowed class actions in public interest.[53] Such an action is labelled as Public Interest Litigation (PIL). PIL is a form of legal proceeding in which redress is sought for injury to the public in general or identified sections of it. It enables claimants to address gross violations of fundamental rights through the exercise of state powers (either by commission or by omission). Basic human rights play an important role in such actions. In particular, the right to life and liberty in Article 21 of the Indian Constitution[54] is often addressed.

The Supreme Court in a historic judgement in *Consumer Education and Research Centre* v. *Union of India*[55] has held that the right to health care and medical care is a fundamental right under Article 21, read with Articles 39(e), 41, 43, and 48-A as it is essential for making the life of the workman meaningful and purposeful with dignity of person. A PIL was filed for the protection of the rights of employees working in the asbestos industry who were suffering from asbestosis. The Court held that the state, be it the Union or the state government or an industry, public or private, is enjoined to take all such action which would promote health, strength, and vigour of the workmen during the period of employment and even after retirement. The Court made it clear that all authorities or even private persons or industries are bound by its order.[56]

In *Paschim Banga Khet Mazdoor Samity* v. *State of West Bengal*[57] the Supreme Court held that the denial of medical assistance by a government hospital to an injured person on the ground of non-availability of beds amounted to violation of the right to life under Article 21 of the Constitution. The Court directed the state to pay compensation to the petitioner.

In *Parmananda Katara* v. *Union of India*[58] the Supreme Court held that it is the professional obligation of all doctors, whether government or private, to extend immediate medical aid to the injured to protect his life without waiting for legal formalities to be complied with by the police. It is the obligation of those who are in charge of the health of the community to protect life. When an accident occurs, doctors are duty-bound to provide essential services. They should not refuse medical treatment.

These decisions point out that every individual has a fundamental right to health care emanating from the right to life under Article 21 of the Constitution. The right to health care is broad enough to encompass the right to reproductive health services. Therefore, young girls' right to health care, which is violated as a consequence of child marriage, is within the purview of Article 21 and the state is obligated to fulfil it. One way to get this right enforced is to obtain a court ruling against the government by initiating public interest litigation before the Supreme Court. So far no such petition has come before the Supreme Court. An argument distinguishing the right to health care from the right to health has also not been made in the Court. The two could be distinguished on the basis of CESCR's General Comment 14 on Health that the right to health embraces other human rights, such as the right to life, human dignity, education, equality, and the right to marry and found a family and are integral components of it.[59] Based on this analysis a PIL could be filed in the Supreme

Court challenging the failure of the government to prohibit child marriage. An argument could be raised that because of child marriage the young brides are forced to suffer many reproductive health problems and thereby their right to health is forfeited.[60]

To bring such a case before the Supreme Court, it is essential to have enough data to convince the Court about the adverse effects of early marriage on the reproductive health of young girls. Until recently, young girls were not the focus group of the government or for that matter even of voluntary organizations.[61] As mentioned in earlier chapters, NFHS has collected some data relating to the age of marriage, maternal mortality, and morbidity. However, there is hardly any community-level research on the after-effects of child marriage on young brides. If a case is to be brought before the Supreme Court, as mentioned before,[62] such data will have to be gathered through scientific research. Once proper homework is done, there is reason to believe that the Supreme Court might hold the government accountable for its failures.

While initiating such a petition before the Supreme Court, reference could be made to the international human rights conventions and the norms, viz., the Children's Convention, the Women's Convention, and the Slavery Convention. The Supreme Court has referred to the Women's Convention and General Recommendation of CEDAW in its celebrated decision in the *Vishaka* case[63] and has declared that the sexual harassment of women at the workplace is a violation of their right to life and right to live with dignity. This decision has paved the way for using international conventions for realizing women's human rights. The precedent has already been well established. A strong argument could be made on the basis of these two conventions for holding the government politically and legally accountable for the injustices of preventable causes of maternal mortality and morbidity caused to young girls.[64] It could be argued that the young girls' right to reproductive health and the right to protection from child marriage are violated by the government's inaction.

The above discussion on the jurisprudence of the Supreme Court of India points out that the fundamental right to health care is part and parcel of the right to life. However, to be more effective and practical, such jurisprudence needs to be transformed either into a specific fundamental right or special legislation. Along with the right to health services, right to health also needs to be part of such legislation. It would provide an opportunity to the people to use it as an instrument for realization of their right to health.

The Indian government has endorsed POA and PLA, which have urged the governments to prohibit practices harmful to health.[65] CEDAW in its concluding observation on the report on India noted with concern that maternal mortality rates and infant mortality rates are among the highest in the world.[66] It recommended that the Government of India adopt a holistic approach to women's health covering their entire life cycle and urged the government to allocate sufficient resources for the country's health programme[67]. However, CEDAW has not directly commented on the sufferings of young brides in its concluding observations. In future it should relate the issue of child marriages with the health of young brides and ask the government to submit relevant information. CEDAW should also ask the government to take actions in the light of its General Recommendation 14.

By referring to the very high percentage of child marriages, which could have a negative impact on their health, CRC has also expressed its concern for the health of adolescents, particularly girls, in its concluding observations on the Indian report.[68] It has recommended that India should strengthen the existing National Reproductive and Child Health Programme, targeting the most vulnerable groups of the population.[69]

CRC has expressed its concern over the high maternal mortality and very high levels of low birth weight and malnutrition among children, including micronutrient deficiencies.[70] It has focussed on limited access to quality public health care facilities, insufficient numbers of qualified health workers, poor health education including exacerbated situation of extreme disparities faced by women and girls, especially in rural areas. CRC has recommended that India should take all necessary steps to adapt, expand, and implement the Integrated Management of Child Illness Strategy, and to pay particular attention to the most vulnerable groups of the population.[71] CRC has also recommended that India should undertake studies to determine the socio-cultural factors which lead to practices such as female infanticide and selective abortions, and to develop strategies to address them.[72] What needs to be seen is how the government responds to these observations.

Rights Affecting the Development of the Girl Child

Besides the unequal situation which results from the biological differences there are other consequences of child marriage on young girl children. They are unable to pursue avenues leading to overall personality development.[73] This results directly from the fact of early marriage as well as from the birth of a child which usually follows soon after the marriage. After childbirth, the life of a woman in the majority of cases changes much more significantly than the life of a man. In most cases girls' education and other social activities come to an end after marriage. These impair career advancement as well as other opportunities of development for them. The problem has been emphasized forcefully by CEDAW in its General Comment 21 on Equality in Marriage and Family Relations, which reads: 'The responsibilities that women have to bear and raise children affect their right to access education, employment, and other activities related to their personal development. They also impose inequitable burdens of work on women.'[74] Men on the other hand do not have to compromise their life plans. They do not stay at home to take care of children. They are not affected in most cases in terms of the ability to work and pursue a career. Therefore, child marriage seriously hampers women's right to education and thereby their ability to develop. Besides right to education, another significant right that is taken away as a result of child marriage is the right to information on which also her development is dependent.

Right to Education and Development

The right to education is articulated in Article 26 of UDHR. It declares:

1. Everyone has the right to education. Education shall be free, at least in the elementary and fundamental stages. Elementary education shall be compulsory ...

2. Education shall be directed to the fullest development of the human personality and to the strengthening of respect for human rights and fundamental freedoms ...

This fundamental right to free and compulsory education is reiterated in Articles 13 and 14 of ICESCR. Article 10 of the Women's Convention is elaborate and spells out the responsibility of state parties in the following terms. It states: 'States Parties shall take all appropriate measures to eliminate discrimination against women in order to ensure them equal rights with men in the field of education and in particular to ensure equality between men and women.' It takes cognizance of the fact that there is a high rate of female student dropout from school and requires state parties to reduce it.[75]

Article 28 of the Children's Convention requires state parties to recognize the right of the child to education on the basis of equal opportunity and requires 'to make primary education compulsory and available free to all'.[76] Article 29(a) mentions explicitly that the education of the child shall be directed to: '[T]he development of the child's personality, talents and mental and physical abilities to their fullest potential.' A reading of these two articles indicates that state parties are bound to impart education in such a way that it would contribute to the holistic development of the child and would make her/him a responsible citizen of the nation. However, in many developing countries, state parties fail to fulfil this obligation. In countries where child marriage of girls is the norm, it becomes both cause and effect of the denial of education to girls.

The right to education is the foremost right for adolescents, particularly for girls, as they are not admitted to school or are forced to drop out due to social, economic, and cultural reasons and gender bias. When schooling is neglected or is not made easily accessible, the right to education and to all other opportunities that education opens up are violated.

The right to education does not merely mean the right to attend school. It provides an opportunity for personal development, for increasing knowledge, and for gaining exposure to the outside world. It increases the potential for becoming economically independent, strengthens decision-making capability, enhances self-confidence and autonomy, delays marriage, and thereby allows development. One can view a strong relation between education and delayed marriage. Therefore, to realize young girls' human rights it is the foremost duty of the states to implement the right to education.

CESCR has expressed in its General Comment 13 that the right to education, like all human rights, imposes three types or levels of obligations on state parties: the obligations to respect, protect, and fulfil.[77] In turn, the obligation to fulfil incorporates both an obligation to facilitate and an obligation to provide. The obligation to respect requires state parties to avoid measures that hinder or prevent the enjoyment of the right to education. For instance, a state must not interfere in sex education provided to adolescents in school.[78] The obligation to protect requires state parties to take positive actions to prevent violation of rights committed by private individuals.

Young girls' right to life and liberty is violated by parents when they force them to marry in their childhood or deny them information about reproductive health. The obligation to fulfil (facilitate) requires states to take positive measures that enable and assist individuals and communities to enjoy the right to education. Finally, state parties have an obligation to fulfil (provide) the right to education. As a general rule, state parties are obliged to fulfil (provide) a specific right in the covenant when an individual or group is unable, for reasons beyond their control, to realize the right themselves by the means at their disposal.

CRC has expressed its concern over the right to education, particularly of girls' education, time and again through its concluding observations.[79] Often the issue is discussed in connection with the need to raise and enforce the legal age at marriage.[80]

Right to Education: India's Obligation

Article 45, one of the directive principles, provides for free and compulsory education for children below the age of fifteen years. It reads:[81] 'The State shall endeavour to provide, within a period of ten years from the commencement of this Constitution, for free and compulsory education for all children until they complete the age of fourteen years.' The Supreme Court of India used this directive principle to expand the interpretation of the legally enforceable fundamental 'right to life' in Article 21 of the Constitution and deciding that the right to life includes the right to education. It said that the right to education meant that a child has a right to free education till the age of fourteen years.[82] In spite of this decision, the directive of compulsory education could not become a reality.

The Indian Constitution was amended in the year 2002. Article 21A, which was added to the part on fundamental rights, provides for free and compulsory education. It reads:[83] 'The State shall provide for free and compulsory education for all children of the age of six to fourteen years in such manner as the State may, by law, determine.' Article 45 was also amended in 2002 and it now reads: 'The State shall endeavour to provide early childhood care and education for all children until they complete the age of six years.' What could not become a reality in the past more than fifty years needs to be done by the states in the coming years. To give every child primary education, there needs to be political and financial commitment. Otherwise, it will remain a distant dream. Mere insertion of the right to education in the chapter on fundamental rights will not make it a reality.

The reason for saying so is that even today 58 per cent of women are illiterate.[84] The dropout rate of girls from school is very high. In the country as a whole, only 68 per cent of the children aged 6–14 are attending school. The proportion is higher for males than for females: 76 per cent for males compared with 59 per cent for females. The gap between girls and boys in school attendance is more pronounced in the rural than in the urban areas, especially for the age goup of 11–14, where only 48 per cent of the rural girls as opposed to 73 per cent of rural boys are in school. Even today, 41 per cent of the school-age girls in India are not attending school.[85]

There are a number of reasons for this scenario. Girls are always given secondary treatment in the family compared to boys. A girl's education is usually not the priority for the parents. They do not understand the all-pervasive importance of education. With the limited resources available to them, parents prefer to give education to sons. When a girl is born in the family, the main concern of the parents is how to marry her off at the earliest possible opportunity when she is still a child. After marriage, though there is no legal prohibition on attending school, it becomes practically difficult for her to attend school due to household responsibilities. Her marriage automatically results in her dropping out of school.

So long as young girls remain unmarried, they are required to take care of their siblings, cook for the family, and do all other domestic chores. The need for developing her vocational skills is not considered essential since her economic independence is never a concern. Earning bread for the family is always thought of as a man's responsibility. On marriage, girls leave their natal home and stay with their husbands' families where they are required to take care of household activities. There is a general understanding that if girls are to be engaged in doing domestic activities there is no need to send them to school, which for them is considered, waste of time, energy, and money.

Besides, the long distance of the school from home is another reason in rural areas for not sending girls to school. Parents are sceptical about the sexuality of their daughters. They have a feeling of insecurity if a girl is required to travel a long distance to go to school, as there is likelihood of either her getting involved with a stranger, or being molested on her way to school. They are afraid of voluntary/forced sexual relationship between girl and a stranger. Instead of giving proper sex education by sending her to school, the alternative that is preferred by the parents is taking the girls out of schools and marrying them off at a younger age.

As discussed earlier, child marriage has serious repercussions on the reproductive health of the young girls. A key condition to make them aware of such bad effects on their reproductive health is to give them information. But the basic education is a precondition to the right to information. They need to be equipped with the basic ability of reading and writing to know about their own reproductive system. Girls must, therefore, be sent to and retained in schools. This would also help delay their marriage.

If a girl is not married off at a young age, she needs to be engaged in some other activities. The best alternative is the school education. However, to send her to school, the parents need to be convinced of the importance of education for girls. At the same time, unless the facilities for education, even in the remote geographical locations, are provided, the right to education would not become a reality. And without essential budgetary allocation and effective legislation, nothing can be achieved in this direction. Equally important is to provide security to the girls on their way to school. Unless care is taken that they are not sexually harassed on their way, the parents would not feel safe to send their girls to school. The law-and-order situation also, therefore, has a great relevance in promoting the girls' right to education.

Some efforts to educate young girls were initiated in India through the Integrated Child Development Schemes (ICDS).[86] ICDS extended its activities to young girls in 1990 with a programme for out-of-school girls in the age group of 11–18 years. It focussed on nutritional supplements and health check-ups. It also focussed on childcare education for adolescent girls. Another scheme, *Balika Samriddhi*,[87] was launched by the Government of India in 1997. The objective of the scheme is to contribute towards a better life for the girl child. It provides for a post-delivery grant or gift for the mother of a girl, on the occasion of her daughter's birth. Annual scholarships to attend middle and high schools are also provided for pursuing higher studies or self-employment.

A multipurpose investment programme with a view to changing attitudes towards girls, their schooling, delaying marriage, and limiting fertility has also been introduced in various states.[88] Rajasthan instituted the first such programme, *Rajyalakshmi*, in 1994. It was followed in Haryana by *Apni Beti, Apna Dhan* (Our daughter, our wealth) and most recently in Karnataka in 1998.

The basic objective of these programmes is to start the process of changing the status of the girl and society's perception of her and to perceive her more as an asset than a liability. Government invests some money in the name of the girl child at the time of her birth. Nobody is allowed to access this money until she turns eighteen and has met the requirements of educational or marital status. Such schemes also have an objective of delaying the age at marriage. Voluntary organizations with the help of international agencies such as United Nations Population Fund and the funding agencies like the Ford Foundation have recently taken up projects for catering to the needs of adolescent girls. These efforts, as welcome as they are, have not yet addressed the problem at the national level. No systemic changes are introduced. The efforts are sporadic and patchy.

One of the major criticisms against these policies and programmes is that the adolescents are perceived as a single homogenous group.[89] In fact, the adolescents are heterogeneous and have differing experiences and needs at any given point of time. The term encompasses a variation of gender, age, needs, marital status, geographic location, and socio-economic status and conditions. Adolescents in India are located in urban, rural, or tribal areas; they are in school, out of school; they are involved in economic activity in formal or informal sectors. There are adolescents who are in marginalized circumstances such as street children and children of sex workers. Some adolescents are unmarried, while other are married, and significant numbers are pregnant or have even given birth before completing eighteen years of age. Their needs have not been addressed so far in an effective and time-bound manner.

CEDAW has also expressed its concern in the concluding observations on India's report for not providing girls with equal access to primary and secondary education. It mentioned that the budgetary allocation for education is still far below India's responsibility with regard to the Beijing PLA.[90] It has urged the government to take affirmative action, set a period, and provide adequate resources for primary and secondary education so as to give girls equal access to education.[91] It called upon the government to make primary and secondary education compulsory by introducing and enforcing relevant regulations.[92]

CRC expressed it's serious concern about the striking disparities with regard to access to education, attendance at primary and secondary levels, and dropout rates between different states, rural and urban areas, boys and girls, the affluent and the poor, and children belonging to scheduled castes and tribes. Welcoming the 83rd Constitutional Amendment Bill concerning the fundamental right to primary education, CRC emphasized the importance of focusing attention on improving the provision and quality of education, especially in view of its potential benefit for addressing various concerns, including the situation of girls.[93] CRC recommended that the state party should develop measures to address the prevailing disparities in access to education; to improve the quality of teacher-training programmes and the school environment.[94] CRC recommended that India should give due regard to the aims of education laid down in Article 29 of the Convention, including tolerance and equality between the sexes, and should consider introducing human rights issues in the school curricula.[95] Now the responsibility is on the government to respond to these recommendations, particularly when the right to education has become a fundamental right. Voluntary organizations working in the field need to pursue their goal till the rights of children, particularly of girl children, are ensured.

Right to Information

The right to seek, receive, and impart information is protected by all the basic human rights conventions. Article 19 of UDHR and ICCPR and Article 13.2 of the Children's Convention declare that everyone has the right to freedom of opinion and expression, which includes the right to seek, receive, and impart information. As mentioned before, the right to education is a prerequisite to the right to information. Unless a girl is educated, she is not able to demand or to make meaningful use of information regarding her health or sexual and reproductive health nor regarding her future development. Child marriage usually denies her the right to education and in turn the right to information. The significance of access to information on reproductive health is reinforced by Article 10 of the Women's Convention. It states that state parties shall take all appropriate measures to eliminate discrimination against women in order to ensure to them equal rights with men in the field of education and in particular to ensure on a basis of equality of men and women '(h) Access to specific educational information to help to ensure the health and well-being of families, including information and advice on family planning.' The Women's Convention also guarantees the right to family planning information in Article 16(1)(e). It directs signatory states to 'ensure on a basis of equality of men and women: 'The same rights to decide freely and responsibly on the number and spacing of their children and to have access to information, education and means to enable them (couples) to exercise these rights.'

Recognizing the frequent difficulty in accessing family planning information and services in rural areas, the Women's Convention in Article 14(2)(b) also emphasizes the need to guarantee access to adequate health care facilities, including information and counselling. At the minimum, the right to information implies a 'negative' obligation or 'obligation of forbearance' on the part of the state not to interfere with a person's ability to seek and receive information. This notion of non-interference arises from the fact that the human rights treaties commonly stipulate a freedom rather than a right to information. However, according to Sandra Coliver there is a positive obligation on the part of the states and it requires governments to impart the information.[96] She further lays emphasis on the rights of adolescents and argues that they have a right to information on an equal basis with older women, and may have an enhanced right to information and counselling tailored to their particular needs.[97] It is the right of adolescents to receive information without any discrimination on the basis of age. However, child marriage denies this right to them.

According to Article 24(f) of the Children's Convention, state parties are required 'to develop preventive health care guidance for parents and family planning education and services'. Unfortunately, the article is not clearly worded. It introduces uncertainty as to whether it is children or their parents to whom the family planning education should be made available. Thereby young persons are not expressly and unambiguously guaranteed the right to access family planning information. However, CRC has on numerous occasions mentioned that information on family planning be made available to adolescents.[98] It has given increasing attention to adolescents on matters of education about sex and family life. CRC has also suggested that sex education be introduced in the school curricula.[99] It has even suggested the content of a sex education curriculum as well as the methodology for communicating the necessary information to adolescents.

CRC has often discussed the issue in connection with the need to raise and enforce the legal age at marriage.[100] CRC has also addressed on a number of occasions the conflict between the parental rights of authority and the children's right to reproductive health information and services.[101] As per the recommendations of CRC, state parties are duty-bound to make provision for imparting reproductive health information to the adolescents.

The right of young girls to receive reproductive health information could also be read into the Women's Convention as discussed earlier. They need to be informed about the high risks involved in untimely pregnancies.

In fact, most of the reproductive health challenges faced by adolescents could well be met if the right to reproductive health information were assured to them. Otherwise, their right to health would be meaningless.

POA reiterated the same rights in favour of young girls. It requested that the response of societies to the reproductive health needs of the adolescents should be based on information that helps them attain a level of maturity required to make responsible decisions.[102] In particular, information and services should be made available to the adolescents to help them understand their sexuality and protect them from unwanted pregnancies, unsafe abortion, STDs including HIV/AIDS, and subsequent risk of infertility.

ICPD's recognition of these rights of the young girls was further endorsed and supported by PLA.[103] In fact, POA and PLA provided life to the letters of international human right conventions. POA urges that training should be given to all who are in a position to provide guidance to young girls concerning responsible sexual and reproductive behaviour—particularly parents and families, communities, schools, mass media, and peer groups.[104]

In this context, it is worth taking a note of the decision of the European Court of Human Rights in *Kjeldsen, Busk Madsen and Pedersen* v. *Denmark*.[105] Some parents took exception to compulsory sex education in state schools. They complained that it violated the state's duty to respect 'the right of parents to ensure such education and teaching in conformity with their own religious and philosophical convictions'. They argued that it violated their right to religious non-discrimination, right to private and family life, and/or the right to freedom and thought, conscience, and religion set out in the European Convention. However, the European Court of Human Rights held that compulsory sex education classes in state schools did not violate any of these rights as the classes were primarily intended to convey useful and correct information.

Right to Information: India's Obligation

The Indian Parliament recently enacted the Freedom of Information Act, 2002. It has not yet come into force. However, the judiciary has held that freedom of speech, recognized under Article 19 of the Constitution, includes the right to information.[106] Unless the right to information is bestowed on the adolescents in connection with their reproductive health, their right to health cannot be realized. The decision of the Supreme Court of India could be used for the fulfilment of young girls' right to information regarding matters of their reproductive health till the law is meaningfully enforced.

As argued by Sandra Coliver, the Indian state in under a positive obligation to impart necessary information to young girls.[107] As emphasized rightly by her, they have a right to information on an equal basis with older women, and also have the enhanced right to information and counselling tailored to their particular needs. The government at present is not providing such information to young girls in any significant way. As a consequence, sexual violence against young girls is on the increase in India. Issues regarding such violence within the family are also being raised quite vehemently. Therefore, providing information to young girls about reproductive health has become extremely relevant and important.

End Notes

[1] See Chapter One at 14.

[2] M.F. Fathalla, 'Women's Health: an Overview' (1994) 46 *International Journal of Gynaecology and Obstetrics*, 105–88.

[3] Article 6 (2).

[4] Rebecca Cook, *Women's Health and Human Rights*, (Geneva: WHO, 1994) at 24.

[5] UN document CCPR/C/21/Rev.1 at Para 5, 19 May 1989.

[6] Ibid.

[7] Rebecca Cook, and M. Fathalla, 'Advancing Reproductive Rights Beyond Cairo and Beijing' (1996) 22 *International Family Planning Perspective* 117.

[8] Principle 1.

[9] S.P. Sathe, *Judicial Activism in India* (New Delhi: Oxford University Press, 2002) 209.

[10] AIR 1984 SC 802.

[11] (1995) 3 SCC 42.

[12] *Arvinder Singh Bagga* v. *U. P.* AIR 1995 SC 117.

[13] 1993 SOL Case No. 098.

[14] *Olga Tellis* v. *Bombay Municipal Corporation*, AIR 1986 SC 180; *Narendra Kumar* v. *State of Haryana* (1994) 2 SC 94.

[15] *Paschim Banga Khet Mazdoor Samity* v. *State of West Bengal* (1996) 4SCC 37.

[16] *Unni Krishnan* v. *State of Andhra Pradesh* 1993 SOL Case No. 051. Every child has a right to free education in India up to the age of fourteen years; *Mohini Jain* v. *State of Karnataka* 1992(5) SLR 1 (SC).

[17] AIR 1989 SC 424.

[18] Though recent data reveal that pregnancy among unwed adolescents is not unheard of.

[19] Statistical data is not available regarding what percentage of married adolescents suffer every year from pregnancy-related complications in India. There is lack of community-based research on the subject. However, the hospital-based research findings show that adolescents who give birth are three times as likely to die in childbirth as are women aged 20–9 under similar circumstances. See Chapter One at 18.

[20] See Chapter One at 17.

[21] See Chapter One at 17–18.

[22] CESCR, General Comment 14, *The Right to the Highest Standard of Health*: E/C.12.2000/4, Para 8, 4 July 2000. Online: UN High Commissioner for Human Rights Web Page (Treaty-bodies database) <www.unhchr.ch> accessed on 18 October 2000, Para 12.

[23] CEDAW, General Recommendation 24, UNGAOR, 1999, Doc. No. A/54/38/Rev-1, Para 29.

[24] Ibid. Para 30.

[25] Ibid. Para 31.

[26] See Chapter One at 17–18.

[27] Constitution of the World Health Organization, in *Basic Documents*, 39th ed. (Geneva: WHO, 1992).

[28] CESCR, General Comment 14, supra note 22, Para 11.

[29] Ibid. CESCR, General Comment 14, Para 8.

[30] Ibid. CESCR, General Comment 14, Para 21.

[31] Ibid., CESCR, General Comment, Para 20.

[32] Lynn P. Freedman, 'Censorship, Women's Health and Human Rights' in Sandra Coliver (ed.), *The Right to Know: Human Rights and Access to Reproductive Health Information* (Philadelphia: Article 19 and University of Pennsylvania Press, 1995) at 7.

[33] M.F. Fathalla, 'Reproductive Health: A Global Overview' (1991) 626 *Annals of the New York Academy of Sciences* 1.

[34] ICPD, Paragraph 7.2.

[35] Bharati Sadasivam, 'The Rights Framework In Reproductive Health Advocacy: A Reappraisal' (1997) 8 *Hastings Women's Law Journal* 313 at 313.

[36] Supra note 23, Para 28.

[37] Leyla Gúlcúr, 'Evaluating the Role of Gender Inequalities and Rights Violations in Women's Mental Health' (2000) 5 *Health and Human Rights Journal* 46.

[38] See for example, L. Dennerstein, J. Astbury, and C. Morse, *Psychological and Mental Health Aspects of Women's Health* (Geneva: WHO, 1993).

[39] Ibid. at 61. Disability-adjusted life years are a quantified measure of the global burden of disease-assessing years of life lost to premature death and recently revised to include years lived with a disability of specified severity and duration.

[40] WHO, *World Health Report* (Geneva: WHO, 1999).

[41] C.J.L. Murray and A. D. Lopez, *The Global Burden of Disease* (Cambridge: Harvard University Press, 1996).

[42] J. Jambunathan, 'Socio-cultural Factors in Depression in Asian Indian Women' (1992) 49 *Social Science and Medicine* 1461, from Gúlcúr, supra note 37 at 55.

[43] F. Fikree and L.I. Bhatti, 'Domestic Violence and Health of Pakistani Women,' (1999) 65 *Gynaecology and Obstetrics* 195.

[44] Concluding Observations of CRC: Kuwait, 19th session, CRC/C/15/Add.96 Para. 28, 26 October 1998.

[45] Concluding Observations of CRC: Ghana, 19th session, 42, UN Doc. RC/C/15/Add.73 Para. 21, 18 June 1997.

[46] Concluding Observations of CRC: Ethiopia, 14th session, UN Doc. CRC/C/15/Add.67 Para. 14, 24 January 1997.

[47] The government declared the policy with a view to having an integrated comprehensive approach towards future development of health services. However, the government never thought of creating a statutory right to health.

[48] See items 20A, 19, 26.

[49] See item 6.

[50] See item 20.

[51] See items 23, 34.

[52] Sathe, supra note 9 at 195–248.

[53] Ibid.

[54] Article 21 of the Indian Constitution: Protection of Life and Personal Liberty: No person shall be deprived of his life or personal liberty except according to procedure established by law.

[55] (1995) 3 SCC 42. Again in *State of Punjab* v. *Mohinder Singh Chawala* AIR 1997 SC 1225, the Supreme Court reiterated that the right to health is an integral part of life and the government has a constitutional obligation to provide health facilities.

[56] In *Kirloskar Brothers Ltd* v. *Employees' State Insurance Corporation* (1996) 2 SCC 682, the Supreme Court reiterated that 'right to health' is a fundamental right and is available not only against the state but even against private industries.

[57] (1996) 4 SCC 37.

[58] AIR 1989 SC 424.

[59] CESCR, General Comment 14, supra note 22, Para 8.

[60] See Carmel Shalev, 'Rights to Sexual and Reproductive Health: ICPD and the Convention on the Elimination of All Forms of Discrimination against Women' (2000) 4 *Health and Human Rights* 39 at 51.

[61] Saroj Nagi, 'Time to Focus on Adolescents says UN Study', *The Times of India*, 9 October 2000.

[62] See above at 191 et al.

[63] *Vishaka* v. *State of Rajasthan* AIR 1997 SC 3011 at 3014–15.

[64] Ann Starrs and Inter-Agency Group for Safe Motherhood, *Report of the Safe Motherhood Action Agenda: Priorities for the Next Decade* (Sri Lanka, 1997) at 10.

[65] Para 277 (d).

[66] CEDAW/C/2000/1/CRP.3/Add, 1 February 2000, Para 49.

[67] Ibid. Para 50.

[68] Ibid. Para 50.

[69] Ibid. Para 51.

[70] CRC/C/15/Add.115, 23/2/2000 (23rd Session) Para 48.

[71] Ibid. Para 49.

[72] Ibid.

[73] Diana D.M. Babor, 'Population Growth and Reproductive Rights in International Human Rights Law' (1999) 14 *Connecticut Journal of International Law* 83 at 95.

[74] Comment on Article 16(1)(e), Para 21.

[75] Article 10(f). The reduction of female student drop-out rates and the organisation of programmes for girls and women who have left school prematurely.

[76] Article 28 (a).

[77] CESCR General Comment 13, E/C.12/1999/10, Para 46, 8 December 1999.

[78] See *Gillick* v. *West Norfolk and Wisbech Area Health Authority and Another* (1985) 3 All ER 402; Jane Pilcher, 'Contrary to Gillick: British Children and Sexual Rights since 1985' (1997) 5 *International Journal of Children's Rights* 299.

[79] For example, see Concluding Observations: Ethiopia.

[80] Cynthia Price Cohen, 'The United Nations Convention on the Rights of the Child: A Feminist Landmark', 1997, 29 *William and Mary Journal of Women and the Law* 29 at 55.

[81] Article 45.

[82] *Unni Krishnan* v. *State of Andhra Pradesh* AIR 1993 SC 2178; *Mohini Jain* v. *State of Karnataka* AIR 1992 SC 1858.

[83] This article was inserted by the Eighty-sixth Amendment to the Constitution in 2002.

[84] International Institute for Population Sciences (IIPS), *National Family Health Survey (NFHS) 1992–93 India* (Mumbai: IIPS, 1995) Table 3.9 at 54.

[85] Ibid. Table 3.10 at 56.

[86] India for South Asia Conference on the Adolescent at New Delhi, UNFPA Country Paper, at 22 (UNFPA, 1998).

[87] T.M. Vijay Bhaskar, 'Balika Samriddhi Yojana' (1997) *Social Welfare* 14.

[88] Ibid. at 25–6.

[89] ICPD + 5 Meeting the Needs of Adolescents at 5.

[90] CEDAW/C/2000/1/CRP.3/Add, 1 February 2000, Para 35.

[91] Ibid. Para 36.

[92] Ibid.

[93] At that time the Eighty-third Constitutional Amendment Bill concerning the fundamental right to primary education was pending before Parliament and it was welcomed by CRC. CRC/C/15/Add.115, 23 February 2000, (23rd Session) Para 56.

[94] Ibid. Para 58.

[95] Ibid. Para 59.

[96] Sandra Coliver, 'The Right to Information Necessary for Reproductive Health and Choice under International Law', in Coliver (ed.) supra note 32 at 38 (58).

[97] Ibid. at 65.

[98] See Corinne A.A. Packer, 'Preventing Adolescent Pregnancy: The Protection Offered by International Human Rights Law', (1997) 5 *International Journal of Children's Rights* 46.

[99] Ibid.

[100] Supra note 80.

[101] See Concluding Observations of CRC: October 30, 1996, 13th Session— (a) Morocco, CRC/C/15/Add.60 Para 13, 25; (b) Slovenia, CRC/C/15/Add.65 Para 10; (c) Nigeria, CRC/C/15/Add.61 Para 13; and (d) Mauritius CRC/C/15.Add.64 Para 13.

[102] Para 6.15.

[103] Para 107 (e) and (g); Para 93–5 of PLA outline the particular problems of adolescent girls with respect to inadequate sexual and reproductive health information. It calls upon states to meet their educational and service needs to enable them to deal in a positive and responsible way with their sexuality.

[104] Para 7.48.

[105] 1 Eur. HR Rep. (1976) 711.

[106] *S.P.Gupta* v. *Union of India* AIR 1982 SC 149; *Secretary, Ministry of Information and Broadcasting* v. *Cricket Association of Bengal* AIR 1995 SC 1236.

[107] See supra note 96 and 97.

7

Strategies and Future Action

CEDAW and CRC: Need for Collaboration

The Women's Convention and the Children's Convention both provide a continuum to human right protection under the international standards. Each guarantees similar sets of rights. Nonetheless, the differences are reflected in the ratification rates and in reservations filed by signatory parties. It is unfortunate that the largest number of reservations have been filed in respect of the Women's Convention.[1] Although reservations are not intended to allow governments to contradict the main thrust of the conventions, in many cases reservations entered by signatory parties have gone against the very principle of non-discrimination. What is interesting is that countries, which have overtly rejected the concept of universal, fundamental human rights of women, have ratified the Children's Convention without reservations in respect of similar provisions.

The Vienna Conference had urged states to withdraw reservations that are contrary to the object and purpose of the conventions or which are otherwise incompatible with international treaty law.[2] CEDAW and CRC have requested state parties to withdraw the reservations through concluding observations on the country reports as well as through the general recommendation.[3] However, neither committee has taken a position that the reservations are incompatible and are, therefore, unacceptable.[4] Committee members of both the conventions, by working in collaboration, could communicate to state about the non-acceptability of incompatible reservations or declarations.

Such a view was also expressed in a meeting organized by the International Women's Right Action Watch (IWRAW) in 1998 at New York.[5] The meeting identified some areas of potential collaboration. Use of the Women's Convention to extend children's rights into adulthood, extension of children's rights to deal with gender-specific rights of girls, right to education, socio-economic rights of girl children, and violence against them were some of the issues. The health of young girls was thought to be the key issue. The complementarity of the two conventions in this regard offers scope for working together.[6] Such joint efforts would make state parties react more responsibly. As a result, solutions to the problem of child marriage could be better achieved in future.

Strengthening International Normative Standards

International human rights law has taken serious cognizance of and has responded to the issue of child marriage. The treaty-monitoring bodies' jurisprudence developed through general recommendations or comments and concluding observations on the country reports demonstrates concern for the issue of child marriage. CEDAW's General Recommendation 21 on 'Equality in Marriage and Family Relations'[7] and HRC's General Comment 28 on 'Equality of Rights between Men and Women'[8] are of particular relevance as both have addressed the issue of child marriage specifically. CEDAW's General Recommendation 19 on Violence against Women,[9] and General Recommendation 24 on Women and Health[10] have both contributed to the development of human rights of young girls.

The committees have rejected cultural arguments as justifications for discriminatory practices and have held governments responsible for private acts. The committees have established the connection between violation of the right to health and child marriages. The concluding observation on the country reports have also addressed the issue of child marriage from the feminist perspective and have asked signatory parties to take appropriate measures, including legal, to remedy the violation of various human rights of girl children because of child marriages. However, still there is room for deepening their understanding and analysis of the issues relating to child marriage and violation of human rights of young girls. The committees could develop their jurisprudence by defining the content and meaning of human rights and addressing the issue more systematically. The committees need to connect the adverse consequences of child marriages on the development of young girls. The committees have not addressed the practice of child marriage as a form of slavery. The legal minimum age for marriage has been defined only by CEDAW, while CRC, HRC, and CESCR are still silent on it. Child marriage has been declared as a harmful traditional practice by CRC in clear terms, and is indirectly referred to by CEDAW but HRC has not commented so far. Child marriage has received uneven attention from different committees. Similarly, the issue has not been addressed with respect to all those countries where the practice is prevalent. The committees can rectify these issues in two ways: by adopting the general recommendations/comments and through improving the concluding observations.

CEDAW and CRC particularly could adopt the general recommendation/comment on child marriage mentioning it as a form of slavery and focussing further on eighteen as the age of marriage, providing free consent of the parties to the marriage, demanding compulsory registration of marriage, and declaring any marriage not in compliance with such conditions illegal and void.[11] Such general recommendation/comment could be used for authoritative interpretation of the broadly worded treaty provisions to advance human rights of young girls in the context of child marriage. It could also work as a tool for state parties to give their periodic reports and for voluntary organizations to give alternative reports to the respective committees, which in turn would help the committees give more comprehensive comments in concluding observations. In addition, the reporting procedure to the treaty-monitoring bodies could be improved by giving substantial field information. UN agencies, such as UNICEF, UNFPA, and WHO, could contribute significantly in reporting to treaty bodies about the factual situation prevalent in a country. Similarly, more voluntary organizations could be involved in understanding the activities of the treaty bodies with the help of international voluntary organizations, and in turn such voluntary organizations could help develop the jurisprudence of these committees by submitting shadow or alternative reports. By adopting all these measures, the performance of state parties could be assessed and the ones failing in compliance could be asked to improve upon it. This in turn would help improve the implementation of human rights of young girls.

Strategies for Implementation of Human Rights at National Level

International human rights law depends for its effective application on international consensus and the implementation of effective means of action at the domestic level.[12] Besides the reporting procedure and complying with the general recommendations/comments and concluding observations on the periodical reports of the state by the treaty bodies, a number of strategies could be adopted for implementation of human rights of young girls in the context of child marriage at the domestic level. Those strategies could include creating awareness about human rights, having a dialogue with the government, and approaching the judiciary and the National Human Rights Commission.[13]

Education and Training

Creating awareness about international human rights jurisprudence through publicity at the national level is one of the most important strategies that needs to be adopted for holding the state accountable for its negligence or inaction in enforcing the rights of young girls. Unless people are made aware about the rights and corresponding obligations of the state, they might not demand concrete actions from the state to remedy injustice done to them. This is particularly true in case of young girls who are vulnerable due to their age, sex, and gender.

Everyone, right from the school children to the members of various departments of the government, needs to be educated about the concept and language of human rights. They could be given training with the help of law teachers and students about how and why human rights are violated and what should be done to prevent further violations.

In the context of child marriage, a special responsibility could be put on certain professionals. For instance, health professionals, law enforcement officials, people's representatives, members of the judiciary, and social workers in non-governmental organizations and in the local community could be trained to address the practice of child marriage from human rights perspective. They in turn, during their day-to-day work, could take action to prevent child marriages.

Building Linkages with the State

Governments are ultimately responsible for shaping and applying international human rights law at the domestic level. Traditionally, voluntary organizations and governments have been divided by mutual suspicion, lack of understanding, and some times even hostility. There is a need to build linkages and understanding between civil society and government. In partnership with the government, voluntary organizations could contribute to the better formulation, implementation, and evaluation of policies and activities. Voluntary organizations could contribute in the process by sharing women's experiences that are either ignored or are not understood by those in power, who generally are men. Both need to work to harmonize and reinforce their objectives.

Judicial Intervention

Denial of human rights could have a negative impact on the judiciary.[14] Continued respect for and acceptance of the exercise of judicial power depends on preserving the perceived and actual fairness and integrity of the system. Absence of an affirmative vision of the judicial role that responds to concerns about fairness and proper allocation of governmental power fuels the political and theoretical attack on legitimacy, which in turn contributes to public perception of judicial illegitimacy. To develop and enhance institutional competence and legitimacy, remedies could be sought against the state through judicial interventions by filing a public interest litigation.[15] A strong brief could be prepared on the basis of various international legal instruments that India has ratified. The Indian state could be motivated to respond to its international obligations through such a petition.

The Supreme Court of India has already created a precedent of referring and using the international instruments and the general recommendations of the monitoring bodies for protection of women's rights.[16] The Court has liberalized Court procedure to accept petitions from organizations challenging the violations of the rights of vulnerable groups including children.[17] The Court has specifically insisted that public officials must act in a manner consistent with the requirements of the Constitution, the Directive Principles of State Policy, and the international treaties ratified by India.[18] The Supreme Court has shown its willingness to immerse itself in administrative detail in order to do justice to disadvantaged groups.[19] Based on this already established public interest litigation jurisprudence, a petition could be filed for the protection of young girl's rights against the practice of child marriage and its impact on their reproductive health and personal development. A favourable decision from the Supreme Court in such a case might be a stepping stone in the process of realization of young girls' human rights. Such a decision could help bring the issue of child marriage in the limelight and could propagate a message that child marriage is a legal wrong.

In addition to public interest litigation, a test case could also be filed in the Supreme Court for claiming exemplary damages on behalf of the victim of a child marriage. Exemplary damages are damages that are given entirely without reference to any proven actual loss suffered by the plaintiff.[20] The reason behind this is to consider the interest of the public as a whole with a view to ensuring that public bodies perform their duties properly, especially where the fundamental rights of citizens are concerned.[21] In case where pregnancy has occurred within the child marriage and where it has resulted in the death of the child wife, the case could be made against the Indian government. It could be argued that due to non-implementation of CMRA by the government, the child marriage took place, which resulted in the loss of life violating the right to life. Thus, if the international law along with the national law and the Constitution are studied carefully, interpreted dynamically, and applied imaginatively to the existing realities, it would provide a basis for the realization of the human rights of young girls and in turn for the desired social change.

The National Human Rights Commission of India and Child Marriage

In addition to the formal judicial system, there is another forum in India that works for the promotion of human rights, namely the National Human Rights Commission (NHRC) established under the Protection of Human Rights Act, 1993. It was established with a view to providing better protection of human rights.[22] NHRC is empowered to inquire into violations of human rights either on receipt of a complaint or *suo motu*, that is to say, on its own initiative, and after investigations, it may recommend to the government that it take proper remedial action.[23] NHRC's function is to review the safeguards provided by the Constitution or any law for the protection of human rights, to recommend measures for their effective implementation, to study treaties and other international instruments on human rights, and to make recommendations for their effective implementation.[24]

NHRC is also expected to undertake and promote research in the field of human rights, spread human rights literacy among various sections of society, and promote awareness of the safeguards available for the protection of these rights through publications, the media, seminars, and other available means.[25] NHRC is required to submit an annual report to the Central government.[26] The Central government then has to lay the reports before each House of the Parliament along with a memorandum of action taken or proposed to be taken on the recommendations of NHRC and the reasons for non-acceptance of the recommendations, if any.[27]

In the context of child marriage, the role that has been played by NHRC needs to be understood. So far, no complaint has been filed before NHRC on the issue of child marriage. However, in the light of repeated reports of child marriages taking place in certain parts of the country, particularly in Rajasthan, despite the long-standing existence of the Child Marriage Restraint Act, 1929, NHRC undertook a study of CMRA and made the following observations:

— The Child Marriage Restraint Act may need to be so amended as to make the offence cognizable and non-bailable;

— There was need to decentralize executive powers and other respon-sibilities in order to sensitize the public and to facilitate reporting on inci-dents of child marriages; there was also a need to devolve powers to voluntary organizations and other responsible persons at the panchayat and village levels in order to prevent child marriages;

— Compulsory primary education, through the provision of incentives and proper infrastructural facilities for schooling, was an important means of reducing and ultimately eliminating the practice of child marriage;

— There should be greater emphasis on the prevention of child marriages rather than on their annulment;

— Compulsory registration of marriages could act as an impediment to child marriage.[28]

However, NHRC did not recommend in 1995 to the Central government that it take immediate steps. The reason was that the National Commission for Women and the Department of Women and Child Development had jointly proposed a Draft Marriage Bill in 1994. The Bill declared child marriage void and made registration of marriages compulsory. NHRC had suggested to the Central government to take early action on the draft bill. However, the Central government responded that it was of the view that only through social and economic uplift of certain sections of society could the practice be eradicated and no further legislative measures were contemplated. The Central government further argued that it would be inappropriate to introduce any form of legislation requiring compulsory registration of marriages since this would impinge on personal laws.[29]

NHRC, however, expressed the view that the response of the Central government amounted essentially to a total disinclination to strengthen or alter the law or see to its better implementation in respect of this very important social and cultural problem.[30] As the Draft Marriage Bill prepared by the National Commission for Women has not made any headway, NHRC has decided to revive its original proposal regarding the amendments to the Child Marriage Restraint Act, 1929. At present, it is preparing a fresh draft on the proposed amendments to CMRA and is intending to pursue it in the period ahead.[31]

Future Action

International agencies have taken account of what has been achieved by international conferences as well as by human rights treaties and of what needs to be done further to achieve the goals of ICPD and FWCW through Cairo+5 and Beijing+5 respectively. Young girls' sexual and reproductive right was one of the major concerns in Cairo+5 as well as Beijing+5. The General Assembly of the United Nations had called a special session to review the progress of POA of ICPD. It designated the Commission for Population and Development (CPD) as Preparatory Committee (Prep Com) to prepare a review report of the implementation of POA of ICPD. The General Assembly asked the United Nations Fund for Population Action (UNFPA) and UN Department of Economic and Social Affairs (DESA) to collaborate with CPD in this effort.

UNFPA organized the Hague Forum at The Hague, the Netherlands, from 8 to 12 February 1999, to review the progress made during the last five years of the ongoing implementation of POA of ICPD. UNFPA prepared the background paper for it. After taking account of developments in all regions during the last five years the report pointed out that despite some progress, much more remains to be done to address continuing gender inequalities that constrain the ability of girls to experience high standards of reproductive and sexual health. Harmful traditional, religious, and cultural attitudes and practices still continue to affect their health. The report suggested the following actions for promoting the sexual and reproductive rights of the adolescents:

— Development of a multi-sectoral reproductive health policy and a national plan for education, vocational training, income-generating opportunities, and sexual and reproductive health information services.

— Enactment and implementation of legislation including removal of restrictive laws.

— Investment in training parliamentarians, legislators, judges, and the media people in the light of ICPD objectives.

— Development of reproductive health programmes based on the sexual and reproductive health needs of adolescents.

— Involvement of voluntary organizations and the private sector in such programmes.

— Development of strategies for addressing emergency reproductive health needs of adolescents.

— Implementation of quality sexual and reproductive health programmes covering basic health care and STD screening and treatment; effective referral services and counselling that addresses sexuality, builds self-esteem; and promotes gender equality; training to develop broad-based life skills including assertiveness and decision making to resist peer group pressures or abusive situations and to manage sexual feeling and overtures, both wanted and unwanted.[32]

The Hague Forum submitted this report to the Prep Com. After reviewing the report the Prep Com prepared its draft report on the key actions needed for further implementation of POA of ICPD. The Prep Com also substantially supported all the above-mentioned recommendations of the Hague Forum. The review report of the Prep Com was discussed in the special session of the General Assembly from 30 June to 2 July 1999. All states expressed their commitments to further implement POA of ICPD in this session.[33] Though there was no direct reference to the issue of child marriage in the key actions, there were many relevant actions for promotion of young girls' human rights. If the Indian government abides by its commitment, it would do justice to the young girls.

The General Assembly of the United Nations also called the twenty-third special session on 'Women 2000: gender equality, development and peace for the twenty-first century' to review the progress of PLA of the Beijing conference from 5 June to 9 June 2000 known as Beijing + 5. It adopted a political declaration and outcome document entitled 'Further actions and initiatives to implement the Beijing Declaration and Platform for Action'.[34]

The General Assembly had asked the Commission on the Status of Women (CSW), with its ten member Bureau, to work as the preparatory committee (prepcom) for the special session with the help of the Division for the Advancement of Women. The prepcom adopted a draft resolution[35] on the basis of informal discussions, formal meetings, and consultation meetings entitled 'Follow-up to the Fourth World Conference on Women and full implementation of the Beijing Declaration and Platform for Action' and subsequently, prepared a document for the special session of the General Assembly.

In the special session, governments and the international community once again reaffirmed their commitment to the Platform for Action and a common development agenda with gender equality as an underlying principle. The outcome document recognized that the efforts towards ensuring women's advancement needed to combine a focus on women's conditions and basic needs with a holistic approach based on equal rights and partnerships, as well as, promotion and protection of all human rights and fundamental freedoms.

It further recognized that policies, programmes, and budgetary processes should adopt a gender perspective on the basis of clear research-based knowledge on the situation of women and girls. The special session reaffirmed the importance of gender mainstreaming in all areas and at all levels and the complementarity between mainstreaming and special activities targeting women. Certain areas were identified as requiring focussed attention. These included education, social services and health, including sexual and reproductive health, violence against women and girls, and the persistent and increasing burden of poverty on women. Certain groups needing special attention were also identified including young girls.

At its fifty-fifth session, the General Assembly called on governments and the United Nations system to take effective action to achieve full and effective implementation of the Beijing Declaration and Platform for Action and the outcome of the twenty-third special session of the General Assembly.[36] It was agreed to focus on the closure of the gender gap in primary and secondary education by 2005 and free, compulsory, and universal primary education for both girls and boys by 2015 to create and maintain a non-discriminatory as well as gender-sensitive legal environment through reviewing legislation with a view to striving to remove discriminatory provisions as soon as possible, preferably by 2005 and to provide universal access to high-quality primary health care throughout the life cycle including sexual and reproductive health care, not later than 2015.[37]

With this background, keeping women's human rights in the centre of focus as against the dominance of men's rights in a men's world is a major goal. Hopefully, the international agencies, monitoring bodies, and civil society will play a significant role in realizing women's human rights.[38]

End Notes

[1] Christine Chinkin, 'Reservations and Objections to the Convention on the Elimination of All Forms of Discrimination against Women', in J.P. Gardner (ed.), *Human Rights as General Norms and a State's Right to Opt Out, Reservations and Objections to Human Rights Convention*, (London: BIICL, 1997) at 64; also see Belinda Clark, 'The Vienna Convention Reservations Regime and the Convention on Discrimination against Women' (1991) 81 *American Journal of International Law* 281; Rebecca Cook, 'Reservations to the Convention on the Elimination of All Forms of Discrimination against Women' (1990) 30 *Virginia Journal of International Law* 643; Michele Brandt and Jeffrey Kaplan, 'The Tension Between Women's Rights and Religious Rights: Reservation to CEDAW by Egypt, Bangladesh and Tunisia' (1995–96) 12 *Journal of Law and Religion* 105.

[2] GENERAL A/CONF.157/23.

[3] For instance, see Concluding Observation on India, CEDAW/C/2000/1/CRP.3/Add.4/Rev.1, 1 Feb 2000, Para 32.

[4] See HRC General Comment 24, Chapter Five, note 64 and accompanying text.

[5] IWRAW, *Women, Children and Human Rights: The CEDAW Convention and the Convention on the Rights of the Child* (Minnesota: University of Minnesota, 1998) at 2.

[6] Kirsten Backstrom, 'The International Human Rights of the Child: Do They Protect the Female Child?' (1996–97) 30 *George Washington Journal of International Law and Economics* 541 at 573–82; Shannon S. Ragsdale and Vanessa D. Campbell, 'Protection of the Female Child: The Mothers of our Future—Case Studies of India, Pakistan, Bangladesh and Sri Lanka' (1999) 7 *Tulsa Journal of Comparative and International Law* 177 at 197.

[7] See Chapter Five, note 27 and accompanying text.

[8] See Chapter Five, note 12 and accompanying text.

[9] See Chapter Five, note 87 and accompanying text.

[10] See Chapter Six, notes 23–25 and accompanying text.

[11] See supra note 7.

[12] See generally, Kathleen Mahony, 'Theoretical Perspectives on Women's Human Rights and Strategies for their Implementation' (1996) 21 *Brooklyn Journal of International Law* 799 at 668–71.

[13] H. Hannum, *Guide to International Human Rights Practice* (Philadelphia: University of Pennsylvania Press, 1992).

[14] Dinah Shelton, *Remedies in International Human Rights Law* (New York: Oxford University Press, (1999) at 50.

[15] S. Sturm, 'A Normative Theory of Public Law Remedies' (1991) 79 *Georgia Law Journal* 1357 at 1403.

[16] *Vishaka* v. *State of Rajasthan* AIR 1997 SC 3011.

[17] *Sheela Barse* v. *Union of India* AIR 1986 SC 1773.

[18] *Sheela Barse* v. *Secretary, Children Aid Society* AIR 1987 SC 656.

[19] See G.L. Peiris, 'Public Interest Litigation in the Indian Subcontinent: Current Dimensions' (1991) 40 *International Comparative Law Quarterly* 66.

[20] Shelton supra note 14 at 74.

[21] *Nilabati Behera* v. *State of Orissa and others* AIR 1993 SC 1960.

[22] Section 3 of the Act. There is also a provision for the establishment of a State Human Rights Commission in every state under Section 20 of the Act.

[23] Sections 12 to 18 of the Protection of Human Rights Act.

[24] Section 12 of the Act.

[25] Ibid.

[26] Section 20(1).

[27] Section 20(2).

[28] NHRC, Annual Report 1995–96.

[29] Memorandum of Action Taken on the Annual Report of NHRC for 1995–96. The government filed the same declaration on Article 16 of the Women's Convention. See NHRC Annual Report, 1996–97.

[30] NHRC, Annual Report 1996–97.

[31] NHRC, Annual Report 1998–99. The Commission to date has not progressed further.

[32] UNFPA, *A Five-Year Review of Progress towards the Implementation of POA of ICPD*, a background paper for the Hague Forum, 8–12 February 1999 at 49–51.

[33] http://www.iisd.ca/population/cpd.32.

[34] A/55/341, 10 June 2000.

[35] E/CN.6/1998/11, during the forty-second session of CSW from 2 to 13 March 1998.

[36] See Resolution A/Res/55/71, 'Follow-up to the Fourth World Conference on Women and full implementation of the Beijing Declaration and Platform for Action and the outcome of the twenty-third special session of the General Assembly.'

[37] http://www.un.org.womenwatch/daw/followup/bfbeyond.html checked on 12th November 2001.

[38] See The NGO Country Report on Beijing +5 from the Indian Women's Movement, *What has changed for Women and Girls in India since 1995?* (The Task Force on Women 2000: India, 2000) at 43–9.

Conclusions

There is a long road from the ideal set out in international human rights documents to the actual realization of the human rights of young girls' especially in the context of child marriage. Achieving this goal would require fundamental changes in ideas and patterns of behaviour, as well as the establishment of mechanisms to monitor and enforce the relevant laws. The International Conference on Human Rights at Vienna, 1993; on Population and Development at Cairo, 1994; and the Fourth World Conference on Women at Beijing, 1995 stand as milestones on the road to women's empowerment and enjoyment of their human rights. Cairo+5 and Beijing+5 meetings have given further momentum to women's empowerment. The goals hereinafter are to develop and refine monitoring and follow-up mechanisms in order to facilitate the long and tedious process of ensuring implementation of women's human rights. Civil society has a critical role to play in the process. The partnership between the government and voluntary organizations is essential for formulation, implementation, and evaluation of policies and development objectives and activities. Voluntary organizations are important voices of people. Their association and networks provide an effective means of focussing local and national initiatives and addressing social, legal, political, and economic developmental concerns. People's participation in the whole process is also extremely significant.

Legal protection is extremely important for the promotion of rights of any powerless, non-vocal, vulnerable group of society. In case of adolescents, it is the responsibility of the national and international community to see that the rights of adolescents are protected, promoted, and ensured through proper legislation. However, it is equally important to keep in mind that mere passing of any law would not achieve its objectives unless it is meaningfully strengthened by other support mechanisms. Finally, one cannot forget that a strong political will is a condition precedent for succeeding in any mission whether at a national or global level. And a meaningful political will can be created only through democratic processes and pressures, for which we all need to work relentlessly.

Women throughout the world lose out by being women. Their power of choice and socializing are frequently thwarted by customs and traditions that are legitimized by a patriarchal society. They are forced to live as appendages and servants of others. But they are bearers of human capabilities—basic powers of choice that make a moral claim for opportunities to be realized and to flourish.[1]

The world community has been slow to address the problem of injustice to women, because it has lacked a consensus on sex-based inequality as an urgent issue of political justice. The outrages suffered every day by millions of women—domestic violence, child sexual abuse and child marriage, inequality before law, poverty, lack of dignity—are not uniformly regarded as ignominious, and the international community has been slow to decide that they are human rights abuses.

I have argued that the traditional exclusion of women from the articulation, development, implementation, and enforcement of human rights has rendered gender issues invisible, and consequently has shielded gender-based abuses from much needed scrutiny. Women's experience not being given the central place in the formulation of laws, or in other words their explicit and implicit exclusion from policy formulation and enforcement of laws, has resulted in denial of justice to women. The flawed public/private dichotomy has historically not taken serious cognizance of wrongs inflicted on women because of their sex.[2]

Notwithstanding these roadblocks in law and life, women have refused to accept, and indeed have fought strongly against, their imposed invisibility and silence. Women have made unrelenting efforts to raise their voices, urge their perspectives, and demand that their needs be met. As a result of the mobilization of women at many levels—from local collectives to regional NGOs, to government programmes, to international agencies, and human rights programmes—women's issues have begun to be addressed and placed on the national and international agenda. The evolution of feminist jurisprudence has offered a theoretical foundation to the women's movement. It has conveyed a message to the world community that the realization of women's human rights requires the incorporation of feminist thought at every level.

In the last five years women have argued for the special needs of adolescent girls who have been excluded so far from the enjoyment of human rights. They are attracting the attention of the international community towards issues that concern individual adolescent girls, such as gender-based discrimination, forced child marriages, sexual harassment within marriage, and denial of reproductive freedom along with denial of right to education and development. The incorporation of women's voices and concerns into the rights discourse has become essential to effect this reformulation of rights. Only such an approach would help develop, expand, and transform the content and meaning of human rights in a manner that would reflect women's realities and include women's perspectives.

I have argued in previous chapters that the issue of child marriage, if approached from such perspective, would make a distinctive contribution to the pragmatic pursuit of gender justice. I have argued unequivocally that practices that harm an individual girl's physical and/or mental well-being are wrong. Many such practices are highly paternalistic, particularly towards women. These discriminatory practices must be condemned and cannot be justified in the name of culture.[3] If an obligation to eliminate barriers to women's equality is modified according to considerations of culture, religion, and/or tradition, then equality can never be achieved.

This is not to say or to suggest that there are no cultural considerations or accommodations to be made when dealing with human rights. On the contrary, factors such as race, nationality, ethnicity, etc., are integral to the human rights construct. However, there is a distinction between accommodating or respecting cultural customs and using culture as a pretext to deny equality, integrity, and dignity to individuals on the basis of sex. I have argued that the cultural practices that take away the rights of girl children are not the right choices to be resorted to.[4]

Liberty is not just a matter of having rights on paper; it requires being in a position to exercise those rights. This requires material and institutional resources, including legal and social acceptance of the legitimacy of the adolescent girls' claim. They need special attention and aid to arrive at a level of capability to achieve goals in the life because for all these decades they have been in a position of traditional deprivation and powerlessness. The state that is responsible for guaranteeing human rights effectively must take adolescent girls' rights more seriously. The state must take into account what the girls do and what they are in a position to do or, in other words, what their opportunities and liberties are.[5]

The discussion in the previous chapters has pointed out how in the name of culture, tradition, and religion girls are married off at a young age by their parents in India. Though child marriage has serious repercussions on the lives of these girls, the practice continues under the guise of giving protection to young girls. While the age at marriage has been rising in India, there are still significant proportions of females that marry by the age of eighteen and even by the age of fifteen. The disparities by region within the country vary to a great extent. I have argued that there exist socio-cultural, legal, and political barriers that have contributed to the continuing low age at marriage. In a traditional patriarchal setting that is age- and gender-stratified, women and girls have relatively less autonomy; their sexuality is controlled, and the prestige of the natal family is believed to be destroyed by even the hint of *impurity* or doubt about the virginity of unmarried girls. In such settings child marriage is seen as a means of ensuring virginity.

In addition, economic considerations play an important role in perpetuating child marriage. Young girls are considered economically unproductive and investment in them is considered similar to 'watering someone else's garden'. Gender disparities are observed in educational attainment and potential economic activity, and this lack of non-domestic alternatives reinforces traditional roles for girls including child marriage. These pervasive socio-cultural norms reinforcing child marriage are compounded by lacunae in the law and lack of commitment to enforcing existing laws.

I have argued that law is an important instrument that regulates and controls human behaviour as well as an important instrument for bringing about the desired change in society. It has a double significance for women. On the one hand, it helps maintain discrimination against them, and on the other hand it helps remove that discrimination. CMRA is one such legislation. CMRA lays down the minimum but different ages of marriage for both the parties. Thereby, it regulates human behaviour, but discriminates against women. At the same time, due to other substantive and procedural lacunae, it has not been able to achieve the prevention of child marriages. I have suggested, therefore, that CMRA needs to be amended to remove the discrimination against women.

I have suggested four principal amendments to CMRA:

— Introduction of a uniform minimum age of marriage of eighteen years for both parties,

— Requirement of free and informed consent of both parties,

— Provision for compulsory registration of marriage, and

— In the absence of compliance with any one of these conditions a marriage would be void.

I have suggested that the enforcement of the provision regarding declaration of child marriages as being void could be postponed for a decade to prepare people to accept the change and provide breathing space to the government to create the necessary support structure that would give unmarried girls alternatives to marriage. I have argued that in the long run this would be beneficial to future generations and society. These amendments would contribute in minimizing the prevalence of the practice of child marriages in India.

I have argued that to bring in a uniform policy, the existing religion-based personal laws of marriage that are contradictory to CMRA also need to be amended. In the absence of compatibility on the issue of a uniform civil code, reforming these laws is the only alternative available. I have pleaded, therefore, for similar changes in the marriage laws too—uniform minimum age of marriage, free and informed consent of the parties, compulsory registration of marriage, and declaration of child marriages as null and void. I have suggested concrete amendments in other relevant laws that would remove the existing discrepancies amongst various laws such as the law of guardianship and the criminal law dealing with the offence of rape. I have also suggested procedural reforms in the law so as to enable its effective implementation. Along with law reforms the government must indicate its commitment to the implementation of these laws through sufficient budgetary provisions.

Legal reforms to a great extent involve changing the habits and behaviour of humans, often contrary to their personal and vested interests. It is not an easy task to achieve such a behavioural change merely through legal reforms. To accomplish such behavioural change requires a combination of incentives to change and disincentives for failure to change. To achieve this we need to create an environment that is open to change. Along with the law reform strategy, therefore, I have also emphasized on providing meaningful alternatives to girls including education, vocational training, and personality development opportunities. In a democratic set-up, civil society has to take the responsibility to make the government work in this direction.

I have argued that child marriage violates the human rights of young girls. Though India has ratified major international conventions such as the Women's and Children's Convention as well as ICCPR, ICESCR, and the Slavery Convention, it has not complied with its obligations under any of these treaties. The state has not looked at the issue of child marriage from the rights perspective. I have attempted to establish a case against the Government of India that the state has committed a breach of duty to respect, protect, and fulfil the rights of young girls by not preventing child marriages in the country. I have analysed the specific articles of these conventions and international norms that have been established by monitoring bodies and international conferences. I have suggested a number of strategies that need to be adopted at national and international levels that would help prevent further violation of human rights of young girls.

I have argued that civil society has an important role in judging the state's actions. NGOs are important voices of people. Their associations and networks provide an effective means of focussing local, national, and international initiatives and addressing social, economic, legal, and developmental concerns. In case of non-compliance with international norms by the state, NGOs can adopt different strategies. Traditionally, NGOs and governments have been divided by mutual suspicion, lack of understanding, and some times even hostility. There is a need to build linkages and understanding between civil society and government. In partnership with the government, NGOs could contribute in better formulation, implementation, and evaluation of policies and activities. Both need to work to harmonize and reinforce their objectives. The way forward is through constructive dialogue.

However, sometimes the confrontationist strategy adopted by NGOs also helps achieve the objective. In recent decades, the Supreme Court of India has built up human rights jurisprudence by extensively relying on Article 21 of the Constitution. Therefore, I have suggested that a public interest litigation should be filed by NGOs in the Supreme Court challenging the lackadaisical attitude of the Indian government towards the issue of child marriage of girls. If the international law along with the Constitution and the national laws are carefully studied, dynamically interpreted, and imaginatively applied to the existing realities, it would provide a basis for realization of adolescent's human rights and in turn for desirable social change. I have argued that a favourable decision from the Supreme Court might be a stepping stone in the process of realization of adolescent's human rights.

I have suggested that such a petition should be filed after doing the proper homework. Integrated research on how laws and the method of their implementation do not take into account the existing socio-cultural constraints, would be significant to establish a strong case before the court. How socio-economic development, female autonomy, legal literacy rates, and gender development index and education influence the age of marriage in a region could be analysed with the existing social science data. Such analysis would help convince the court to take commitment from the government to respect and protect the rights of young girls.

I have argued through the preceding pages that the cultural practice of child marriage tolerated by the Indian state has to be challenged on the basis of the feminist method of 'asking the woman question'. The existing laws, their enforcement, and judicial interpretations have failed to take into account women's feelings and opinions and their perspective. Lawmakers have not asked what women want and why and so have treated them unequally and caused injustice to them. Society has ignored their experiences and sufferings while fixing social, legal, and cultural norms. In a public interest litigation, while challenging the tolerance of the practice of child marriages by the state, the human rights violation arguments should be founded on this feminist approach.

Social changes that encourage women to marry and bear children somewhat later are largely positive for women and for society as a whole. Women have greater opportunity to realize their rightful aspirations and attain their full potential to contribute to the economic, social, and political life of their communities. At the same time, delays in marriage raise fears that women may enter into sexual relationships outside marriage, which will defy or undermine their communities' religious and cultural norms, as sexual activity and fertility is legitimized in Indian culture only through marital relations. Recently, concern has been expressed about increasing sexual activity among unmarried adolescents in India.[6] Thus even if we succeed in postponing marriages, such relationships can expose young people to the risks connected to premarital sexual activity for longer periods of time and thereby increase the risk of unintended pregnancies and births out of wedlock.

It is imperative therefore to provide young women with the information, skills, and necessary services to protect themselves against accidental pregnancy, and protect themselves, their partners, and their unborn children against diseases. The health care system in India is bureaucratized and male dominated with a hierarchical top-down approach. To date, women's voices have largely been missing from the health policy debate. There is a growing concern among advocates of women's health that women's views and perspectives must be incorporated in policies and programmes that are designed for them. In order to effectively integrate information regarding sexuality and counselling with reproductive health programmes in a gender-sensitive way, not only is it important to make this an explicit job responsibility of all service providers at various levels of the health care system, but also to sensitize all health planners and service providers to gender issues. I have argued, therefore, that a long-term process of gender sensitization and training is needed to effect social change within the present rigid bureaucratic system.[7]

I have suggested that reproductive health programmes must be redesigned to enhance access and improve the quality of service, particularly from the perspective of the user. There is a need to focus specially on adolescent girls. As studies of gender and development increasingly bring power relations into the discussion about policy development, the social significance of age as well as gender should also be incorporated as the most significant dimension of social distinction.[8] Understanding the requirements of working with girl children would take us a long way towards grasping the meaning of shift from family planning to reproductive health. The government, NGOs, and the private sector must work in partnership to promote reproductive health policies and programmes. I have argued for a paradigm shift in such programmes. It is essential that strong advocacy efforts to involve and empower a range of different constituencies be carried out with a view to catalysing a process of networking with a number of organizations so that the reproductive health ideology and the ethos could be effectively internalized. If we do not prepare ourselves, we would be risking the lives of future generations to an unimaginable extent.

Opting to give girls in marriage at young age is not a wise alternative. A nation's fate lies in the strengths and aspirations of its youth. And increased educational opportunities for young women, who are almost half of the youth population of the world, play a pivotal role in building and maintaining a society's well-being. If nations recognize the importance of making such commitments, enormous changes in the conditions of life for all are possible.[9]

In conclusion, we can say that legal protection is extremely important for the promotion of rights of any powerless, non-vocal, vulnerable groups like adolescent girls. It is the responsibility of the national and international community to see that rights of adolescents are promoted and protected through proper legislation. However, it is equally important to keep in mind that mere passage of any law will not be able to achieve its objectives unless it is meaningfully strengthened by other support mechanisms.[10] Finally, one cannot forget that a strong political will is a condition precedent to succeed in any mission whether at a national level or the global level. And a meaningful political will can be created only through democratic processes and pressures. All of us, including academicians, researchers, representatives at the national, international, intergovernmental, and non-governmental levels, and activists in various fields, need to work together relentlessly, utilizing an interdisciplinary approach to the rights construct, to ensure justice for young girls.

End Notes

[1] Martha C. Nussbaum, *Women and Human Development—The Capabilities Approach* (Cambridge University Press, 2000) at 298.

[2] Kathleen Mahony, 'Theoretical Perspectives on Women's Human Rights and Strategies for their Implementation' (1996) 21 *Brooklyn Journal of International Law* 799 at 605.

[3] Sonia Correa, *Population and Reproductive Rights* (New Delhi: DAWN and Kali for Women, 1994) at 76–84.

[4] Celestine Nyamu, 'How should Human Rights and Development Respond to Cultural Legitimisation of Gender Hierarchy in Developing Countries' (2000) 41 *Harvard International Law Journal* 381.

[5] Nussbaum, supra note 1 at 54.

[6] Shireen Jejeebhoy, 'Adolescent Sexual and Reproductive Behaviour: A Review of the evidence from India' in Radhika Ramasubban and Shireen Jejeebhoy (eds), *Women's Reproductive Health in India* (New Delhi: Rawat Publications, 2000) 40 at 47–58.

[7] Saroj Pachauri, 'Defining a Reproductive Health Package for India: A Proposed Framework', in Maitreyi Krishnaraj, Ratna Sudarshan, and A. Sheriff (eds), *Gender, Population and Development* 310–39 (New Delhi: Oxford University Press, 1998) 310 at 334.

[8] Margaret E. Greene, *Watering the Neighbour's Garden: Investing in Adolescent Girls in India* (New Delhi: Population Council, 1997) at 4. See generally Naila Kabeer, *Reversed Realities: Gender Hierarchies in Development Thought* (London: Verso, 1994).

[9] The Alan Guttmacher Institute, *Into A New World, Young Women's Sexual and Reproductive Lives*, (New York: The Alan Guttmacher Institute, 1998) at 6–7.

[10] There are few schemes of the government that are not enforced effectively. See Greene, supra note 8 at 21–6.

Select Bibliography

Books and Journal Articles

Agarwala, S.N., *Age at Marriage in India*, Bombay: Kitab Mahal Publishing Ltd., 1962.

Agnes, Flavia, 'Protecting Women against Violence? Review of A Decade of Legislation, 1980–9' (1992) 27 *Economic and Political Weekly* WS 19.

Alan Guttmacher Institute, *Into A New World, Young Women's Sexual and Reproductive Lives*, New York: The Alan Guttmacher Institute, 1998.

Anderson, J.N.D. (ed.), *Changing Law in Developing Countries*, London: George Allen and Unwin, 1963.

An-Naím, Abdullahi A., 'State Responsibility under International Human Rights Law to change Religious and Customary Law', in Rebecca Cook (ed.), *Human Rights of Women*, Philadelphia: University of Pennsylvania, 1994, p. 167.

Anti-Slavery International, Submission made to the Committee on the Rights of Child, *Role of the Family in the Promotion of the Rights of the Child*, General Discussion Day, 10 October, London: Anti-Slavery International, 1994.

Askari, Ladan, 'The Convention on the Rights of the Child: The Necessity of Adding a Provision to Ban Child Marriage', (1998) 5 *Journal of International and Comparative Law* (1998) 123.

Atwood, Stephen J., and Hussein, Julia, 'Adolescent Motherhood: Priorities and Next Steps', (1997) 43 *Journal of Family Welfare* 8.

Babor, Diana D.M., 'Population Growth and Reproductive Rights in International Human Rights Law', (1999) 14 *Connecticut Journal of International Law* 83.

Backstrom, Kirsten 'The International Human Rights of the Child: Do They Protect the Female Child?' (1996–7) 30 *George Washington Journal of International Law and Economics* 541.

Banerjee, Gooroo Dass, *Hindu Law of Marriage and Stridhan*, Calcutta: Thacker, Spink and Co. 1879.

Bartlett, Katharine T., 'Feminist Legal Methods', (1990) 103 *Harvard Law Review* 829.

Barua, Alka and Kathleen Kurz, 'Reproductive Health-seeking by Married Adolescent Girls in Maharashtra, India', (2001) 9 *Reproductive Health Matters* 53.

Baxi, Upendra, *Towards a Sociology of Indian Law*, New Delhi: Satvavahan Publication, 1986.

Bayefsky, Anne, 'The Principle of Equality or Non-discrimination in International Law', (1990) 11 *Human Rights Law Journal* 1.

Bhadra, Mita, 'Changing Age at Marriage of Girls in India', in Mita Bhadra (ed.), *Girl Child in Indian Society*, New Delhi: Rawat Publication, 1999, 120.

Bhaskar, Vijay T.M., 'Balika Samriddhi Yojana', (1997) *Social Welfare* 14.

Bhatia, J., and John Cleland, 'Self-Reported Symptoms of Gynaecological Morbidity and Their Treatment in South India', (1995) 26 *Studies in Family Planning* 208.

Bhende, Asha, 'A Study of Sexuality among Adolescent Girls and Boys in Underprivileged Groups in Bombay', (1994) 55 *Indian Journal of Social Work* 557.

Bilyeu, Amy Small, 'Trokosi—the Practice of Sexual Slavery in Ghana: Religious and Cultural Freedom vs. Human Rights', (1999) 9 *Indiana International and Comparative Law Review* 457.

Bose, Ashish, 'North-South Divide in India's Demographic Scene', (2000) 35 *Economic and Political Weekly* 1698.

Brandt, Michele and Jeffrey Kaplan, 'The Tension Between Women's Rights and Religious Rights: Reservation to CEDAW by Egypt, Bangladesh and Tunisia' (1995–6) 12 *Journal of Law and Religion* 105.

Brown, Sarah, 'Feminism, International Theory, and International Relations of Gender Inequality', (1988) 17 *Millennium* 461.

Brownlie, Ian, *System of Nations: State Responsibility*, Oxford: Clarendon Press, 1983.

Bunch, Charlotte, 'Women's Rights as Human Rights: Toward a Re-Vision of Human Rights', (1990) 12 *Human Rights Quarterly* 486.

Bunting, Annie, *Particularity of Rights, Diversity of Contexts: Women, International Human Rights and the Case of Early Marriage* (unpublished doctoral thesis, 1999).

Buvinic, M., 'The Cost of Adolescent Childbearing: Evidence from Chile, Barbados, Guatemala and Mexico', (1998) 29 *Studies in Family Planning* 201 at 208.

Byrnes, Andrew, 'Enforcement through International Law and Procedure' in Rebecca Cook (ed.), *Human Rights of Women*, Philadelphia: University of Pennsylvania, 1994, p. 195.

Chandra, Sudhir, *Enslaved Daughters Colonialism, Law and Women's Rights*, New Delhi: Oxford University Press, 1998.

Charlesworth, Hilary Chinkin, Christin, and Wright, Shelley, 'Feminist Approaches to International Law' (1993) 85 *American Journal of International Law* 613.

Chhabra, S., 'A Step towards helping mothers with unwanted pregnancies' (1992) 3 *Indian Journal of Maternal and Child Health* 41.

Chinkin, Christine, 'Reservations and Objections to the Convention on the Elimination of All Forms of Discrimination against Women', in J.P. Gardner (ed.), *Human Rights as General Norms and a State's Right to Opt Out: Reservations and Objections to Human Rights Convention*, London: BIICL, 1997, p. 64.

Clark, Belinda, 'The Vienna Convention Reservations Regime and the Convention on Discrimination against Women' (1991) 81 *American Journal of International Law* 281.

Cohen, Cynthia and Per Miljeteig Olssen, 'Status Report: United Nations Convention on the Rights of the Child' (1991) 8 *New York Law School Journal of Human Rights* 367.

Cohen, Cynthia, 'The United Nations Convention on the Rights of the Child: A Feminist Landmark' (1997) 29 *William and Mary Journal of Women and the Law* 29.

Coliver, Sandra, 'The Right to Information Necessary for Reproductive Health and Choice under International Law', in Sandra Coliver (ed.), *The Right to Know: Human Rights and Access to Reproductive Health Information*, Philadelphia: Article 19 and University of Pennsylvania Press, 1995, p. 38.

Commonwealth Secretariat and Interights, *Developing Human Rights Jurisprudence: Conclusions of Judicial Colloquia on the Domestic Application of International Human Rights Norms*, London: Commonwealth Secretariat, 1992.

Connors, Jane, 'General Human Rights Instruments and their Relevance to Women', in Andrew Byrnes, et al. (eds), *Advancing the Human Rights of Women*, UK: Commonwealth Secretariat, 1997, 27.

Cook, Rebecca, 'Reservations to the Convention on the Elimination of All Forms of Discrimination against Women' (1990) 30 *Virginia Journal of International Law* 643.

Cook, Rebecca, 'International Protection of Women's Reproductive Rights' (1992) 24 *New York University Journal of International Law and Politics* 645.

Cook, Rebecca, 'State Accountability under the Convention on the Elimination of Discrimination against Women', in Rebecca Cook (ed.), *Human Rights of Women*, Philadelphia: University of Pennsylvania Press, 1994, 228.

Cook, Rebecca, 'State Responsibility for Violation of Women's Human Rights' (1994) 7 *Harvard Human Rights Journal* 125.

Cook, Rebecca, *Women's Health and Human Rights*, Geneva: WHO, 1994.

Cook, Rebecca, 'Women's International Human Rights Law: The Way Forward', in Rebecca Cook (ed.), *Human Rights of Women*, Philadelphia: University of Pennsylvania, 1994, p. 3.

Cook, Rebecca and Bernard Dickens, 'Recognising Adolescents' "evolving capacities" to exercise choice in reproductive healthcare', (2000) 70 *International Journal of Gynaecology and Obstetrics* 13.

Cook, Rebecca and Bernard Dickens, et al., *Advancing Safe Motherhood Through Human Rights*, Geneva: World Health Organization, 2001.

Cook, Rebecca and M. Fathalla, 'Advancing Reproductive Rights Beyond Cairo and Beijing' (1996) 22 *International Family Planning Perspective* 117.

Cook, Rebecca and M.F. Fathalla, 'Duties to Implement Reproductive Rights' (1998) 67 *Nordic Journal of International Law* 1.

Correa, Sonia, *Population and Reproductive Rights*, New Delhi: DAWN and Kali for Women, 1994.

Crenshaw, Kimberlé, 'Demarginalizing the Intersection of Race and Sex: A Black Feminist Critique of Antidiscrimination Doctrine, Feminist Theory and Antiracist Politics' (1989) *University of Chikago Legal Forum* 139.

Crenshaw, Kimberlé, 'Mapping the Margins: Intersectionality, Identity Politics and Violence against Women of Colour' (1991) 43 *Stanford Law Review* 124.

Dagne, Hail Gabriel, 'Early Marriage in Northern Ethiopia', (1994) 4 *Reproductive Health Matters* 35.

Das, Sanjay and Prasamita Mohanty, 'Adolescent Girl and Education', in Sunil Mehra (ed.), *Adolescent Girl: An Indian Perspective*, New Delhi: Mamta Publication, 1995, p. 85.

Dennerstein, L., J. Astbury, and C. Morse, *Psychological and Mental Health Aspects of Women's Health*, Geneva: WHO, 1993.

Department of Women and Child Development, Ministry of Human Resource Development, Government of India, 'Demographic Profile and Future Strategies for Development of the Girl Child in India' (1995) 25 *Social Change* 24.

Dhagamwar, Vasudha, *Law, Power and Justice*, Bombay: Tripathi, 1974.

Dhagamwar, Vasudha, *Uniform Civil Code*, New Delhi: Indian Law Institute, 1990.

Diwan, Paras, *Law of Marriage and Divorce*, New Delhi: Wadhwa Publication, 1996.

Diwan, Paras, *Modern Hindu Law: Codified and Uncodified*, Allahabad: Allahabad Law Agency, 1993.

Dugal, Ravi, *Population and Family Planning Policy: A Critique and a Perspective*, Bombay: CEHAT, 1994.

Dyson, Tim and Mick Moore, 'On Kinship Structure, Female Autonomy, and Demographic Behaviour in India' (1983) 9 *Population and Development Review* 35.

Eaton, M., 'Patently Confused: Complex Inequality and *Canada* v. *A.G. Canada*' (1994) 1 *Review of Constitutional Studies* 203.

Efiong and Banjoko, 'The Obstetric performance of Nigerian primigravidgae aged 15 and under' (1975) 82 *British Journal of Obstetric and Gynaecology* 228.

Erikson, Rosemary and Simpson Rites, *Use of Social Science Data in Supreme Court Decisions*, Chicago: University of Illinois, 1998.

Fathalla M.F., 'Reproductive Health: A Global Overview' (1991) 626 *Annals of the New York Academy of Sciences* 1.

Fathalla, M.F., 'Women's Health: An Overview', (1994) 46 *International Journal of Gynaecology and Obstetrics* 105.

Fikree, F. and L.I. Bhatti, 'Domestic Violence and Health of Pakistani Women' (1999) 65 *Gynaecology and Obstetrics* 195.

Forum on Early Marriage, *Early Marriage: Whose Right to Choose?*, UK Forum on Marriage, 2000.

Freedman, Lynn P., 'Censorship, Women's Health and Human Rights' in Sandra Coliver (ed.), *The Right to Know: Human Rights and Access to Reproductive Health Information*, Philadelphia: Article 19 and University of Pennsylvania Press, 1995, p. 7.

Freedman, Lynn P., 'Human Rights and Women's Health', in M. Goldman and M. Hatch (eds), *Women and Health*, New York: Academic Press, 1999, p. 428.

Freeman, M.D.A., *The State, the Law and the Family*, London: Tavistock, 1984.

Friedman, Elisabeth, 'Women's Human Rights: The Emergence of a Movement' in Julie Peters and Andrea Wolper (eds), *Women's Rights Human Rights*, New York: Routledge, 1995, p. 19.

Ganatra, B.R., et al., 'Too far, too little, too late: A community-based case-control study of maternal mortality in rural west Maharashtra, India' (1998) 76 *Bulletin of the World Health Organization* 591.

Gangrade, K.D., 'Social Development and the Girl Child' (1995) 25 *Social Change* 70.

George, A., 'Understanding sexuality from the perspective of poor women of Bombay', 1993, Paper presented at workshop on Sexual Aspects of AIDS/STD Prevention in India.

Ghosh, Shohini, 'Deviant Pleasures and Disorderly Women' in Ratna Kapur (ed.), *Feminist Terrains in Legal Domains*, New Delhi: Kali, 1996, p. 150.

Goonesekere, Savitri, *Child, Law and Justice*, New Delhi: Sage, 1996.

Gopalan, C., 'Women and Nutrition in Developing Countries: Considerations' in H.M. Wallace and K. Giri (eds), *Health Care of Women and Children in Developing Countries* 1990, 252.

Greene, Margaret E., *Watering the Neighbour's Garden: Investing in Adolescent Girls in India*, New Delhi: Population Council, 1997.

Gúlcúr, Leyla, 'Evaluating the Role of Gender Inequalities and Rights Violations in Women's Mental Health' (2000) 5 *Health and Human Rights Journal* 46.

Hannum, H., *Guide to International Human Rights Practice*, Philadelphia: University of Pennsylvania Press, 1992.

Henkin, Louis, 'Where are we going from here?' in Martin (ed.), *International Human Rights Law and Practice: Cases, Treaties and Materials*, Cambridge: Kluwer Law International, 1997, 21.

Hernandez, Berta E., 'To Bear or Not to Bear: Reproductive Freedom as an International Human Right' (1991) 17 *Brooklyn Journal of International Law* 309.

Hernandez-Truyol and Berta Esperanza, 'Women's Rights as Human Rights—Rules, Realities and the Role of Culture: A formula for Reform' (1996) 21 *Brooklyn Journal International Law* 605.

Hidaytullah, M. (ed.), *Mulla's Principles of Mahomedan Law*, 19th ed., Bombay: N.M. Tripathi, 1990.

Hobcraft, John, 'Delay Marriage and First Birth', Background Paper for the WHO Technical Consultation on Safe Motherhood, Geneva: WHO, 1997.

Hossain, Sara, 'Women's Rights and Personal Laws in South Asia' in Rebecca Cook (ed.), *Human Rights of Women*, Philadelphia: University of Pennsylvania Press, 1994, 465.

India, Country Paper, South Asia Conference on Adolescents, July 1998 at 9.

International Institute for Population Sciences (IIPS) and ORC Marco, *National Family Health Survey (NFHS-2) 1998–99 India*, Mumbai: IIPS, 2000.

International Institute for Population Sciences (IIPS) and ORC Marco, *National Family Health Survey (NFHS-2) 1998–99 India*, 'Summary of Findings', Mumbai: IIPS, 2000.

International Institute for Population Sciences (IIPS), *National Family Health Survey (NFHS) 1992–93 India*, Mumbai: IIPS, 1995.

International Institute for Population Sciences (IIPS), *National Family Health Survey (NFHS) 1992–93 Rajasthan*, Mumbai: IIPS, 1995.

International Planned Parenthood Federation, *Charter on Sexual and Reproductive Rights*, New York: IIPF, 1995.

IWRAW, *Women, Children and Human Rights: The CEDAW Convention and the Convention on the Rights of the Child*, Minnesota: University of Minnesota, 1998.

Jabbi, M.K., 'Child Marriages in Rajasthan' (1986) 16 *Social Change* 3.

Jambunathan, J., 'Socio-cultural Factors in Depression in Asian Indian Women' (1992) 49 *Social Science and Medicine* 1461.

Jejeebhoy, Shireen, 'Adolescent Sexuality and Fertility' (1996) 447 *SEMINAR* 16.

Jejeebhoy, Shireen, 'Adolescent Sexual and Reproductive Behaviour: A Review of the evidence from India', in Radhika Ramasubban and Shireen Jejeebhoy (eds), *Women's Reproductive Health in India*, New Delhi: Rawat Publications, 2000, p. 40.

Jejeebhoy, Shireen, 'Reproductive Health Information in India: What are the Gaps?' (1999) 34 *Economic and Political Weekly* 3075.

Jejeebhoy, Shireen, 'Safe Motherhood in India: Priorities for Social Science Research', in Radhika Ramasubban and Shireen Jejeebhoy (eds), *Women's Reproductive Health in India*, New Delhi: Rawat Publications, 2000, p. 134.

Jejeebhoy, Shireen, 'The Importance of Social Science Research in the Promotion of Sexual and Reproductive Choice of Adolescents' (1999) 18 *Medicine and Law* 255.

Kabeer, Naila, *Reversed Realities: Gender Hierarchies in Development Thought*, London: Verso, 1994.

Kamminga, *Inter-State Accountability for Violations of Human Rights*, Philadelphia: University of Pennsylvania Press, 1992.

Kanitkar, Tara, 'National Family Health Survey: Some Thoughts' (1999) 34 *Economic and Political Weekly* 3081.

Kapadia, K.M., *Marriage and Family in India*, 3rd ed., New Delhi: Oxford University Press, 1992.

Kapur, Ratna, 'Guest Editorial' (1993) 1 *National Law School Journal Special Issue on Feminism and Law* viii.

Kapur, Ratna and Brenda Cossman, 'Women, Familial Ideology and the Constitution: Challenging Equality Rights', in Ratna Kapur (ed.),

Feminist Terrains in Legal Domains, New Delhi: Kali for Women, 1996, p. 61.

Kapur, Ratna and Brenda Cossman, *Subversive Sites: Feminist Engagements with Law in India*, New Delhi: Sage Publications, 1996.

Karkal, Malini, 'Invisibility of the Girl Child in India' (1991) 52 *Journal of Social Work* 5.

Karkal, Malini and Irudaya Rajan, 'Age at Marriage: How Much Change' (1989) 24 *Economic and Political Weekly* 505.

Karowitz, Leo, 'Law and the Single Girl' in *Women and the Law: The Unfinished Protection* (1969) 11.

Khan, M.E., et al., 'Sexual Violence within Marriage' (1996) 447 *SEMINAR* 32.

Koeing, Michael and Gillian Foo, 'Patriarchy, Women's Status and Reproductive Behaviour in Rural North India' (1992) 21 *Demography India* 145.

Kosambi, Meera, 'Girl Brides and Socio-legal Changes, Age of Consent Bill (1891) Controversy' (1991) 26 *Economic and Political Weekly* 1857.

Kosambi, Meera, 'Gender Reform and Competing State Controls over Women: The Rukhmabai Case, 1884–88' (1995) 29 *Contributions to Indian Sociology*.

Kosambi, Meera, 'Women's Emancipation and Equality—Pandita Ramabai's Contribution to Women's Cause' (1988) 23 *Economic and Political Weekly WS* 38.

Kumari, Ranjana, 'Rural Female Adolescence: Indian Scenario' (1995) 25 *Social Change* 177.

Kurian, N.J., 'Widening Regional Disparities in India Some Indicators' (2000) 35 *Economic and Political Weekly* 538.

Lai, Sarah and Ralph Regan, 'Female Sexual Autonomy and Human Rights' (1995) 8 *Harvard Human Rights Journal* 201.

Lassen, Nina, 'Slavery and Slavery-Like Practices: United Nations Standards and Implementation' (1988) 57 *Nordic Journal of International Law* 197.

Laurie, Zabin and K. Kiraguk, 'The Health Consequences of Adolescent Sexual and Reproductive Behaviour in Sub-Saharan Africa' (1998) 29 *Studies in Family Planning* 216.

Lettenmaier, et al., 'Mothers' lives matter: Maternal Health in the community' (1988) *Population Report Series* (L-7).

Levesque, Roger J.R., 'Sexual Use, Abuse and Exploitation of Children: Challenges in Implementing Children's Human Rights' (1994) 60 *Brooklyn Law Review* 959.

Lewis, Hope, 'Between Irua and Female Genital Mutilation: Feminist Human Rights Discourse and the Cultural Divide' (1995) 8 *Harvard Human Rights Journal* 1.

Liskin, L., et al., 'Youth in the 1980s: Social and Health Concerns', (1985) 13 *Population Report* (M9) 349.

MacKinnon, Catherine, 'Feminism, Marxism, Method and the State: An Agenda for Theory' (1987) 7 *SIGNS* 515.

Mahmood, Tahir, 'Marriage-Age in India and Abroad—A Comparative Conspectus' (1980) 22 *Journal of Indian Law Institute* 38.

Mahmood, Tahir, *Muslim Law of India*, New Delhi: Allahabad Agency, 1990.

Mahony, Kathleen, 'Canadian Approaches to Equality Rights and Gender Equality in the Courts', in Rebecca Cook (ed.), *Human Rights of Women*, Philadelphia: University of Pennsylvania Press, 1994, p. 437.

Mahony, Kathleen, 'Theoretical Perspectives on Women's Human Rights and Strategies for their Implementation' (1996) 21 *Brooklyn Journal International Law* 799.

Mamdani, Masuma, 'Adolescent Reproductive Health: Experience of Community-Based Programmes', in Saroj Pachauri (ed.), *Implementing Adolescent Reproductive Health Agenda for India: The Beginning*, New Delhi: Population Council, 1998, p. 263.

Mane, Purnima, 'Socialisation of Indian Women in their Childhood: An Analysis of Literature' (1991) 52 *Indian Journal of Social Work* 81.

Mayer, Ann Elizabeth, 'Cultural Particularism as a bar to Women's Rights: Reflections on the Middle Eastern Experience', in Julie Peters and Wolper Andrea (eds), *Women's Rights Human Rights*, New York: Routledge, 1995, p. 176.

Mensch, Barbara, et al., *The Uncharted Passage*, New York: Population Council, 1998.

Minow, Martha, 'Forward: Justice Engendered' (1987) 101 *Harvard Law Review* 10.

Mitra, Ashok, 'Levels of Regional Developments', in *Census of India*, Part I, New Delhi: Govt of India, 1961.

Mossman, Mary Jane, 'Feminism and Legal Method: The Difference it Makes' (1986) 3 *Australian Journal of Law and Society* 30.

Mukhopadhyay, M. and Sliver Shackles, *Women and Development in India*, Oxford: Oxfam, 1984.

Mulay, Sanjeevanee, 'Demographic Transition in Maharashtra, 1980–93' (1999) 34 *Economic and Political Weekly* 3063.

Murphy, John, 'Introduction to Universal Declaration of Human Rights' in Carol E. Lockwood, et al. (eds), *The International Human Rights of Women*, New York: American Bar Association, 1998, p. 138.

Murray, C.J.L. and A.D. Lopez, *The Global Burden of Disease*, Cambridge: Harvard University Press, 1996.

Murty, K.S.N., 'Marriage of Hindu Minors' (1969) *All India Report Journal* 72.

NGO Country Report on Beijing +5 from the Indian Women's Movement, *What has changed for Women and Girls in India since 1995?*, The Task Force on Women 2000: India, 2000.

Nagi, Saroj, 'Time to Focus on Adolescents, says UN Study', *The Times of India*, 9 October 2000.

National Academy of Science, *In Her Lifetime: Female Morbidity and Mortality in sub-Saharan Africa*, Washington DC: National Academy of Science, 1996.

Nowak, Manfred, *U.N. Covenant on Civil and Political Rights: CCPR Commentary*, Kehl: N.P. Engel Publisher, 1993.

Nussbaum, Martha C., *Women and Human Development—The Capabilities Approach*, New York: Cambridge University Press, 2000.

Nyamu, Celestine, 'How should Human Rights and Development Respond to Cultural Legitimisation of Gender Hierarchy in Developing Countries' (2000) 41 *Harvard International Law Journal* 381.

Opsahl, Torkel, 'The Human Rights Committee', in Philip Alston (ed.), *The United Nations and Human Rights: A Critical Appraisal*, Oxford: Clarendon Press, 1992, p. 431.

Pachauri, Saroj and A. Jamshedji, 'Risks of Teenage Pregnancy' (1983) 37 *Journal of Obstetrics and Gynaecology* 477.

Pachauri, Saroj, 'Defining a Reproductive Health Package for India: A Proposed Framework', in Maitreyi Krishnaraj, Ratna Sudarshan, and A. Sheriff (eds), *Gender, Population and Development*, New Delhi: Oxford University Press, 1998, p. 310.

Packer, Corinne A.A., 'Preventing Adolescent Pregnancy: The Protection offered by International Human Rights Law' (1997) 5 *International Journal of Children's Rights* 46.

Parashar, Archana, *Women and Family Law Reforms in India: Uniform Civil Code and Gender Equality*, New Delhi: Sage, 1992.

Pathak, K.B. and F. Ram, 'Adolescent Motherhood: Problems and Consequences' (1993) 39 *Journal of Family Welfare* 17.

Peiris, G.L., 'Public Interest Litigation in the Indian Subcontinent: Current Dimensions' (1991) 40 *International Comparative Law Quarterly* 66.

Pendse, Vinaya, 'Maternal Deaths in an Indian Hospital: A Decade of (No) Change', in Berer Marge and Ravindran Sundari (eds), *Safe Motherhood Initiatives: Critical Issues*, New York: Reproductive Health Matters, 1999, p. 119.

Phadke, Y.D., *Shodh Bal Gopalancha* (in Marathi), Pune: Sri Vidya Prakashan, 1993.

Pilcher, Jane, 'Contrary to Gillick: British Children and Sexual Rights since 1985' (1997) 5 *International Journal of Children's Rights* 299.

Pound, R., *Social Control through Law*, London: Oxford University Press, 1942.

Qadeer, Imrana, 'Reproductive Health: A Public Health Perspective' (1998) 33 *Economic and Political Weekly* 2675.

Ragsdale, Shannon S. and Vanessa D. Campbell, 'Protection of the Female Child: The Mothers of our Future—Case Studies of India, Pakistan, Bangladesh and Sri Lanka' (1999) 7 *Tulsa Journal of Comparative and International Law* 177.

Rajyalakshmi, C., 'Socio-cultural Roots of Child Marriages' (1990) 20 *Social Change* 38.

Ramachandran, P., 'Nutrition in Pregnancy' in C. Gopalan, and S. Kaur (eds), *Women and Nutrition in India*, New Delhi: Nutrition Foundation of India, 1989, p. 93.

Rao, Arati, 'Politics of Gender and Culture in International Human Rights' in Julie Peters and Andrea Wolper (ed.), *Women's Rights Human Rights*, New York: Routledge, 1995, p. 169.

Ravindran, Sundari T.K., 'Engendering Health' (2000) 489 *Seminar* 34.

Ray, Rajat, *Social Conflict and Political Unrest in Bengal: 1875–1927*, New Delhi: Oxford University Press, 1984.

Reaume, Denise, 'What is distinctive about feminist analysis of law?: A Conceptual Analysis of Women's Exclusion from Law' (1996) 2 *Legal Theory* 265.

Reddi, P., et al., 'Adolescent Pregnancy' (1993) 43 *Journal of Obstetrics and Gynaecology of India* 764.

Rehof, Lars Adam, *Guide to the Travaux Préparatoires of the United Nations Convention on the Elimination of All Forms of Discrimination against Women*, Amsterdam: Martinus Nijhoff Publisher, 1993, p. 184.

Rhode, Deborah, 'The "Woman's Point of View"' (1988) 38 *Journal of Legal Education* 39.

Romany, Celina, 'Women as Aliens: A Feminist Critique of the Public/Private Distinction in International Human Rights Law' (1993) 6 *Harvard Human Rights Journal* 87.

Rustogi, Preet, 'Identifying Gender Backward Districts Using Selected Indicators' (2000) 35 *Economic and Political Weekly* 4276.

Rwezaura, Bart, 'Protecting the Rights of the Girl Child in Commonwealth Jurisdictions', in Andrew Byrnes (ed.), *Advancing the Human Rights of Women: Using International Human Rights Standards in Domestic Litigation*, London: The Commonwealth Secretariat, 1997, p. 114.

Sadasivam, Bharati, 'The Rights Framework In Reproductive Health Advocacy: A Reappraisal' (1997) 8 *Hastings Women's Law Journal* 313.

Sagade, Jaya, 'Uniform Civil Code' (1991) 43 *Social Action* 501.

Sarkar, Tanika, 'Colonial Lawmaking and Lives/Deaths of Indian Women Different Readings of Law and Community' in Ratna Kapur (ed.), *Feminist Terrains in Legal Domains*, New Delhi: Kali for Women, 1996, p. 210.

Sathe, A.G., 'The Adolescent in India: A Status Report' (1987) 34 *Journal of Family Welfare* 11.

Sathe, S.P., *Judicial Activism in India*, New Delhi: Oxford University Press, 2002.

Sathe, S.P., *Towards Gender Justice*, Bombay: S.N.D.T. Women's University, 1993.

Senanayake, Pramilla, 'Adolescent Fertility and Teenage Pregnancy', in Helen M. Wallace, et al. (eds), *Health Care of Women and Children in Developing Countries* 651.

Sethi, Geeta, 'AIDS and the Adolescent Girl' in Sunil Mehra (ed.), *Adolescent Girl: An Indian Perspective*, New Delhi: Mamta Publication, 1995, p. 53.

Shalev, Carmel, 'Rights to Sexual and Reproductive Health: ICPD and the Convention on the Elimination of All Forms of Discrimination against Women' (2000) 4 H*ealth and Human Rights* 39.

Sharma, Adarsh, 'Socio-Cultural Practices Threatening the Girl Child' (1995) 25 *Social Change* 94.

Sharma, V., et al., 'Can Married Women Say No to Sex' (1998) 44 *Journal of Family Welfare* 1.

Shelton, Dinah, *Remedies in International Human Rights Law*, New York: Oxford University Press, 1999.

Sheppard, Colleen, 'Grounds of Discrimination: Towards an Inclusive and Contextual Approach' (2001) 80 *The Canadian Bar* 893.

Singh, B.P., *Women, Birth Control and the Law*, New Delhi: Deep and Deep Publisher, 1993.

Singh, Kirti and Divya Kapur, 'Law, Violence and the Girl Child' (2001) 5 *Health and Human Rights Journal* 8.

Singh, Susheela, 'Adolescent Childbearing in Developing Countries: A Global Review' (1998) 29 *Studies in Family Planning* 118.

Singh, Susheela, et al., 'Early Marriage Among Women in Developing Countries' (1996) 22 *International Family Planning Perspectives* 148.

Sivaramayya, B., 'Towards Equality: The Long Road Ahead', in A. Dhanda (ed.), *Essays in Honour of Lotika Sarkar*, Bombay: Tripathi, 1999, p. 387.

Smart, C., *Feminism and the Power of Law*, London: Routledge, 1989.

Sohn, 'The New International Law: Protection of Rights of Individuals Rather then States' (1982) 32 *American University Law Review* 1.

Srinivasan, K., 'Fertility Proximate Determinants' in J.K. Satia and Shireen Jejeebhoy (eds), *The Demographic Challenge*, New Delhi: Oxford University Press, 1991, p. 36.

Srivastava, K., 'Socio-Economic Determinants of Child Marriage in Uttar Pradesh' (1983) 12 *Demography India* 59.

Stark, Barbara, 'Introduction to International Covenant on Economic, Social and Cultural Rights', in Carol E. Lockwood, et al. (eds), *The International Human Rights of Women*, New York: American Bar Association, 1998, p. 215.

Starrs, A., *The Safe Motherhood Action Agenda: Priorities for the Next Decade. Report on the Safe Motherhood Technical Consultation*, New York: Family Care International, 1998.

Starrs, Ann, and Inter-Agency Group for Safe Motherhood, *Report of the Safe Motherhood Action Agenda: Priorities for the Next Decade*, Colombo, 1997.

Sturm, S., 'A Normative Theory of Public Law Remedies' (1991) 79 *Georgia Law Journal* 1357.

Sullivan, Donna, 'The Public/Private Distinction in International Human Rights Law' in Julie Peters and Andrea Wolper (eds), *Women's Rights Human Rights*, New York: Routledge, 1995, p. 126.

Tayabji, F.B., *Muslim Law*, 4th ed., Bombay: N.M. Tripathi, 1968.

Taylor, Debbie, 'Servile Marriages: Institutional Slavery' (1994) 24 *Anti-Slavery Report* 24.

Tinker, Anne, 'Making Newborn Lives a Priority' (2001) Issue 3 *International Federation of Gynaecology and Obstetrics* (*FIGO*), no page.

Treitel, Andrew, 'Conflicting Traditions: Muslim Sharia Courts and Marriage Age Regulation in Israel' (1995) 26 *Columbia Human Rights Law Review* 403.

Uberoi, Patricia, 'Hindu Marriage Law and the Judicial Construction of Sexuality', in Ratna Kapur (ed.), *Feminist Terrains in Legal Domains*, New Delhi: Kali, 1996, p. 184.

Willimas, Joan C., 'Deconstructing Gender' in Katherine Bartlett and Roseanne Kennedy (eds), *Feminist Legal Theory: Readings in Law and Gender*, Boulder, Co.: Westview Press, 1991, 112.

Government of India Documents

Bengal Government Judicial, McLeod's Medical Report on Child Wives, NF J C/17Proceedings 104–17, June 1893.

Census Report of India, 1991

Government of Gujarat, *Report of the Suicide Inquiry Committee*, 1964.

Government of India, *Report of the Age of Consent Committee*, 1929.

Government of India, *Report of the Committee on the Status of Women in India—Towards Equality*, 1974.

National Human Rights Commission, Annual Report, 1996–97.

National Human Rights Commission, Annual Report, 1998–99.

The Gazette of India, 15 December 1977, Part II, S.2.

International Documents

1919 Treaty of Saint-German-en-Laye.

Beijing Platform for Action, *Report of the Fourth World Conference on Women*, Beijing, September 1995, UN Doc A/CONF.177/20 (1995).

CEDAW, A/51/38, 9 May 1996, Concluding Observations on the combined initial, second and third periodic reports of Ethiopia.

CEDAW, A/53/38, 14 May 1998 (19th Session), Concluding Observations on the report of Indonesia.

CEDAW, C/1998/II/L.1/Add.6, 7 July 1998 Concluding Observations on the report of The Republic of Nigeria.

CEDAW, C/1998/II/L.1/Add.8, 8 July 1998 (19th Session), Concluding Observations on the report of The Republic of Korea, Bangladesh, Chile, Cyprus.

CEDAW, C/2000/1/CRP.3/Add, 1 February 2000.

CEDAW, *General Recommendation 19*, Violence against Women, UN GAOR, 1992, Doc. No. A/47/38.

CEDAW, *General Recommendation 21*, UN GAOR, 1994, Doc. No. A/47/38.

Committee on Economic, Social and Cultural Rights (hereinafter CESCR) General Comment 13, E/C.12/1999/10, para 46, 8 December 1999.

CESCR, General Comment 14, *The Right to the Highest Standard of Health*: E/C.12/2000/4, 4 July 2000.

Committee on the Elimination of Discrimination against Women (hereinafter CEDAW), January 2000, *Response to Questions on India's First Report on CEDAW*, Permanent Mission of India to the UN, New York, 2000.

Concluding Observations of Committee on Rights of Children (hereinafter CRC) on India: CRC/C/15/Add.115, 23 February 2000.

Concluding Observations of CRC: Ethiopia, CRC/C/15/Add.67, 24 January 1997.

Concluding Observations of CRC: Ghana, CRC/C/15/Add.73, 18 June 1997.

Concluding Observations of CRC: Guatemala, CRC/C/Add.58, 7 June 1996.

Concluding Observations of CRC: India, CRC/C/15/Add.115, 23 February 2000.

Concluding Observations of CRC: Indonesia, CRC/C/15 Add.7, 18 October 1993.

Concluding Observations of CRC: Kuwait, CRC/C/15/Add.96, 26 October 1998.

Concluding Observations of CRC: Lebanon, CRC/C/Add.54, 7 June 1996.

Concluding Observations of CRC: Mauritius, CRC/C/15.Add.64, 30 October 1996.

Concluding Observations of CRC: Morocco, CRC/C/15/Add.60, 30 October 1996.

Concluding Observations of CRC: Nepal, CRC/C/15/Add.57, 7 June 1996.

Concluding Observations of CRC: Nigeria, CRC/C/15/Add.61, 30 October 1996.

Concluding Observations of CRC: Nigeria, CRC/C/Add.54, 9 September 1995.

Concluding Observations of CRC: Slovenia, CRC/C/15/Add.65, 30 October 1996.

Concluding Observations of HRC on India: CCPR/C/79/Add.81, 4 August 1997.

Constitution of the World Health Organization, in *Basic Documents*, 39th ed., Geneva: WHO, 1992.

Convention on Consent to Marriage, Minimum Age for Marriage and Registration of Marriages, 1962.

Convention on the Elimination of all Forms of Discrimination Against Women, G.A. Res. 34/180, UN GAOR, 34th Session., No.46 at 193, UN Doc.A/39/45 (1979) (entered into force, 3 September 1981).

Convention on the Rights of the Child, G.A. Res. 44/25 (XLIV), UN GAOR, 44th Session, Supp. No. 49 at 167, UN Doc. A/44/49 (1989) (entered into force September 1990).

Forced Labour Convention, 1930.

Human Rights Committee, General Comment 14, UN GAOR 1990, UN Doc. A/45/38.

Human Rights Committee, General Comment 19, UN GAOR 1990, UN Doc. A/45/38.

Human Rights Committee, General Comment 28, UN GAOR 2000, UN Doc.A/55/40.

ICPD + 5 Forum, The Hague, *Interpreting Reproductive Health*, Geneva: WHO, 1999.

International Conference on Population and Development, Plan of Action.

International Covenant on Civil and Political Rights.

International Covenant on Economic, Social and Cultural Rights.

Maastricht Guidelines on violation of economic, social and cultural Rights.

Slavery Convention, 1926.

Supplementary Convention on the Abolition of Slavery, the Slave Trade, and Institutions and Practices Similar to Slavery, 1956.

UN Treaty Collection: Treaty Reference Guide.

UN Yearbook 1951.

UN Yearbook 1956.

UN, Department of International Economic and Social Affairs, *Adolescent Reproductive Behaviour: Evidence from Developing Countries*, Vol. II, New York: UN, 1989.

UNDP Report on Human Development, 2000.

UNFPA, *A Five-Year Review of Progress towards the Implementation of POA of ICPD*, a background paper for The Hague Forum, 8–12 February 1999.

UNICEF, New York, 'Too Many Teen Brides', in *The Progress of Nations 1998*—for global information regarding the extent of child marriage.

UNICEF: 'Child Marriages Must Stop', Press Release on 8 March 2001.

United Nations Charter.

United Nations Optional Protocol to the Convention on the Elimination of All Forms of Discrimination against Women, UN Doc. A/Res/54/4.

United Nations, International Human Rights Instruments, Compilation of General Comments and General Recommendations Adopted by Human Rights Treaty Bodies, HRI/Gen/1/Rev.2, 29 March 1996.

Universal Declaration of Human Rights.

Vienna Convention on the Law of Treaties, 1993.

WHO, *Safe Motherhood: Health Day 1998: Delay Childbearing*.

World Health Organization, *World Health Report*, Geneva: WHO, 1999.

World Health Organization, *Maternal Mortality: A Global Fact Book*, Geneva: WHO, 1991.

World Health Organization, *Obstetric Fistulae: A Review of Available Information*, Geneva: WHO, 1991.

World Health Organization, *The Health of Young People: A Challenge and a Promise*, Geneva: WHO, 1993.

World Health Organization, United Nations Children's Fund, and United Nations Population Fund, *Maternal Mortality in 1995. Estimates developed by WHO, UNICEF and UNFPA*, Geneva: WHO, 2001.

List of Cases

Abdul Aziz v. *Bombay* AIR 1954 SC 321.   xlv

All India Imam Organization v. *Union of India & Ors.* 1993   178
     SOL Case No. 098.

Ayyah Pillai v. *Manik Pillai* (1965) 1 Madras Law Journal   71
     172.

Bandhua Mukti Morcha v. *Union of India,* 1984(2) SCR 67.   178

Bhagwat Sarup v. *Emperor* AIR 1945 All 306.   71

Birupakshya Das v. *Kunju Behari* AIR 1961 Orissa 104.   71

Consumer Education and Research Centre v. *Union of India*   178, 189
     (1995) 3 SCC 42.

Dadaji Bhikaji v. *Rukhmabai* IX Indian Law Reporter   64
     (Bombay Series) 529 (1885).

Durga Bai v. *Kedarmal* 1980 HLR (Raj.) 166.   102

Durjyodhan v. *Bengabati Devi* AIR 1977 Ori. 36.   102

Emperor v. *Fulbhai Bhulbai* AIR 1940 Bom. 363.   71

Ghulam Bhik v. *Rustom Ali* AIR 1949 East Punjab 354.   71

Gillick v. *West Norfolk and Wisbech Area Health Authority*   206
     and Another (1985) 3 All ER 402.

Jwala Prasad v. *Emperor* AIR 1934 All 331.   71

Katari Subba Rao v. *Katari Seetha Mahalakshmi* AIR 1994   102
     AP 364.

Kirloskar Brothers Ltd v. *Employee's State Insurance Corporation*   205
     (1996) 2 SCC 682.

Lila Gupta v. *Laxmi Narain* AIR 1978 SC 1351.   75, 102

Maneka Gandhi v. *India* AIR 1978 SC 597.   109

Mohd. Ahmed Khan v. *Shah Bano Begum* AIR 1985 SC 945. 107

Mohini Jain v. *State of Karnataka* AIR 1992 SC 1858. 203, 206

Moore v. *Valsa* 1 (1992) DMC 55. 103

Mt Jalsi Kaur v. *Emperor* AIR 1933 Patna 471. 71

Munshi Ram v. *Emperor* AIR 1936 All. 11. 71

Narendra Kumar v. *State of Haryana* (1994) 2 SC 94. 202

Nilabati Behera v. *State of Orissa and others* AIR 1993 SC 219
1960.

Nizamuddin v. *Huseni* AIR 1960 MP 212. 105

Olga Tellis v. *Bombay Municipal Corporation*, 1985 202
Supplement (2) SCR 51.

Panchireddi v. *Ganapatlu* AIR 1975 AP 193. 61, 102

Parmananda Katara v. *Union of India* AIR 1989 SC 424. 178, 190

Paschim Banga Khet Mazdoor Samity v. *State of West Bengal* 190, 202
(1996) 4SCC 37.

Pirmohammad Kukaji v. *The State of MP* AIR 1960 MP 24. 105

Premi v. *Daya Ram* AIR 1965 HP 15. 102

Public Prosecutor v. *Thammanna Rattayya* AIR 1937 Madras 71
490.

Queen Empress v. *Huree Mohan Mythee* XVIII Indian Law 64, 65
Reporter (Calcutta) 49 (1891).

Rabindra Prasad v. *Sita Devi* AIR 1986 Patna 128. 102

Ram Baran v. *Sital Pathak* AIR 1939 All. 340. 71

Rambhau v. *Rajaram* AIR 1956 Bom. 250. 71

Sagar v. *State* AIR 1968 AP 165. 66

Sahib Ali Biswas v. *Jinnatan Nahar* AIR 1960 Cal. 717. 105

Sheela Barse v. *Secretary*, Children Aid Society AIR 1987 SC 108, 219
656.

Sheela Barse v. *Union of India* AIR 1986 SC 1773. 108, 219

Sivanandy v. *Bhagavathyamma* AIR 1962 Mad. 400. 71

State of Punjab v. *Mohinder Singh Chawla* AIR 1997 SC 1225. 205

Sowmitri Vishnu v. *Union of India* AIR 1985 SC 1618. xlv

Sushila Gothala v. *State of Rajasthan* AIR 1995 SC 90. 109

Unni Krishnan v. *State of Andhra Pradesh* AIR 1993 SC 2178. 203, 206

Usman v. *Budhu* AIR 1942 Sind 92. 105

Venkataramana v. *State* AIR 1977 AP 43. 61, 102

Vishaka v. *State of Rajasthan* AIR 1997 SC 3011. 128

X. and Y. v. *The Netherlands*, 1985 European Court of Human Rights Series A, Vol. 91. 128

Yusuf v. *State of Bombay* AIR 1954 SC 321. 66

Index

Abortion 19
  unsafe 19, 201
Adolescent fertility 15
Adolescent girl
  evolving capacity 123
Age at marriage 44, 111
  same age of bride and bridegroom
  87
Age of consent 35–8, 40–3, 63
Asking the woman question *See also*
  feminist method

Bangalore Principles 116
Beijing *See also* UN International
  Conference
Beijing Platform of Action (PLA)
  116, 141, 177, 192, 201, 217
Beijing +5 141, 142, 148, 216, 221
Brandeis Brief 92

Cairo *See also* UN International
  Conference
Cairo +5 221
Cairo Programme of Action (POA)
  116, 141, 177, 186, 192, 201, 215,
  216
CEDAW (Committee on Elimination
  of Discrimination against Women)
  112, 116, 121, 127, 137, 144–52,
  154, 158, 159, 163, 182, 187, 191–
  3, 198, 208–10

General Recommendation 148,
  151
General Recommendation 19
  150, 152, 154, 209
General Recommendation 21
  137, 151, 193, 209
General Recommendation 24
  209
Child Marriage *See also* Personal
  Laws
  consequences of 14–22
    epidemiological context 14–
    21
  custom of 4, 41, 55, 59
  demographic context 4–7
  development of girl child and
    xxvii, 14–24, 35, 175–202
  domestic violence xxv, xxxviii,
    151
  health of girl child and 14–21
  Human rights approach xxxv–
    xxxvii, 125
  International Human Rights
    111–31
  judicial approach 60–3
  law relating to 36
  legal effect 52, 87, 88
  meaning of xxxvi
  mental health and 20, 186–7
  punishment for 47, 48
  rape 38, *See also* Rape Law

reasons for   7–14
sexual violence   95, 180
term   xxvi
validity of   52, 53
violence   22, 125, 151
void, need to declare child
    marriage   54–7
Child Marriage Restraint Act
    (CMRA)   xxiv, xxv, 36, 43–52,
143, 144, 159, 162
Children's Convention   xxxvi, xxxvii,
133
    Article 1   159
    Article 2   139, 156
    Article 3   5, 155
    Article 6   176, 177
    Article 10   193
    Article 12   155, 159
    Article 13   199
    Article 18   154
    Article 19   155
    Article 24   154, 155, 181, 200
    Article 28   194
    Article 29   194
    evolution of   121, 122
Christian Law of Marriage   80
Civil Law of Marriage   82
Committee on Rights of Children
    (CRC)   112, 137, 139, 147, 148,
154, 156–9, 163, 187, 192, 195,
198–200, 207–10, 213
Consent
    of parties   xxvi, 58
        consent without force   78
        free consent   35, 37, 41,
        58, 59, 78–80, 82, 86, 88,
        100
        under HMA   77, See also
        Marriage
Constitution of India
    Article 14   142
    Article 15   142

Article 51   115
Article 253   115
Development   47, 175–7, 179, 180,
186, 187, 193
    rights affecting   192–201
Different ages at marriage   44, 45
Dimensions of problem of child
    marriage   1–34
Discrimination against women
    definition   133

Early marriage   xxvii, See also child
    marriage
Education   45, 47, 56, 57, 147, 182,
184, 187, 190, 193–9
    right to   46, 180, 193–9
Employments, skills for   45

Female genital mutilation (FGM)
157
Feminist Legal Method   xxix
Feminist method   xxviii–xxxiv
    asking the woman question
    xxix–xxxi, 8, See also woman
    question
Feminist perspective   xxix, 144,
159
Forced marriage   xxvii, 147, 159, See
    also Child marriage, Early marriage

Gender   23, 119, 141, 142, 143,
147, 148, 150, 151, 154, 159,
165
    norms   22
    See also sex and gender
General Comments adopted by
    Human Rights Treaty Bodies   See
    also Human Rights Committee
    (HRC)
General Recommendations Adopted
    by Human Rights Treaty Bodies
    See also CEDAW

Girl child
    focus on   xxvii
Guardianship
    Hindu law   83–5

Health, right to   181–7, *See also*
    reproductive health
Hindu Marriage Act   75–83, 87
Hindu Minority and Guardianship
    Act   83–5, 90
Human Rights
    approach   xxxv–xxxvii
    evolution of   117
    violation of   132–74
Human Rights Committee (HRC)
    112, 138, 139, 146–8, 154, 158–60,
    163, 165, 166, 209
        General Comment 8   160
        General Comment 19   154
        General Comment 28   138,
        209

ICCPR   xxxvi, 112, 117, 118, 122,
    124, 133, 134
ICESCR   xxxvi, 112, 116, 118, 122,
    133, 134
Indian Majority Act   xxvii
Infant mortality   20, 177, 181, 192
Information, right to   199

Legal method   xxviii
Life, right to   175–80

Marriage
    civil law in India   82
    consent regarding   35, 137–9,
        142–4, 149, 150, 152, 154,
        156, 161, 164
    in India   3–4
    See also personal laws of marriage
    registration   82, 89
    right to marry   148–57, 184

Marriage convention   xxxvi, 1,
    123
Maternal morbidity   17, 19, 179
Maternal mortality   15, 16, 125,
    175, 177, 183, 188, 191, 192
Mental health   20, 186–7
Muslim Law of Marriage   79–80

National Commission for Women
    54, 59
National Family Health Survey
    (NFHS)   4, 5, 7, 12, 18, 19, 20,
    90, 91, 191
National Health Policy   188
National Human Rights Commission
    (NHRC)   213–15

Obligation of Government
    to fulfil rights   115
    to protect rights   115
    to respect rights   114
Optional Protocol to Women's
    convention   112, 120, 121

Parsi Law of Marriage   81–2
Patriarchy   7–10, 21, 22, 25
Personal laws of marriage   75–82
    See also Hindu Marriage Act
    See also Muslim Law of Marriage
    See also Christian Law of Marriage
    See also Parsi Law of Marriage
Public Interest Litigation   92–3, 96,
    178, 180, 181, 189–90, 226, 227

Rape law   35–8, 40–2, 63–4, 74, 86,
    89
Registration of marriage   59–60
Reproductive health   xxv, 13–15, 18,
    21–6, 36, 46, 47, 60, 63, 92, 93, 95,
    113, 125, 126, 142, 143, 168, 181–
    4, 186–8, 190, 191, 194, 196, 197,
    199–202, 208, 212, 215–17

right to   186
Restitution of Conjugal Rights   39,
  40
Role of Law   97–100

Sarda Act   42, 43
Sarda Bill   42, 43
Sex and gender   133, 134, 135, 140,
  141, 144
Sexual activity
  early   2, 3
Sexual harassment of women   116
Sexuality   23–5
  control over   9, 10
Slavery Convention   2, 123–6
  Article 1   163
  Article 2   164
  evolution of   123, 124
Special Rapporteur
  on violence against women   157
  on traditional practices   157
Spouse, right to choose   137
STD and HIV/AIDS   18, 19, 21,
  23, 24, 180, 187

UDHR   111, 112, 116–18, 122,
  134, 148, 159, 176, 181, 193,
  199
UN International Conferences   113,
  115, 215, 226
  on Human Rights at Vienna
    113, 140, 151, 208, 221
  on Population and Development
    at Cairo (ICPD)   113, 116,
    221
  on Women at Beijing (FWCW)
    113, 116, 140, 141, 148, 216,
    221
Unsafe abortion   19–20

Vesico-vaginal fistula (VVF)   14, 15,
  18

Victimization of girl child, preventive
  measures   55–7
Vienna   See also UN International
  conference
Virginity   xxvii, 9, 52, 56, 224
Violation of Human Rights by custom
  of child marriage   132–74
  rights affecting reproductive
    health   175
  right to be free from slavery   163
    India's obligation   165
  right to education and
    development   192, 193–5
    India's obligation   195–9
  right to equality   132, 134, 137,
    154
    India's obligation   142, 143
  right to health   181–7
    India's obligation   188–92
  right to information   199–201
    India's obligation   201, 202
  right to liberty and security   159,
    162
    India's obligation   162
  right to life   175–8
    India's obligation   178–81
  right to marry and found a family
    148
    India's obligation   157
  right to non-discrimination
    on ground of age   132, 133,
      139, 140
    on ground of sex and gender
      133, 135, 140
Violence against women   xxxvi, 97,
  98, 116, 142, 150–2, 157, 182, 209,
  217, 222

Woman question   xxix–xxxi, 8, 36,
  45, 62
Women's Convention   xxxvi, 58, 59,
  112, 133–40

Article 1   133, 150, 160
Article 2   136, 140, 152
Article 3   134, 152, 161, 162
Article 5   134, 136, 140, 144,
   152
Article 10   152, 199

Article 12   182
Article 14   200
Article 16   137, 144–6, 148,
   149, 151, 152, 154, 157, 158,
   199
   evolution of   118–21